THE IRREPRESSIBLE
CHURCHILL

THE IRREPRESSIBLE
CHURCHILL

WINSTON'S WORLD, WARS & WIT

Selected and compiled with historical commentary
by
Kay Halle

CONWAY

To the memory of
Sir Winston Churchill

A Conway book

First published in hardback in Great Britain in 1985
First paperback edition published in 1987

This edition published in 2010 by
Conway
an imprint of Anova Books Ltd.
10 Southcombe Street
London W14 0RA
www.anovabooks.com
www.conwaypublising.com

Distributed in the U.S. and Canada by
Sterling Publishing Co., Ltd
387 Park Avenue South
New York, NY 10016-8810

British Library Cataloguing in Publication Data:
A CIP catalogue record for this book is available from the British Library.

ISBN 9781844861194

10 9 8 7 6 5 4 3 2 1

Reproduction by SX Composing DTP
Printed and bound by Toppan Leefung Printing Ltd, China

CONTENTS

In my belief,
you cannot deal
with the most
serious things
in the world
unless you
also understand
the most amusing.

—Winston S. Churchill

PROLOGUE

When I first saw Winston Churchill he was standing on a delicate Adam Chair in the drawing room of Chartwell, his manor house in Kent. Clad in coveralls and muddy boots, he was in the act of replacing the candles of a great Waterford crystal chandelier, as there had been an electric power failure just before his son Randolph and I arrived at tea time. As we entered the drawing room we found Mrs Churchill, literally at her husband's feet, miraculously resisting all temptation to rail at the mud-encased boots on the satin-covered chair. As I reached up to shake Mr Churchill's hand, he had just put a match to the last in the sparkling chandelier, and I caught his cherubic face aglow in the candlelight as he looked down from his perilous perch. His first words were those of a small boy gazing in wonderment at his birthday cake: 'Isn't it just like Berkeley Square?' It was the autumn of 1931, and he was referring to John L. Balderston's then current play, a provocative treatment of time and space, acted out in a candlelit eighteenth-century London drawing room.

Zipped into his twentieth-century work clothes, Mr Churchill was a picture in contrasts as he stumped down off the gilt chair. Before we had come upon him, he had been working in his fields, supervising the construction of a very modern system of ponds and lakes which filled and emptied by electrically controlled locks of his own design, to hold his Golden Orfe, a species of carp. After the disarming circumstances of our introduction, I knew why he had been called a nonconformist traditionalist.

All during that brimful weekend there was much coming and going of political figures. High-powered debates ranged over the whole field of human endeavour with, of course, Mr Churchill the central figure. He was then busy preparing an important speech before Parliament on the Statute of Westminster, a Bill which extended Dominion status to include a wider range of self-government.

Soon after our arrival he showed me his bedroom, arranged with the Spartan simplicity that marked Napoleon's campaign headquarters—iron pallet and all. As his room was close by mine and as soundproof as a cranberry box, I could hear him during much of the night, tramping up and down, talking his speech into the long pier glass which served as the backboard for these practice runs. Around two o'clock in the morning he summoned his close assistant, Brendan Bracken*—'Winston's faithful

---

* Brendan Bracken, 1901–1958; Parliamentary Private Secretary to W.S.C., 1940–1941; Minister of Information, 1941–1945; First Lord of the Admiralty, May to August, 1945.

chela' [the word for *disciple*, in India], as Stanley Baldwin[†] called him—to try to spike or refute his arguments. Then followed the fugue of their voices until early morning.

It was also at the time of the Round Table Conference, and Mr Churchill was disturbed over the discussions about India, opposing the argument that some were making that India should be promised eventual Dominion status. This had caused Conservative Party chieftains to descend on Chartwell in a last-minute effort to try to persuade him to change his mind. They felt he would be driving himself out of the Conservative councils by this unpopular stand, at the very time his voice should be their strongest and most persuasive. Some also feared that he might be about to lead a revolt of Conservative Members of Parliament, dissatisfied with Baldwin's leadership, as Mr Churchill's India position found strong support inside the Tory Party.

All during my visit it was not only the projection and capacity of Mr Churchill's intellect wrestling with the great issues that captivated me, but also the verbal felicity and ingenuity with which he transposed his thoughts into so many striking phrases and word pictures, blowing them into the air like so many coloured bubbles. Unforgettable barbs and humorous images punctuated the flow of his talk, at the end of which friend or foe, situation or himself would be dropped unceremoniously through the trap door of his unique improvisations. Of this gift, his mother, Lady Randolph Churchill, wrote, 'We could see and understand everything [the Boer War] with the help of Winston's graphic tongue.'

From Lord Randolph must have come the biting wit, the instinct for the jugular, the insult in full dress, and a genius for the cut and thrust of Parliamentary debate, all so much an accepted tradition of the House of Commons. Uncanny prescience, a creative brilliance and elemental drive also seemed a legacy from his father.

Lord Salisbury,[†] during one of his Premierships, vowed, 'I could do very well with two departments, in fact I have four—the Prime Ministership, the Foreign Office, the Queen [Victoria], and Randolph Churchill—and the burden of them increases in that order.'

Lady Randolph had a similar reputation for her own quick thrusts. Bernard Shaw once turned down one of her invitations to dine, replying, 'Certainly not! What have I done to provoke such an attack on my well-known habit?' 'I know nothing about your habits,' Lady Randolph retorted. 'I hope they are not as bad as your manners.'

On another occasion Lord and Lady Randolph were invited to dine on a Sunday at Marlborough House with the Prince of Wales, later Edward VII. Knowing that it was a day of rest for servants they came in a public conveyance, called a 'Queen's

---

[†] Stanley Baldwin, Conservative Prime Minister and First Lord of the Treasury, 1923–1924, 1924–1929, 1935–1937.
[†] Lord Salisbury, Robert Cecil, 1830–1903; third Marquis.

carriage,' instead of their own brougham. When it came time to leave, the Prince accompanied his guests to the door. As Lady Randolph's scruffy looking hired four-wheeler drew up, the Prince handed her into it with the tease, 'Your conscience is better than your carriage.' 'Is it not, Sir, the Queen's carriage?' she flashed back. 'How can I have a better?'

I remember one family lunch at Chartwell in 1931. Mr Churchill sat at the head of his table in Renaissance splendour in an open-throated silk shirt, a velvet smoking jacket and slippers with WSC threaded in gold on the toes. In front of him stood a bottle of *Pol Roger* champagne, his favourite vintage. Later in World War II Madame Pol Roger is said to have allocated the remaining output of that particular year for his use in gratitude for his part in the liberation of France. Twenty years later, he was to name one of his race horses Pol Roger. There was also a Napoleon brandy at his side, from which he supplied us all. The flame of a candle set in a Georgian silver candlestick kept his cigar lighted.

His beautiful wife 'Clemmie,' his son Randolph, and Diana, Sarah and Mary, his daughters, were around him. Flouting British custom, little Mary had not been packed off to the nursery, but added her exuberance to the coziness and warmth of the group. Three 'young gentlemen,' assistants and researchers, were also lunching with us, as Mr Churchill was then in the middle of his monumental biography of his ancestor, John Churchill, the first Duke of Marlborough, who delivered the European continent from the expansionist schemes of Louis XIV. Mr Churchill told me he particularly selected his 'young gentlemen' for their differing political views as he enjoyed and profited from their arguments, which he liked to provoke.

As I had just visited Blenheim Palace, we talked of that 'Great Pile' of over 320 rooms, set in 2,700 acres of parks and gardens, begun on June 18, 1705, the gift of a grateful Queen Anne and British nation to Marlborough. It had been designed by the playwright-architect Sir John Vanbrugh, and Mr Churchill liked to quote Vanbrugh's epitaph, written by poet Abel Evans:

> *Under this stone, Reader, survey*
> *Dead Sir Vanbrugh's house of clay.*
> *Lie heavy on him,*
> *Earth! for he*
> *Laid many heavy loads on thee!*

Though he was born at Blenheim, Mr Churchill loved best his own simple manor house, Chartwell, bought with earnings from his history of World War I.

The magnificence of Blenheim in contrast to his adored Chartwell led Mr Churchill to quote a poem attributed to Alexander Pope, *Upon the Duke of Marlborough's House at*

Woodstock, written in 1714.

> *See, Sir, here's the grand approach,*
> *This way is for his Grace's coach;*
> *There lies the bridge, and here's the clock;*
> *Observe the lion and the cock,*
> *The spacious court, the colonnade,*
> *And mark how wide the hall is made!*
> *The chimneys are so well design'd,*
> *They never smoke in any wind.*
> *This gallery's contrived for walking,*
> *The windows to retire and talk in;*
> *The council-chamber for debate,*
> *And all the rest are rooms of state,*
>   *Thanks, Sir, cried I, 't is very fine,*
> *But where d'ye sleep, or where d'ye dine?*
> *I find by all you have been telling*
> *That 't is a house, but not a dwelling.*

To add to the lively scene that day at lunch, an assortment of Churchill pets played a continual game of tag under the table between the guests' legs while a favourite marmalade-coloured cat, Tango, kept rubbing against Mr Churchill's receptive leg. Noticing the hypnotic attraction my foot held for his French poodle, he explained, 'I see that Rufus (I) is showing a marked preference for American shoe leather!'

At that time, the American Ambassador to London, Charles Dawes, a mid-westerner, was making news in England by refusing to wear knee breeches to the Court, hanging Navajo Indian blankets on the Embassy walls and disguising the comedian Leon Errol as a waiter to play practical jokes on the guests at an Embassy dinner. Moreover, the Ambassador stood by the Prohibition law of the United States and served no alcohol at the American Embassy. Mr Churchill liked everything about Mr Dawes except that. 'Your Ambassador is a typical American,' he told me. 'He comes from the heart of your country. He is not one of those who would be more British than the British. I admire him and dine with him every week. But on leaving your Embassy I always repair immediately to my Club, where I order each of the wines and brandy of which I was deprived at his table.' One of Mr Churchill's most endearing qualities was daring to be himself.

As on all visits to Chartwell, the flow of conversation that day continued high-powered and uninhibited, sparkling from the oldest to the youngest around the table. Everything everyone said seemed exciting. At one point there was such a verbal traffic jam Mr Churchill roared at his brilliant and voluble son: 'Randolph, lie down,' and, 'don't interrupt me while I'm interrupting!'

During these pyrotechnics my eyes wandered over to a painting which hung over the buffet. I took it to be a seventeenth-century Dutch still life. Catching my interested glance, Mr Churchill lit up. 'It's *my* bottlescape, I painted it,' he bubbled. Then, after a longer second look at the painting, I spied a contemporary lamp nestling in the clutch of bottles and lifted my glass to toast him.

In 1931, he had hit the very bottom of his political fortunes. He was out of office, warning his country and the world of the mortal peril in the prospect of German rearmament. It was then that he said of himself, 'Here I am, after almost thirty years in the House of Commons, after holding many of the highest office of state. Here I am, discarded, cast away, marooned, rejected and disliked.' But that day at Chartwell, surrounded by his family, secretaries and friends, not a single sign of any inner anguish was apparent.

At one point the conversation turned to party politics, and Mr Churchill used the word, 'ratting,' which by my expression he judged I had not understood. 'I can give you no better example of what it means to "rat" the party,' he said, 'than to use myself as an illustration. I ratted the Conservatives by going across the floor to join the Liberals, and again to return to the Conservatives. During these switches I won several high Cabinet posts. Though some of my friends were shocked, these "rats" turned out to be most felicitous. After one "rat," Stanley Baldwin made me Chancellor of the Exchequer. You know,' he continued with a naughty twinkle, 'the family motto of the House of Marlborough from which I descend is *Faithful but Unfortunate*. But I, by my enterprise, nay daring, have reversed the motto, to *Faithless but Fortunate*.'

This union of the pound and the dollar was originated by the Hon. Winston Churchill and permitted to me during a joint to Chartwell. He requested me to transmit it to my father as a token of the currency of the future. Franklin Roosevelt. Oct. 1st 1933

UNION OF THE POUND AND THE DOLLAR

On a later visit to Chartwell on October 8, 1933, James Roosevelt, the President's eldest son, was among the guests. It was not long after his father's first inaugural. Mr Churchill and Mr Roosevelt had not yet become 'the good companions' they later became as they had met only fleetingly at a dinner at Gray's Inn* in London long years before, during World War I when President Roosevelt was Assistant Secretary of the Navy and Mr Churchill was Minister of Munitions.

After dinner on this particular weekend Mr Churchill initiated a guessing game, drawing from each of us a confession of our fondest wish. His guests fumbled and qualified their answers. But when the question was put to him, he shot back without a flicker of hesitation, 'I wish to be Prime Minister and in close and daily communication by telephone with the President of the United States. There is nothing we could not do if we were together.' Then, turning to a secretary, he called for a piece of paper on which he inscribed the insignias of a pound and a dollar sign intertwined.† 'Pray, bear this to your father from me,' he said to James Roosevelt. 'Tell him this must be the currency of the future.'

'What will you call this new currency, Sir?' asked young Roosevelt.

'The sterling dollar,' said Mr Churchill.

'What, Sir, if my father should wish to call it the dollar sterling?' grinned Roosevelt.

'It's all the same, we are together,' beamed Mr Churchill.

Ten years later, in May of 1943, in the middle of World War II, at a lunch at the British Embassy in Washington, Mr Churchill told his British and American wartime associates, 'I could see small hope for the world unless the United States and the British Commonwealth worked together in fraternal association. I believed that this could take a form which would confer on each advantages without sacrifice. I should like the citizens of each, without losing their present nationality, to be able to come and settle and trade with freedom and equal rights in the territory of the other. There might be a common passport or a special form of passport or visa. There might even be some common form of citizenship, under which citizens of the United States and of the British Commonwealth might enjoy voting privileges after residential qualification and be eligible for public office in the territories of the other, subject, of course, to the laws and institutions there prevailing.'‡

---

* One of the Inns of court where British trial lawyers have their offices.

† In Kenneth Pendar's *Adventure in Diplomacy*, p. 156, he recounts a conversation with W.S.C. eleven years later on the same subject. 'In speaking of an economic currency and eventual common currency for the two countries [Britain and the US], he picked up a pencil and on the back of a scrap of paper drew the £-shaped symbol of the pound sterling with the dollar sign superimposed on it saying, "This is as I see it—the money of the future—the dollar sterling."'

‡ See *The Second World War*, Vol. IV, p. 806.

Although this dream has yet to be realized, he was one step nearer his goal twenty years later, on April 9, 1963, when President John F. Kennedy[§] proclaimed him the first Honorary American Citizen by an Act of the full Congress of the United States.

During sixty-two illustrious years in the House of Commons Winston Churchill's humorous digs, his immortal wit and deadly humour have more than once illumined the contemporary history he has helped to make. 'Chamberlain has a lust for peace,' and 'France though armed to the teeth is pacifist to the core,' will forever illuminate a tragic period in history.

When the terrible events that he foresaw with uncanny prescience finally catapulted him into the Premiership in 1940, he called his military staff and advisers together. It was on the heels of the fall of France and the *Luftwaffe* was poised to strike his 'Island Kingdom.' He listed the grim facts to his dispirited colleagues and growled, 'Gentlemen, we are alone. I must say the moment invigorates ME remarkably.'

On the back of the chair of each of his military chiefs in the underground War Cabinet Room was a name card. All except Mr Churchill's. In front of his place was a square of cardboard. 'Please understand,' it said, 'that there is no depression in this House and we are not interested in the possibilities of defeat. They do not exist. Victoria R.I.' On September 15, 1940, he asked an aide how many Spitfires there were in reserve and was told none. He directed, 'Then we must press forward the attack.' That night he received the news that the RAF had shot down 180 planes, losing under 40, in a battle in the skies which he likened to 'Waterloo . . . on a Sunday.' The tide had turned against the *Luftwaffe*.

Nine years later, on March 31, 1949, after the 'Narzeez' had been smashed, I was invited to tea with Mr and Mrs Churchill at the Ritz Hotel in Boston before Mr Churchill spoke to an audience of the Massachusetts Institute of Technology. Zipped into a pin-striped siren suit giving him the appearance of 'a third hand on a private yacht,' he joined his guests—the late Bernard Baruch, and Harvard's then President, Dr. James Conant and his wife. We sat around a circular table crammed with a complete British tea of plates of buttered scones, sandwiches, pastries, marmalades, tea and rare old whiskies. This particular selection of spirits, produced for Mr Churchill, had been willed to the Massachusetts Institute of Technology by Colonel Edward Green, the son of enormously rich Hetty Green, with the provision that it be used only 'for a very special occasion.' As Mr Churchill took his place at the table he raised a pale-amber glassful of Scotch whisky and toasted, 'This glorious gift, my tea!' Before joining us he had learned that the Americans were erecting a monument in the desert at Alamogordo to those who died in Hiroshima. Swinging around in his chair and fixing us with his unblinking X-ray eyes, he questioned, 'Do the Americans have

§ John Fitzgerald Kennedy, 1917–1963; thirty-fifth President of the US.

a bad conscience because the atom bomb was dropped?' I answered that very many did. Thereupon he proceeded to the defence of the action, referring to the bomb as the 'only deterrent now to the Soviets.' When his son Randolph suggested that saturation bombing was an almost equal horror, Mr Churchill then described in unforgettable words such bombings over Germany, with tears brimming in his extraordinary eyes. At that moment I remembered an account of his mother's visit to Prince Bismarck* in 1893, when she noted, 'His great dog fixed his fierce eyes on mine in so persistent a manner that I became alarmed and thought he was going to spring upon me; but Prince Bismarck reassured me, saying, "He is looking at your eyes because he has not seen any like them."

Mr Churchill went on, 'Tens of thousands of lives were extinguished in one night. Old men, old women, little children, yes, yes—children about to be born—and—and pushie cats.' In spite of his sombre, cumulative listing of the innocent victims of war's savagery, this surprising climax inspired suppressed giggles around the table. Like a flash he turned on us and in deadly earnest explained, 'When I mentioned 'pushie cats' I would not have you think I take them lightly.' (Nor did he take his pigs lightly. 'Dogs look up to men, cats look down on them, but pigs just treat us as equals,' he would say.) It was thus that I learned of the exalted position reserved in his heart for pussy cats—indeed for all animals, fish and fowl—even butterflies. It is perhaps why animal imagery points up so much of his wit and humour.

But it is the broad gauge of that wit and humour that encompassed the grim, majestic, audacious, ironic, sarcastic, derisive, droll, mocking, insinuating, punning, corrosive, contemptuous, iconoclastic, nimble, mordant, self-condemning, self-derisive, disrespectful to himself as well as others—all of it irrepressible. On it he impaled not only his opponents but many a luckless colleague in the House. And there were those healing cracks dropped like depth charges in the middle of tense War Cabinet meetings which inspired the belly laughs that unclenched many a grimly locked jaw and uncreased many a worried countenance.

So instinctive was his gift he seemed sublimely unaware of it. If he were reminded later of some apposite gem he would look in blank amazement. 'The staggering thought,' wrote A. P. Herbert, 'is that this unmatched Parnassian spring is bubbling all the time; the sad thought is that there is not Boswell† with a ready urn to catch, keep and bottle it.'

Long after my first visits to Chartwell I leafed through notes I kept in my little book of that 'unmatched Parnassian spring' that recreated so vividly the climate of that

---

* Prince Otto von Bismarck, 'the Iron Chancellor,' Prussian statesman, 1815–1898; first Chancellor of the German Empire.
† James Boswell, Scottish lawyer; biographer of Dr. Samuel Johnson.

period. Ever since, I have been adding each new Churchillian gem to those earlier ones until they have swelled into a book-size collection.

But that spring bubbled so endlessly for ninety years, and the literary and verbal output and history that inspired it was so immense, that some witticisms are bound to have escaped this urn. I have tried in this collection to exclude all examples that were falsely attributed, though Mr Churchill confessed to as much delight with them as those that were authentic, filing them away in his elephantine memory for re-use. This has made the search for the true sources and his own words an exhilarating pursuit. 'Ear-witness' will designate certain of his witticisms told me by mutual friends. As Mr Churchill went through so many changes of title during his many lives—holding all major Cabinet offices except Secretary of State for Foreign Affairs, and being twice Prime Minister, I shall refer to him throughout the rest of this book as W.S.C.

Kay Halle, Washington, D.C.

A. P. Herbert (Independent Member of Parliament):
Sir Winston Churchill, who, at any time, in any conditions, in any company, on any subject, with never a fault of taste or tact, can make laughter when he wills. And you can't say fairer than that. If he had done nothing else, . . . he could, and would, have made himself famous in this field alone.[*]

Harold Macmillan (Conservative Member of Parliament; Prime Minister, 1957–1963):
Perhaps the most endearing thing about him in private talk, in Cabinet, in the House of Commons, was his Puckish humour, his tremendous sense of fun, and the quick alternation between grave and gay.

Woodrow Wyatt (Labour Member of Parliament):
There are the looks magnanimous, contemptuous, indifferent, very bored, mischievous, sombre, despairing, arrogant. Only one look is missing: the look apologetic. When he gets up to go—the vitality of the House goes with him. It subsides like a reception after the champagne is finished.

Herbert Elliston (Late editor of The Washington Post*):*
Churchill will live if only in his witticisms. And these will be the stock of conversation in all countries for a long time to come. They are as much of a revelation of character as anything he said or did—as much, also, of an influence among men. In wartime they passed by word of mouth all over the world wherever men were struggling with the aggressor and planning a new life in liberty. They lightened the burdens of the dispirited and were quoted as the words of a champion.

Hugh Massingham (Political writer, The Sunday Telegraph*):*
It used to be one of the pleasures of my life to watch him preparing to make a joke at a public meeting. One always knew it was coming. His own laughter began somewhere in the region of his feet. Then a leg would twitch; the bubble of mirth was slowly rising through the body. The stomach would swell; a shoulder, heave. By this time

---

[*] From *Independent Member* by A.P. Herbert, p. 239.

the audience would be convulsed, although it had no idea what the joke was going to be. Meanwhile, the bubble had ascended a little further and had reached the face; the lips were as mobile and expressive as a baby's. The rich, stumbling voice would become even more hesitant. And finally there would be the explosion, the triumphant sentence of ridicule.

President Franklin D. Roosevelt
To a Former Naval Person* (January 31, 1942):
It's fun to be in the same decade with you.

CHURCHILL
Some back the Seer
Others the Statesman
Still others the Soldier
To get the top honours
When no longer here,
And 'Time starts to cheer;
Rightly or wrongly
I'm backing the small boy
Of three score and ten,
Who put out his tongue
At the dread Mountain-den
In the days of the Fear
—I fancy him strongly.

Ralph Hodgson—from 'Flying Scrolls,'
London, 1958

* President Roosevelt's wartime code-name for W.S.C.

THE YEAR
1874

Winston Leonard Spencer Churchill was born prematurely at Blenheim Palace on November 30, 1874, in the thirty-seventh year of Queen Victoria's reign, when men still lived who were born before the French Revolution and had fought against Napoleon. W.S.C.'s American mother, Jennie Jerome, was one-eighth Iroquois Indian.* His father, Lord Randolph Churchill, was the second son of the seventh Duke of Marlborough. Though W.S.C. fought in 1898 in the Sudan in the last great British cavalry charge in which lances were used as weapons, in 1945 he was jointly responsible in principle with President Truman† for dropping the atomic bomb on Japan. In the year of W.S.C.'s birth, the Civil War in America had been over almost ten years. General Ulysses Grant was in his second term as President and Alfred, Lord Tennyson was Poet Laureate of England. Trains, ships and horses were the only means of travel. Electricity, radio, television and telephones were unknown, though eight years later W.S.C.'s father and mother were the first to install electricity in their London home at 28 St. James's Place. The Liberal, William Gladstone, had been Prime Minister for six years before W.S.C.'s birth. In 1874, Benjamin Disraeli became Conservative Prime Minister. From 1851 to 1881 Britain's population rose from 27.5 million to 35 million. The Industrial Revolution brought the drive for expansion and subsequent social reforms. Karl Marx was developing his Socialist philosophy in London from his *Communist Manifesto*. Italy and Germany had each unified. Prince Otto von Bismarck was attempting to quell the Kaiser's ambitions. The French, recovering from the terrible Prussian siege that forced them to a diet of rats, had lost Alsace-Lorraine and suffered the Germans' victory march down the Champs Élysées.

* W.S.C.—¹⁄₁₆ Iroquois Indian. Mother, Jennie Jerome—⅛ Iroquois Indian. Grandmother, Mrs Clara Hall Jerome—¼ Iroquois Indian (wife of Leonard Jerome—Banker, patron of the arts, part owner of *The New York Times*, abolitionist, amateur boxer and explorer, yachtsman and Father of the American Turf). Great-grandmother, Mrs Clarissa Wilcox Hall—½ Iroquois Indian. Great-great-grandmother, Mrs Anna Baker Wilcox—Full Iroquois Indian—b. May 27, 1761; m. in Macedon, N.Y. d. in Macedon, N.Y., December 28, 1813.
† Harry S Truman, 33rd President of the United States, 1945–1953.

CHILDHOOD | 1874-1886

30ᵀᴴ NOVEMBER 1874	W.S.C. born at Blenheim Palace, prematurely.
1876	To Ireland with his father (who served *his* father, the seventh Duke of Marlborough, Viceroy of Ireland, as his Secretary).
FEBRUARY 1880	John Strange Churchill, Winston's brother, born.
28ᵀᴴ APRIL 1880	*New Government, William Gladstone, Liberal Prime Minister,* of whom W.S.C. later wrote, '. . . what gradually made him the most controversial figure of the century was his gift of rousing moral indignation both in himself and in the electorate.'
1881	To St. James's School at Ascot where he was beaten and his health broke.
1882	To Brighton for his weak chest and to a school run by two ladies. Suffered double pneumonia.
24ᵀᴴ JUNE 1885	*New Government, Lord Salisbury, Conservative Prime Minister.* His father, Lord Randolph, became Secretary of State for India, aged thirty-six.
6ᵀᴴ FEBRUARY 1886	*New Government, Gladstone, Liberal Prime Minister.*
3ᴿᴰ AUGUST 1886	*New Government, Lord Salisbury, Conservative Prime Minister.* His father, Lord Randolph, became Chancellor of the Exchequer, aged thirty-seven (and resigned that same year).

SIR WINSTON CHURCHILL AT BLENHEIM PALACE

W.S.C.: At Blenheim I took two very important decisions: to be born and to marry. I am happily content with the decision I took on both those occasions.*

---

* From *A History of the English-Speaking Peoples*.

1876–1879

A ROVING COMMISSION[*]

The Little Lodge was his home in Dublin.

W.S.C.: It was at 'The Little Lodge' I was first menaced with Education. The approach of a sinister figure described as 'the Governess' was announced . . . We toiled each day . . . [When] the Governess was due to arrive . . . I took to the woods . . . Hours passed before I was retrieved . . . We continued to toil every day . . . at . . . figures . . . But the figures were tied into all sorts of tangles and did things to one another which it was extremely difficult to forecast with complete accuracy. You had to say what they did each time they were tied up together . . . In some cases these figures got into debt with one another: you had to borrow one or carry one, and afterwards you had to pay back the one you borrowed.

A ROVING COMMISSION

W.S.C.: My nurse, Mrs Everest, was nervous about the Fenians.[†] I gathered these were wicked people and there was no end to what they would do if they had their way. On one occasion when I was out riding on my donkey, we thought we saw a long dark procession of Fenians approaching. I am sure now it must have been the Rifle Brigade out for a route march. But we were all very much alarmed, particularly the donkey, who expressed his anxiety by kicking. I was thrown off and had concussion of the brain. This was my first introduction to Irish politics!

A ROVING COMMISSION

On a visit to Emo Park outside Dublin as a small child.

W.S.C.: The central point in my memory is a tall white stone tower which we reached after a considerable drive. I was told it had been blown up by Oliver Cromwell. I understood definitely that he had blown up all sorts of things and was therefore a very great man.

---

[*] I have used the title under which I first read the book. In his own country it was published as *My Early Life*. K.H.

[†] Secret Irish revolutionary organization.

1881

His form master at St. James's School led him to an empty classroom and asked him to learn the first declension of the Latin word for table—mensa. The master returned.

W.S.C.: What does 'O table' mean?

Master: 'O table' is the vocative case . . . You would use it in speaking to a table.

W.S.C.: But I never do.

1882

BATTLE

At the end of one school day he lined up with other students to report their day's demerits.

W.S.C.: Nine.

Schoolmistress: Nine—seems even too much for you, Winston.

W.S.C.: The word I used was *nein*, German for no.

AMID THESE STORMS

At school at Brighton, seeing a Punch *cartoon of the American Civil War.*

W.S.C.: First of all, Mr. Punch was against the South, and we had a picture of a fierce young woman, Miss Carolina, about to whip a naked slave, a sort of Uncle Tom, with a kind of scourge which, not being yet myself removed out of the zone of such possibilities, I regarded as undoubtedly severe. I was all for the slave.

---

* Again, this is the American title. In Britain it was published as *Thoughts and Adventures*.

YOUTH | 1887–1895

APRIL **1888**	Entered Harrow, lowest boy in the lowest form.
18TH AUGUST **1892**	*New Government, William Gladstone, Liberal Prime Minister.*
DECEMBER **1892**	Left Harrow. Won Public Schools' Fencing Competition. Fell thirty feet from a tree at Bournemouth. Unconscious for three days, made a slow recovery.
1893	Sent to a crammer in London for six months—where his tutor, Captain James, is said to have concluded, 'That lad couldn't have gone through Harrow, he must have gone under it.'
28TH JUNE **1893**	Entered Royal Military College, Sandhurst, as a cavalry cadet.
3RD MARCH **1894**	*New Government, Lord Rosebery, Liberal Prime Minister.*
DECEMBER **1894**	Passed out of Sandhurst, eight in a class of 150.
24TH JANUARY **1895**	His father, Lord Randolph, died.

1888

A ROVING COMMISSION

W.S.C.: If the reader has ever learned any Latin prose he will know that at quite an early stage one comes across the Ablative Absolute . . . I was often uncertain whether the Ablative Absolute should end in 'e' or 'i' or 'is' or 'ibus', to the correct selection of which great importance was attached. Dr Welldon seemed to be physically pained by a mistake being made in any of these letters. I remember that later on Mr Asquith* used to have just the same sort of look on his face when I sometimes adorned a Cabinet discussion by bringing out one of my few but faithful Latin quotations. It was more than annoyance, it was a pang. Moreover, Headmasters have powers at their disposal with which Prime Ministers have never yet been invested.

---

* Not merely Prime Minister, but one of the leading classical scholars of his generation at Oxford.

1890

LORD RANDOLPH CHURCHILL

At sixteen, in a letter to his mother, Lady Randolph Churchill.
W.S.C.: I am getting terribly low in my finances. You say I never write for love but always for money. I think you are right but remember that you are my banker and who else have I to write to? Please send me 'un peu' [a little].

1892

A ROVING COMMISSION

W.S.C.: I am all for the Public Schools [private schools, in the US] but I do not want to go there again.

A ROVING COMMISSION

After he had fallen from a tree at Bournemouth and ruptured his kidney, his father, Lord Randolph Churchill, brought a surgeon to his son's side.
W.S.C.: But for a year I looked at life around a corner. They made a joke about it in those days at the Carlton Club. 'I hear Randolph's son met with a serious accident. 'Yes, playing a game of Follow my Leader.'—'Well, Randolph is not likely to come to grief in that way!'

1893

A ROVING COMMISSION

On History
W.S.C.: . . . before I went back to school, my father set out to examine me upon it. The period was Charles I. He asked me about the Grand Remonstrance; what did I know about that? I said that in the end the Parliament beat the King and cut his head off. This seemed to me the grandest remonstrance imaginable.

A ROVING COMMISSION

On the subject of mathematics after passing into Sandhurst after three tries.
W.S.C.: Of course I had progressed far beyond vulgar Fractions and the Decimal System. We were arrived in an 'Alice-in-Wonderland' world, at the portals of which stood 'A Quadratic Equation'. This with a strange grimace pointed the way to the Theory of Indices, which again handed on the intruder to the full

rigours of the Binomial Theorem. Further dim chambers lighted by sullen, sulphurous fires were reputed to contain a dragon called the 'Differential Calculus'. But this monster was beyond the bounds appointed by the Civil Service Commissioners who regulated this stage of Pilgrim's heavy journey. We turned aside not indeed to the uplands of the Delectable Mountains,* but into a strange corridor of things like anagrams and acrostics called Sines, Cosines and Tangents. Apparently they were very important, especially when multiplied by each other, or by themselves! They had also this merit—you could learn many of their evolutions off by heart. There was a question in my third and last Examination about these Cosines and Tangents in a highly square-rooted condition which must have been decisive upon the whole of my after life. It was a problem. But luckily I had seen its ugly face only a few days before and recognized it at first sight.

I have never met any of these creatures since . . . I am assured that they are most helpful in engineering, astronomy and things like that. It is very important to build bridges and canals and to comprehend all the stresses and potentialities of matter, to say nothing of counting all the stars and even universes and measuring how far off they are, and foretelling eclipses, the arrival of comets and such like. I am very glad there are quite a number of people born with a gift and a liking for all of this; like great chess-players who play sixteen games at once blindfolded and die quite soon of epilepsy. Serve them right! I hope the Mathematicians, however, are well rewarded. I promise never to blackleg their profession nor take the bread out of their mouths.

and

W.S.C.: I had a feeling once about Mathematics, that I saw it all—Depth beyond Depth was revealed to me—the Byss and the Abyss. I saw, as one might see the transit of Venus—or even the Lord Mayor's Show, a quantity passing through infinity and changing its sign from plus to minus. I saw exactly how it happened and why the tergiversation was inevitable: and how the one step involved all the others. It was like politics. But it was after dinner and I let it go!

---

* From *Pilgrim's Progress*, allegory by John Bunyan, published 1678.

A ROVING COMMISSION
On a career.

W.S.C.: . . . I might have gone into the Church and preached orthodox sermons in a spirit of anxious contradiction to the age. I might have gone into the city and made a fortune. I might have gravitated to the bar and persons might have been hanged through my defence.

A ROVING COMMISSION
On riding.

W.S.C.: I enjoyed the riding-school thoroughly, and got on—and off—as well as most . . . Horses were the greatest of my pleasures at Sandhurst . . . Young men have often been ruined through owning horses, or through backing horses, but never through riding them; unless of course they break their necks, which, taken at a gallop, is a very good death to die.

1894

NEWSPAPER REPORT, THE TIMES
With fellow Sandhurst cadets he protested a ruling that ladies of light virtue and young people be kept from meeting, conversing and refreshing themselves with liquors on the Promenade of the Empire Theatre in Leicester Square. W.S.C. made a speech in the Promenade objecting to the stifling of Britain's freedoms, and wrote a letter to The Times entitled 'Prudes on the Prowl.'
Whereupon Mandell Creighton, the then Bishop of London, wrote to The Times: *'I never expected to see the heir of Marlborough being greeted by a flourish of strumpets.'*

CORRESPONDENT-SOLDIER | 1895–1900

1ST APRIL 1895	Gazetted to the 4th Queen's Own Hussars.
2ND JULY 1895	*New Government, Lord Salisbury, Conservative Unionist Prime Minister.*
NOVEMBER 1895	Visited Cuba to study the fighting between Spain and the Cuban rebels. Wrote first article (published December 6) for the *Daily Graphic*.
1896, 1897	Left for India with the 4th Queen's Own Hussars as a Second Lieutenant; played polo; discovered historians Thomas Macaulay and Edward Gibbon. Active service with Malakand Field Force on the Northwest Frontier. Sent dispatches to the *Daily Telegraph*.
1898	Joined Lord Kitchener's Expedition up the Nile to reconquer the Sudan, with commission to write dispatches for London *Morning Post*.
14TH MARCH 1898	Published first book, *The Story of the Malakand Field Force*, sarcastically referred to as 'A Subaltern's Advice to the Generals.'
2ND SEPTEMBER 1898	Took part in charge of Twenty-first Lancers at Battle of Omdurman.
1ST DECEMBER 1898	Sailed to India to rejoin his regiment.
1899	Returned to India, played polo with winning team, a game he compared to 'thrashing a cobra with a riding crop.' Rejoined 4th Queen's Own Hussars in India. Captained team that won the inter-regiment polo competition, making three of its four goals with right elbow strapped to his side after an accident to shoulder. Resigned commission in the Army to enter politics. Made first political speech to the Primrose League at a Conservative fête at Claverton Manor, near the city of Bath.
JULY 1899	Stood as a Conservative at a by-election at Oldham, and was defeated.
OCTOBER 1899	Went to Boer War in South Africa as war correspondent for the *Morning Post*.
6TH NOVEMBER 1899	Published *The River War*.
15TH NOVEMBER 1899	Captured by Boers two weeks after arrival.
13TH DECEMBER 1899	Escaped from Pretoria into Portuguese East Africa and thence to Durban. Temporarily rejoined Army. Took part in relief of Ladysmith. Visited Ladysmith with his mother, Lady Randolph.
1900	Accepted a commission in South Africa Light Horse.

3ᴿᴰ FEBRUARY 1900	Published *Savrola* in the United States. (English edition published ten days later.)
15ᵀᴴ MAY 1900	Published *London to Ladysmith via Pretoria*.
5ᵀᴴ JUNE 1900	Entered captured Pretoria. Studied Commando operations, which he referred to as 'butcher and run.'

1895

THE WORLD CRISIS, 1911–1914

W.S.C.: In the year 1895 I had the privilege, as a young officer, of being invited to lunch with Sir William Harcourt.* In the course of a conversation in which I took, I fear, none too modest a share, I asked the question, 'What will happen then?' 'My dear Winston,' replied the old Victorian statesman, 'the experiences of a long life have convinced me that nothing ever happens.' Since that moment, as it seems to me, nothing has ever ceased happening.

A ROVING COMMISSION

As a war-correspondent for the Daily Graphic *in Cuba.*
W.S.C.: I was soon awakened by firing . . . A bullet ripped through the hatch of our hut; another wounded an orderly just outside. I should have been glad to get out of my hammock and lie on the ground. However, as no one else made a move, I thought it more becoming to stay where I was. I fortified myself by dwelling on the fact that the Spanish officer whose hammock was slung between me and the enemy's fire was a man of substantial physique; indeed one might almost have called him fat. I have never been prejudiced against fat men . . . Gradually I dropped asleep.

1896

A ROVING COMMISSION

On religion.
W.S.C.: My various readings . . . led me to ask myself questions about religion. Hitherto I had dutifully accepted everything I had

---

* Sir William Harcourt, statesman; Home Secretary, 1880–1885; Chancellor of the Exchequer, 1886, 1892–1894, 1894–1895.

been told . . . I had always had to go once a week to Church . . . All this was very good. I accumulated in those years so fine a surplus in the Bank of Observance that I have been drawing confidently upon it ever since. Weddings, christenings, and funerals have brought in a steady annual income, and I have never made too close enquiries about the state of my account. It might well even be that I should find an overdraft.

A ROVING COMMISSION

At a dinner for the Prince of Wales, later Edward VII.
W.S.C.: I realized that I must be on my best behaviour—punctual, subdued, reserved—in short, display all the qualities with which I am least endowed.

A ROVING COMMISSION

On wrenching his shoulder while disembarking at the Sassoon Dock in Bombay Harbour.
W.S.C.: I scrambled up all right, made a few remarks of a general character, mostly beginning with the earlier letters of the alphabet.

A ROVING COMMISSION

As a young Lieutenant of twenty-one gazetted to the Fourth Queen's Own Hussars in India, being entertained by Lord Sandhurst, the Governor of Bombay.
W.S.C.: We . . . enjoyed a banquet of glitter, pomp and iced champagne . . . His Excellency, after the health of the Queen Empress had been drunk and dinner was over, was good enough to ask my opinion upon several matters, and considering the magnificent character of his hospitality, I thought it would be unbecoming in me not to reply fully. I have forgotten the particular points of British and Indian affairs upon which he sought my counsel: all I can remember is that I responded generously. There were indeed moments when he seemed willing to impart his views; but I thought it would be ungracious to put him to so much trouble; and he very readily subsided.

A ROVING COMMISSION

On drink. With The Malakand Field Force in India.

W.S.C.: Wishing to fit myself for active service conditions I overcame the ordinary weakness of the flesh. By the end of five days I had completely overcome my repugnance to the taste of whisky. Nor was this a momentary acquirement. On the contrary the ground I gained in those days I have firmly entrenched, and held throughout my whole life. Once one got the knack of it, the very repulsion from the flavour developed an attraction of its own, and to this day, although I have always practised true temperance, I have never shrunk when occasion warranted it from the main basic standing refreshment of the white officer in the East.

1897 A ROVING COMMISSION

His first political speech was given to the Conservative Primrose League at Claverton Manor, situated in a park near Bath, now serving as the American Museum in Britain. Although he had been allotted only fifteen minutes to speak, he planned to use twenty-five.

W.S.C.: One must not yield too easily to the weaknesses of audiences. There they were; what could they do? They had asked for it and they must have it.

also

SPEECH

In that first speech.

W.S.C.: England would gain far more from the rising tide of Tory democracy than from the dried-up drain-pipe of Radicalism.

1898 A ROVING COMMISSION

On the eve of joining the 20,000 British and Egyptian forces under Lord Kitchener* fighting in the Sudan to break the hold of the Moslem Dervishes, followers of the Mahdi led by his successor, the Khalifa.

W.S.C.: The President of the Physical Research Society extracted

---

* Horatio Herbert Kitchener, 1st Earl Kitchener of Khartoum, 1850–1916; Sirdar (Commander in Chief) of the British forces in Egypt.

rather unseasonably a promise from me after dinner to 'communicate' with him, should anything unfortunate occur.

EAR-WITNESS

In the Battle of Omdurman in the Sudan involving 60,000 lance-laden Moslem Dervishes (who lost 10,000 dead, 16,000 wounded and 5,000 prisoners while British and Egyptian losses were 482 killed and wounded), finding himself in the midst of a battle of whirling Dervishes.

W.S.C.: (*shouting to a fellow officer*): This is no place for Christians! *also*

A ROVING COMMISSION

Looking back on the cavalry charge at Omdurman—the last important such military charge of recent times.

W.S.C.: It is a shame that war should have flung all this aside in its greedy, base, opportunist march, and should turn instead to chemists in spectacles and chauffeurs pulling levers of airplanes or machine guns.

EAR-WITNESS

Glenway Wescott says on an English country weekend, W.S.C. and Somerset Maugham took a walk together.

W.S.C.: Maugham, I've been observing you and listening to you. You are intelligent, you express yourself well. You will go far. So shall I. Now I would like to have an understanding with you. If you will not talk against me, I will not talk against you.

1899   GREAT CONTEMPORARIES

Dining in Calcutta with the British Viceroy, Lord Curzon, one of his mother's friends.

Lord Curzon: I presume it will not be long before we hear you declaim in the House of Commons?

W.S.C.: (*after thought*): Though greatly hampered by inability to compose at the rate necessary for public speaking, I was strongly of the same opinion myself.

A ROVING COMMISSION

British Winston Churchill to American Winston Churchill.

London, 7 June 1899

Mr Winston Churchill presents his compliments to Mr Winston Churchill, and begs to draw his attention to a matter which concerns them both. He has learnt from the Press notices that Mr Winston Churchill proposes to bring out another novel, entitled *Richard Carvel*, which is certain to have a considerable sale both in England and America. Mr Winston Churchill is also the author of a novel now being published in serial form in *Macmillan's Magazine*, and for which he anticipates some sale both in England and America. He also proposes to publish on the 1st of October another military chronicle on the Soudan War. He has no doubt that Mr Winston Churchill will recognize from his letter—if indeed by no other means—that there is grave danger of his works being mistaken for those of Mr Winston Churchill. He feels sure that Mr Winston Churchill desires this as little as he does himself. In future to avoid mistakes as far as possible, Mr Winston Churchill has decided to sign all published articles, stories, or other works, 'Winston Spencer Churchill', and not 'Winston Churchill' as formerly. He trusts that this arrangement will commend itself to Mr Winston Churchill, and he ventures to suggest, with a view to preventing further confusion which may arise out of this extraordinary coincidence, that both Mr Winston Churchill and Mr Winston Churchill should insert a short note in their respective publications explaining to the public which are the works of Mr Winston Churchill and which those of Mr Winston Churchill. The text of this note might form a subject for future discussion if Mr Winston Churchill agrees with Mr Winston Churchill upon the style and success of his works, which are always brought to his notice whether in magazine or book form, and he trusts that Mr Winston Churchill has derived equal pleasure from any work of his that may have attracted his attention.

Windsor, Vermont

June 21, 1899

Mr Winston Churchill is extremely grateful to Mr Winston Churchill for bringing forward a subject which has given Mr Winston Churchill much anxiety. Mr Winston Churchill appreciates the courtesy of Mr Winston Churchill in adopting the name of 'Winston Spencer Churchill' in his books, articles, etc. Mr Winston Churchill makes haste to add that, had he possessed any other names, he would certainly have adopted one of them. The writings of Mr Winston Spencer Churchill (henceforth so called) have been brought to Mr Winston Churchill's notice since the publication of his first story in the 'Century.' It did not seem then to Mr Winston Churchill that the works of Mr Winston Spencer Churchill would conflict in any way with his own attempts at fiction.

The proposal of Mr Winston Spencer Churchill to affix a note to the separate writings of Mr Winston Spencer Churchill and Mr Winston Churchill—the text of which is to be agreed on between them—is quite acceptable to Mr Winston Churchill. If Mr Winston Spencer Churchill will do him the favour of drawing up this note, there is little doubt that Mr Winston Churchill will acquiesce in its particulars.

Mr Winston Churchill, moreover, is about to ask the opinion of his friends and of his publishers as to the advisability of inserting the words 'The American,' after his name on the title-page of his books. Should this seem wise to them, he will request his publishers to make the change in future editions.

Mr Winston Churchill will take the liberty of sending Mr Winston Spencer Churchill copies of the two novels he has written. He has a high admiration for the works of Mr Winston Spencer Churchill and is looking forward with pleasure to reading *Savrola*.

and

The two Churchills still caused a certain confusion, especially after the American honoured the Englishman with a banquet.

W.S.C.: When a year later I visited Boston, Mr Winston Churchill was the first to welcome me. He entertained me at a very gay banquet of young men, and we made each other complimentary speeches. Some confusion however persisted; all my mails were sent to his address and the bill for the dinner came in to me. I need not say that both these errors were speedily redressed.

SPEECH

Electioneering.

Walter Runciman (*W.S.C.'s Liberal opponent*): I have not been a swashbuckler around the world.

Candidate W.S.C. (*Conservative*): And I do not belong to a Radical Party composed of prigs, prudes and faddists.

A ROVING COMMISSION

After a defeat in which he lost by 1,300 votes.[*]

W.S.C.: I returned to London with those feelings of deflation which a bottle of champagne or even soda water represents when it is half emptied and left uncorked for a night.

A ROVING COMMISSION

Sailing on the 'Dunottar Castle' as the Morning Post's war correspondent to the Boer War with Sir Redvers Buller, Commander-in-Chief of the battle forces, on board.

W.S.C.: Buller was a characteristic British personality. He looked stolid. He said little, and what he said was obscure . . . He had shown himself a brave and skilful officer in his youth and . . . was regarded as a very sensible soldier . . . Certainly he was a man of considerable scale. He plodded on from blunder to blunder and from one disaster to another, without losing either the regard of his country or the trust of his troops, to whose feeding as well as his own he paid serious attention.

A ROVING COMMISSION

From East London to Durban in South Africa in an Antarctic gale on a 150-ton steamer.

W.S.C.: . . . I thought the little ship would be overwhelmed amid the enormous waves or else be cast away upon the rocks which showed their black teeth . . . But all these misgivings were quickly dispelled by the most appalling paroxysms of seasickness . . . I remembered that Titus Oates[†] lived in good health for many years

---

[*] G. W. Steevens reporting W.S.C.'s earliest efforts on the platform: '. . . he talks and talks and you can hardly tell when he leaves off quoting his one idol Macaulay and begins his other, Winston Churchill.'
[†] Titus Oates, English fabricator of a supposed Catholic Plot to massacre Protestants, burn London and assassinate the King. Though pilloried, flogged and imprisoned for life, he was pardoned when William of Orange ascended to the throne.

after his prodigious floggings, and upon this reflection, combined with a firm trust that Providence would do whatever was best, were founded such hopes as I could still retain.

NEWSPAPER REPORT, MANCHESTER GUARDIAN

On the armoured train from Estcourt to Chieveley Junction on which he was travelling as a war correspondent for the Morning Post, *when ambushed by the Boers and summoned to surrender by a horseman who may have been Louis Botha.**

W.S.C.: Keep cool, men! This will be interesting for my paper!

also

EAR-WITNESS

After the armoured car was derailed, injuring several travellers, the civilian engineer suffered a shrapnel wound.

W.S.C.: *(to the choleric engineer)*: Be calm! Nobody is ever wounded twice on the same day.

LONDON TO LADYSMITH VIA PRETORIA

On his failure to bribe the sentries to help him to escape.

W.S.C.: The truth is that the bribery market in the Transvaal has been spoiled by the millionaires. I could not afford with my slender resources to insult them [the sentries] heavily enough.

also

His letter to Mr. de Souza, Secretary of War, South African Republic, from the States Model Schools Prison.

10 December 1899

Sir,

I have the honour to inform you that as I do not consider that your government have any right to detain me as a military prisoner, I have decided to escape from your custody. I have every confidence

---

* Louis Botha, South African soldier-statesman; first Prime Minister of Union of South Africa. 1910–1919.

† Over a decade later W.S.C. recommended the Albert Medal for the engineer and fireman of the train.

in the arrangements I have made with my friends outside, and I do not therefore expect to have another opportunity of seeing you. I therefore take this occasion to observe that I consider your treatment of prisoners is correct and humane, and that I see no grounds for complaint. When I return to the British lines I will make a public statement to this effect. I have also to thank you personally for your civility to me, and to express the hope that we may meet again at Pretoria before very long, and under different circumstances. Regretting that I am unable to bid you a more ceremonious or a personal farewell.

I have the honour to be, Sir, Your most obedient servant,
Winston Churchill
later

EAR-WITNESS

Forty-seven years later, in November, 1946, at a White House dinner with President Truman, Jan Smuts[*], who had been the senior legal official of the South African Republic, told of receiving a letter from W.S.C. protesting his capture as a war correspondent, and asking for release from prison. But he escaped before General Smuts could comply. Later they met and became fast friends.*

W.S.C.: Because you were so slow I made nine thousand pounds!
General Smuts: Nine thousand pounds!
W.S.C.: That's what I was paid for the story of my escape.

EAR-WITNESS

After his capture in the Boer War he joined the South African Light Horse and grew a moustache. Before leaving for South Africa a friend of his mother told him she neither cared for his politics nor his moustache.

W.S.C.: Madame, I see no earthly reason why you should come in contact with either.[†]

---

[*] Jan Christian Smuts, Boer general, 1900–1902; Prime Minister of South Africa; 1919–1924 and 1939–1948; was made a British field marshal in 1941, on Churchill's recommendation.
[†] Lady Lytton once said, 'The first time you meet Winston you see all his faults, and the rest of your life you spend in discovering his virtues.'

A ROVING COMMISSION

During the relief of Ladysmith near Mt. Spion Kop.

W.S.C.: The night was chilly. Colonel Byng [later Lord Byng of Vimy] and I shared a blanket. When he turned over I was in the cold. When I turned over I pulled the blanket off him and he objected. He was the Colonel. It was not a good arrangement. I was glad when morning came.

A ROVING COMMISSION

His compassion for the vanquished.

W.S.C.: I have always urged fighting wars and other contentions with might and main till overwhelming victory, and then offering the hand of friendship to the vanquished. Thus, I have always been against the Pacifists during the quarrel, and against the Jingoes at its close. Many years after this South African incident, Lord Birkenhead* mentioned to me a Latin quotation which seems to embody this idea extremely well. *Parcere subjectis et debellare superbos*†, which he translated finely, 'Spare the conquered and war down the proud'. I seem to have come very near achieving this thought by my own untutored reflections. The Romans have often forestalled many of my best ideas, and I must concede to them the patent rights in this maxim.

and

W.S.C.: I was once asked to devise an inscription for a monument in France. I wrote, 'In war, Resolution. In defeat, Defiance. In victory, Magnanimity. In peace, Goodwill'. The inscription was not accepted. It is all the fault of the human brain being made in two lobes, only one of which does any thinking, so that we are all right-handed or left-handed; whereas, if we were properly constructed, we should use our right and left hands with equal force and skill according to circumstances. As it is, those who can win a war well can rarely make a good peace, and those who could make a good peace would never have won the war. It would perhaps be pressing the argument too far to suggest that I could do both.

---

* F. E. Smith, first Earl of Birkenhead; Lord Chancellor, 1919–1922; Secretary of State for India, 1924–1928; a close friend of Churchill.
† Virgil, *Aeneid*, Book VI: 'The Roman's Duty'.

NEWSPAPER REPORT, BOER WAR—A DISPATCH TO THE LONDON MORNING POST

On guerrilla warfare.

W.S.C.: The individual Boer, mounted in suitable country, is worth three to five regular soldiers . . . There is plenty of room here for a quarter of a million men . . .more irregular corps are wanted. Are the gentlemen of England fox hunting? Why not a Leicestershire Light Horse?

LONDON TO LADYSMITH VIA PRETORIA

On refusing to be inoculated against enteric fever.

W.S.C.: But if they will invent a system of inoculation against bullet wounds I will hasten to submit myself.

and

On the fortunes of war.

W.S.C.: . . .The bullet is brutally indiscriminating, and before it the brain of a hero or the quarters of a horse stand exactly the same chance to the vertical square inch.

IAN HAMILTON'S MARCH

Failing to learn of an intended plan of campaign from senior officers.

W.S.C.: It is wonderful how well men can keep secrets they have not been told.

IAN HAMILTON'S MARCH

On his decision to travel to Cape Town.

W.S.C.: At Stormberg I changed my mind, or, rather—for it comes to the same thing and sounds better—I made it up.

IAN HAMILTON'S MARCH

On the position of a war correspondent.

W.S.C.: 'All the danger of war and one-half per cent the glory': such is our motto, and that is the reason why we expect large salaries.

CONSERVATIVE, THEN LIBERAL, POLITICIAN | 1900–1914

Anecdotes are the gleaming toys of House of Commons history.
—Winston S. Churchill

JULY 1900	Returned to England a hero. Eleven different Constituencies wanted him to stand for them.
JULY 1900	His mother married her second husband—George Cornwallis-West.
1ST OCTOBER 1900	Elected Conservative Member of Parliament for Oldham in General Election.
12TH OCTOBER 1900	Published *Ian Hamilton's March*.
16TH DECEMBER 1900	Gave first lecture in New York City on American tour which earned him £10,000. Introduced by Mark Twain, 'By his father, he is an Englishman; by his mother, an American. Behold the perfect man.'
1901	Liberals were in Opposition, the Parliamentary Labour Party a year old. Queen Victoria died. United States: President William McKinley assassinated, Theodore Roosevelt became President.
JANUARY 1901	W.S.C. took his seat in Parliament.
18TH FEBRUARY 1901	Made his maiden speech.
13TH MAY 1901	Attacked the Army Estimates.
12TH JULY 1902	*New Government, Arthur Balfour, Conservative* [Unionist] *Prime Minister.*
28TH MAY 1903	Attacked Joseph Chamberlain (Colonial Secretary) on his proposed policy of Protection. Published *Mr Broderick's Army*.
21ST MARCH 1904	A large number of Unionists (Conservatives) left the Chamber of the House when W.S.C. rose to speak.
31ST MAY 1904	After growing disagreement with the Balfour Government over Joseph Chamberlain's proposed policy of Protection, W.S.C. crossed the Floor of the House to join the Liberal Party.
5TH DECEMBER 1905	*New Government, Sir Henry Campbell-Bannerman, Liberal Prime Minister.*

2ND JANUARY 1906	Published *Lord Randolph Churchill*, acclaimed by Lord Rosebery 'One of the first dozen, perhaps the first half dozen biographies in the language.' Elected Liberal Member of Parliament for North-West Manchester in General Election. First political office, Under-Secretary of State for the Colonies.
1907	Sworn in as a Privy Councillor. Toured Cyprus, and East Africa (British East Africa, now Kenya; Uganda; Sudan; and Egypt) as Under-Secretary of State for the Colonies.
MARCH 1908	Published *My African Journey*.
8TH APRIL 1908	*New Government, Herbert H. Asquith, Liberal Prime Minister.*
24TH APRIL 1908	Joined Asquith's Cabinet as President of the Board of Trade. Defeated at Manchester in by-election caused by his taking office.
23RD MAY 1908	Elected to represent Dundee.
12TH SEPTEMBER 1908	Married Miss Clementine Hozier at St. Margaret's Church, Westminster.
1909	First daughter, Diana, born July 11.
SEPTEMBER 1909	Attended manoeuvres of the German Army near Würzburg and examined German labour exchanges.
NOVEMBER 1909	Published *Liberalism and the Social Problem*.
JANUARY 1910	Published *The People's Rights*. Re-elected Liberal Member for Dundee. Appointed Home Secretary. Sent force of Metropolitan Police (troops held in reserve) to avoid bloodshed during Welsh coal mining strike called 'Tonypandy incident,' which won him unpopularity with Trade Unions. Re-elected Liberal Member for Dundee.
1910–11	Leading advocate of David Lloyd George's 'People's Budget'. Proposed increasing income tax to level inequities of wealth and to finance social welfare. House of Lords threw out Budget. Prime Minister Asquith threatened to swamp House of Lords with 400 more Liberal-minded peers. Bill passed limiting veto power of Lords. W.S.C. fought against veto of the House of Lords. Played leading role in employment opportunities of Labour Exchanges and establishment of impartial trade boards for fixing more equitable rates of pay, hours, old age pensions and sickness insurance.
3RD JANUARY 1911	As Home Secretary paid surprise visit to the 'Battle of Sidney Street,' where police and sixty of the Scots Guard battled two anarchist assassins in an East End House on Sidney Street.
28TH MAY 1911	Son Randolph born.
AUGUST 1911	Called out the military on occasion of a railway strike.

13TH AUGUST 1911	Became a member of the Committee of Imperial Defence and circulated to the Cabinet an uncannily prophetic memorandum on 'Military Aspects of the Continental Problem,' which proved to be correct, though called 'silly' at the time by the Generals.
25TH OCTOBER 1911	Became First Lord of the Admiralty. Turned Navy from coal to oil burning and advanced from 13.5-inch gun to the 15-inch.
1912	Modernized Navy and set up Royal Naval Flying Corps, later the Fleet Air Arm. Learned to fly. Instructed Naval engineers to explore idea of designing an armoured car to scale trenches, later called a tank or 'Winston's folly.'
1913	Elected an Elder Brother of Trinity House, ancient British organization established 'for relief of and increase and augmentation of shipping of this realm of England.'
17TH JUNE 1914	Secured Parliamentary approval to buy control of Persian oil to supply naval ships newly converted to oil from coal.
28TH JUNE 1914	Assassination of Austrian Archduke Franz Ferdinand at Sarajevo. Preoccupation with Home Rule for Ireland diverted British attention from the Balkan crisis.
JULY 1914	Prevented dispersal of Home Fleet after practice mobilization.
1ST AUGUST 1914	Ordered mobilization of Fleet with approval of the Prime Minister; sent North Sea squadrons to battle stations.
MARCH–APRIL 1915	Naval and military operations against the Turkish Narrows (Gallipoli).
MAY 1915	Initially successful, but stalled, largely due to the fault of commanders on the spot. However, Churchill held responsible. After the set back at Gallipoli, resigned as First Lord of the Admiralty. Appointed Chancellor of the Duchy of Lancaster, in Prime Minister Asquith's new Coalition Government.
11TH NOVEMBER 1915	Resigned to join Army in France.
1916	Served with Royal Scots Fusiliers. Returned to politics in England.
1917	Appointed Minister of Munitions.

1900   EAR-WITNESS

In Chicago on a speaking tour after the Boer War. English-Irish relations were at their worst low. Discovering the balconies filled with Irish-born, pro-Boer workingmen who began shouting abuse, he changed gears in describing a Boer War action.

W.S.C.: And in this desperate situation the Dublin Fusiliers arrived, trumpeters sounded the charge and the enemy were swept from the field. [Suddenly the balconies grew silent, then thundered with cheers.]

A ROVING COMMISSION

On the first money he earned from an American lecture tour, after escaping from a Boer prison camp.

W.S.C.: I sent my ten thousand pounds to my father's old friend, Sir Ernest Cassel,* with the instruction, 'Feed my sheep'. He fed the sheep with great prudence. They did not multiply fast, but they fattened steadily, and none of them ever died. Indeed from year to year they had a few lambs; but these were not numerous enough for me to live upon. I had every year to eat a sheep or two as well; so gradually my flock grew smaller, until in a few years it was almost entirely devoured. Nevertheless, while it lasted, I had no care.

SAVROLA

From his only novel, Savrola, *a pseudo-biographical romance set in an imaginary kingdom, written when he was twenty-three.*

W.S.C.: It is hard, if not impossible, to snub a beautiful woman; they remain beautiful and the rebuke recoils.

and

W.S.C.: Amid the smoke he saw his peroration a high thought and a fine simile, expressed in that correct diction which is comprehensible even to the most illiterate, and appeals even to the simplest . . .

His ideas began to take the form of words to groups themselves into sentences: he murmured to himself; the rhythm of his own language swayed him: instinctively he alliterated . . .

and

W.S.C.: The room, in the grey light with its half-empty glasses and full ashtrays, looked like a woman, no longer young, surprised by

---

* Sir Ernest Cassel, 1852–1921; banker; philanthropist; father of Lady Louis Mountbatten.

THE AUTHOR OF
SAVROLA IN 1900

an unsympathetic dawn in the meretricious paints and pomps of
the previous night.

THE RIVER WAR

Commenting on Sir Evelyn Baring's[*] and General Gordon's[†] desire to use
Zobeir Pasha to hold the tribes to the north from the Mahdi. They could not be
sure that he could be relied on to rescue the Egyptian garrisons in the Sudan.
W.S.C.: The Pasha was vile but indispensable.

THE RIVER WAR

On religious fanaticism.

W.S.C.: What the horn is to the rhinoceros, what the sting is to the wasp, the Mohammedan faith was to the Arabs of the Soudan—a faculty of offence or defence.

THE RIVER WAR

On the rejoicing of the Mahdi's wives after his death.

W.S.C.: Since they were henceforth to be doomed to an enforced and inviolable chastity, the cause of their satisfaction is as obscure as its manifestation was unnatural.

THE RIVER WAR

On the Egyptian soldiers of the 1880s.

W.S.C.: It is beyond dispute that the Egyptian is not a fighting animal.

THE RIVER WAR

On the Sudanese soldier.

W.S.C.: At once slovenly and uxorious, he detested his drills and loved his wives with equal earnestness.

THE RIVER WAR

On the town of Suakin.

W.S.C.: The numerous graves of Greek traders—a study of whose epitaphs may conveniently refresh a classical education—protest that the climate of the island is pestilential.

---

* Sir Evelyn Baring, 1841–1917, first Earl of Cromer; British Agent and Consul-General 'advising' the British-occupied Egyptian Government; known as 'Sir Over Baring'. Of his position, Churchill wrote, 'His status was indefinite; he might be nothing; he was in fact everything.'

† Charles George Gordon, 'Chinese Gordon', 1833–1885, British soldier, humanitarian, and enemy of slavery. Took part in capture of Peking, 1860–1862; Governor of Equatorial Africa (–); and Governor General of the Sudan, 1877–1880. Killed by the Mahdi's soldiers during the evacuation of the Sudan. Because the relief expedition of Khartoum arrived two days too late, Prime Minister Gladstone was widely blamed for his death.

THE RIVER WAR

On the building of the Desert Railway in the Sudan.

W.S.C.: From the growing workshops at Wadi Halfa the continued clatter and clang of hammers and the black smoke of manufacture rose to the African sky. The malodorous incense of civilization was offered to the startled gods of Egypt.

THE RIVER WAR

Comparing American and British railway engines in the Sudan.

W.S.C.: The American engines were sooner delivered and £1,000 cheaper. They broke down rarely . . . The fact that they were considerably faster soon won them a good reputation on the railway, and the soldier who travelled to the front was as anxious to avoid his country's locomotives as to preserve its honour.

THE RIVER WAR

On building a great dam at Aswan to irrigate the desert, a plan which had been opposed because the ancient Egyptian temples of Abu Simbel along the Nile would be submerged.

W.S.C.: Because a few persons whose functions are far removed from those which may benefit mankind—profitless chippers of stone, rummagers in the dust-heaps of the past—have raised an outcry . . . the sacrifice of water—the lifeblood of Egypt—is being offered up. The State must struggle and the people starve, in order that professors may exult and tourists find some space on which to scratch their names.

THE RIVER WAR

W.S.C.: He spoke nothing but Arabic: I only one word of that language. Still we conversed fluently. By opening and shutting my mouth and pointing to my stomach, I excited his curiosity, if not his wonder. Then I employed the one and indispensable Arabic word 'Baksheesh!'* After that all difficulties melted away.

---

* A hand-out.

THE RIVER WAR

On his capture of an Arab he thought to be an enemy who turned out to be an Arab employed by British intelligence.

W.S.C.: Naturally several young gentlemen saw fit to be facetious on the subject. Mr Lionel James, *Reuters* correspondent, even proposed to telegraph some account of this noteworthy capture. But I prevailed on him not to do so, having a detestation of publicity.

THE RIVER WAR

Urging that all soldiers should use pistols in war.

W.S.C.: It will be said that the troopers, getting flurried, would shoot each other. That is very likely. A certain loss of life is inseparable from war, and it makes little difference whether a man is shot by his own side or cut down by the other. But even the rawest recruit in the moment of extreme agitation has a distinct preference for shooting his enemies rather than his friends.

THE RIVER WAR

On honours and decorations after a war.

W.S.C.: The fountain of honour is of notoriously uncertain flow. There are occasions when it throws abundant waters high into the air, and all the crowd are bathed in the invigorating flood. There are other seasons when a solitary jet, passing over expectant heads, strikes some obscure individual standing afar off, to his own intense astonishment no less than of those who have watched his actions. And there are also periods . . . when the spout gives forth nothing— not even to those who suck assiduously.

The men who managed the reconquest of the Soudan were from the very first determined that, although the Ancient Egyptians compelled the Israelites to make bricks without straw, their descendants should not persuade British officers to make war without medals.

1901

A ROVING COMMISSION

On his maiden speech, February 18.

W.S.C.: I learned that . . . Lloyd George* . . . had a moderately phrased amendment . . . but whether he would move it was not certain . . . I gathered that I could . . . have the opportunity of following him . . . I . . . came with a quiverful of arrows of different patterns and sizes, some of which I hoped would hit the target.

The hour arrived . . . Mr Lloyd George . . . soon became animated and even violent . . . I constructed in succession sentence after sentence to hook on with after he should sit down. Each . . . became . . . obsolete. A sense of alarm and even despair crept across me . . . Then Mr [Thomas Gibson] Bowles [the member sitting next to him] whispered 'You might say "instead of making his violent speech without moving his moderate amendment, he had better have moved his moderate amendment without making his violent speech" . . .'

I was up before I knew it, and reciting Tommy Bowles's rescuing sentence. It won a general cheer . . . I could already see the shore . . . till I could scramble up the beach, breathless physically, dripping metaphorically, but safe . . . The usual restoratives were applied and I sat in a comfortable coma till I was strong enough to go home.

A ROVING COMMISSION

Later that day, on meeting Lloyd George in the House of Commons Smoking Room.

Lloyd George: Judging from your sentiments you are standing against the Light.

W.S.C.: (*who had been attacking his own Conservative Party's stereotyped attitude toward the Boer War*): You take a singularly detached view of the British Empire.

HOUSE OF COMMONS

On the clever phrase Thomas Bowles whispered to him for his maiden speech.

* David Lloyd George, 1863–1945; Liberal statesman; Prime Minister, 1916–1922.

W.S.C.: It is difficult to avoid the conclusion that the moderation of the Amendment was the moderation of the hon. Member's political friends and leaders, and that the bitterness of his speech is all his own.

HOUSE OF COMMONS

Responding in the House of Commons to Colonel William Kenyon-Slaney, who had called him a traitor.

W.S.C.: I have noticed when political controversy becomes excited, persons of choleric dispositions and limited intelligences are apt to become rude. If I was a traitor, at any rate I was fighting the Boers in South Africa when Kenyon-Slaney was slandering them at home. I had the honour of serving in the field for our country while this gallant fire-eating Colonel was content to 'kill Kruger with his mouth'* in the comfortable security of England.

AMID THESE STORMS

On Christianity

W.S.C.: . . . this . . . was only a single instance of our duty to preserve the structure of humane, enlightened, Christian society. Once the downward steps are taken, once one's moral and intellectual feet slipped upon the slope of plausible indulgence, there would be found no halting-place short of a general Paganism and Hedonism, possibly agreeable from time to time in this world of fleeting trials and choices.

AMID THESE STORMS

Endorsing Pears Soap.

W.S.C.: Englishmen and Americans are divided by an ocean of salt water but united by a bath tub of fresh water and soap.

---

* Stephanus J. P. Kruger, 1825–1904; President of Transvaal, 1883–1900; known as 'Oom [Uncle] Paul'. The reference is to Kipling's lines:
  'When you've shouted "Rule Britannia", when you've sung "God save the Queen"
  'When you've finished killing Kruger with your mouth . . .'

1902

The editor of the Morning Post *allowed him to look over one of his speeches before it went to press, and was startled when W.S.C. struck out the word 'Cheers' at the end of the quotation and substituted, 'Loud and prolonged applause.'*

EAR-WITNESS

On the difference between a candidate and a Member of Parliament.
W.S.C.: One stands for a place—the other sits for it.

EAR-WITNESS

On politics.
W.S.C.: He is asked to stand, he wants to sit and he is expected to lie.
and
Q.: Mr. Churchill, what brought you into politics?
W.S.C.: Ambition.
Q.: What keeps you there?
W.S.C.: Anger.
At a later press conference.
Q: What are the desirable qualifications for any young man who wishes to become a politician?
W.S.C.: It is the ability to foretell what is going to happen tomorrow, next week, next month, and next year—and to have the ability afterwards to explain why it didn't happen.
and
W.S.C.: Never stand so high upon a principle that you cannot lower it to suit the circumstances.
and
Q.: Do politics mean more to you than any other pursuit?
W.S.C.: Politics are almost as exciting as war and quite as dangerous.
Q.: Even with the new rifle?
W.S.C.: Well, in war you can only be killed once, but in politics many times.
and
W.S.C.: Politics is a profession without any superannuation scheme. Till you are 60 you are a 'young man of promise'. In the sixties you

are in your noon-day prime. In the seventies you begin to be an elder statesman, and at 80 or thereafter, if you live so long, they come to carry you in a bath-chair to the exercise of the highest responsibilities.

1903 · EAR-WITNESS

W.S.C., with Lord Hugh Cecil, mobilized rebellious fellow back-benchers into a group called 'The Hughlighans' (named after Lord Hugh) to discuss issues, wine and food. This convivial group of House of Commons independents resisted tariff reform and dared to move against the stream.

W.S.C. · (*on their credo*): We shall dine first and consider our position afterwards. It shall be High Imperialism nourished by a devilled sardine.

A ROVING COMMISSION

On Joseph Chamberlain* who spoke in his behalf when he stood for Oldham in July, 1899 and lost.

W.S.C.: He loved the roar of the multitude, and with my father could always say, 'I have never feared the English Democracy'. The blood mantled in his cheek, and his eye as it caught mine twinkled with pure enjoyment. I must explain that in those days we had a real political democracy, led by a hierarchy of statesmen, and not a fluid mass distracted by newspapers.

EAR-WITNESS

When Joseph Chamberlain scuttled historic Free Trade principles in favour of Birmingham protection.

W.S.C.: Mr Chamberlain loves the working man, he loves to see him work.

---

* Joseph Chamberlain, 1836–1914; British statesman; leader of Liberal Unionists in Parliament; father of Austen and Neville Chamberlain.

HOUSE OF COMMONS
On the danger of a Tariff lobby in politics.
W.S.C.: A new Party will arise like perhaps the Republican Party of the United States of America—rich, materialist, and secular—whose opinion will turn on tariffs, and who will cause the lobbies to be crowded with the touts of protected industries.

HOUSE OF COMMONS
On his growing discontent with his Tory colleagues.
W.S.C.: They are a class of right honourable Gentlemen—all good men, all honest men—who are ready to make great sacrifices for their opinions, but they have no opinions. They are ready to die for the truth, if they only knew what the truth was.

1905

EAR-WITNESS
When he changed to the Liberal Party in 1904 over Army Reform and Free Trade, he was called the 'Blenheim rat': (The Blenheim spaniel, named after the Churchill family palace, was then a very popular little dog).
W.S.C.: I did not exactly, either by my movement or my manner, invite any great continuing affection.

EAR-WITNESS
Turning away from the views of his father, Lord Randolph Churchill.
W.S.C.: Tory Democracy is a Democracy which supports the Tories.
and
W.S.C.: The Tory fault—a yearning for mediocrity.

LORD RIDDELL'S INTIMATE DIARY
Years later, on May 30, 1923, to Lord Riddell, when Stanley Baldwin thought of inviting W.S.C. to join the Conservative Government.*
W.S.C.: I am what I have always been—a Tory Democrat. Force of circumstances has compelled me to serve with another party, but

---

* George Allardice Riddell, first Baron, 1865–1934; English newspaper proprietor.

my views have never changed, and I should be glad to give effect to them by rejoining the Conservatives.

EAR-WITNESS

Also in 1923. He had survived the long process of leaving the Conservatives only to join the Liberals and later, in 1931, rejoin the Conservatives.

W.S.C.: Anyone can rat, but it takes a certain amount of ingenuity to re-rat.*

HOUSE OF COMMONS

On the night of May 10, 1940, bombs destroyed the House of Commons. More than two years later, on October 28, speaking from the House of Lords, temporary home of the House of Commons, W.S.C. moved that the House be rebuilt.

W.S.C.: There are two main characteristics of the House of Commons which will command the approval and the support of reflective and experienced Members. They will, I have no doubt, sound odd to foreign ears. The first is that its shape should be oblong and not semi-circular. Here is a very potent factor in our political life. The semi-circular assembly, which appeals to political theorists, enables every individual or every group to move round the centre, adopting various shades of pink according as the weather changes. I am a convinced supporter of the party system in preference to the group system. I have seen many earnest and ardent Parliaments destroyed by the group system. The party system is much favoured by the oblong form of Chamber. It is easy for an individual to move through those insensible gradations from Left to Right, but the act of crossing the Floor is one which requires serious consideration. I am well informed on this matter, for I have accomplished that difficult process, not only once but twice. Logic is a poor guide compared with custom. Logic, which has created in so many countries semi-circular assemblies which have buildings which give to every member, not only a seat to sit in, but often a desk to write at, with a lid to bang, has proved fatal to

---

* Sir Charles Dilke's response to W.S.C.'s disappointment in the Liberal Party. 'You had better watch out, Winston. The rat may leave the sinking ship once, but not twice. The second time you're done for.'

parliamentary government as we know it here in its home and in the land of its birth . . .

We owe a great debt to the House of Lords for having placed at our disposal this spacious, splendid hall. We have already expressed in formal Resolution our thanks to them. We do not wish to outstay our welcome. We have been greatly convenienced by our sojourn on these red benches and under this gilded, ornamented, statue-bedecked roof. I express my gratitude, and my appreciation of what we have received and enjoyed, but

> 'Mid pleasures and palaces though we may roam, Be it ever so humble, there's no place like home.*

and

Later, on November 9, 1951, as Prime Minister a second time, speaking at a Lord Mayor's Banquet in the rebuilt Guildhall which had been partly destroyed by German bombs.

W.S.C.: This is the first occasion when I have addressed this Assembly here as Prime Minister. The explanation, my Lord Mayor, is convincing. When I should have come as Prime Minister the Guildhall was blown up, and before it was repaired I was blown out. I thought at the time they were both disasters!

also

EAR-WITNESS

(on another ratter)

W.S.C.: Lord Jowitt† has brought disgrace to the name of rat.

EAR-WITNESS

His comments in the House of Commons Smoking Room when a Conservative member stood as a Liberal in a by-election.

W.S.C.: The only instance of a rat swimming *towards* a sinking ship.

---

* W.S.C.'s last words uttered in the old Chambers of the House of Commons: 'I feel sure we have no need to fear the tempest. Let it roar, and let it rage! We shall come through.'

† William Allen Jowitt, 1st Earl Jowitt, 1885–1957. Liberal MP 1922–24, re-elected 1929; immediately joined Labour Party to become Attorney General, 1929–32; left Labour Party to join National Government, 1931; campaigned against University seats and then tried to be elected from one; rejoined Labour Party, 1939; held post in Churchill coalition; Lord Chancellor, 1945–51.

EAR-WITNESS

Disagreeing with Joseph Chamberlain on Protectionism at the National Liberal Club.

W.S.C.: The country thought Mr [Joseph] Chamberlain . . . was a prophet with a message. They found him a politician groping for a platform.

NEWSPAPER REPORT, THE TIMES

On Arthur Balfour in a speech at Manchester on January 28.*

W.S.C.: I am not surprised that Mr Balfour has declared that he does not intend to dissolve Parliament. Abdications have often taken place in the history of the world, but if you look back on the course of history you will see that they have usually been made by masculine not feminine monarchs. Kings have abdicated but never Queens, and it is one of the attractive qualities of Mr Balfour that his nature displays a certain femininity. No doubt it is that element in his nature which prompts him to cling to office on any terms as long as it is possible to do so.

also

LORD RIDDELL'S INTIMATE DIARY

After David Lloyd George remarked that he heard that Arthur Balfour was dominating the League of Nations.

W.S.C.: (*to Lord Riddell*): If you wanted nothing done, Arthur Balfour was the best man for the task. There was no one equal to him.

also

GREAT CONTEMPORARIES

On Arthur Balfour, the Prime Minister.

W.S.C.: I saw a furious scene in the House of Commons when an Irish member, rushing across the floor in a frenzy, shook his fist for a couple of minutes within a few inches of his face. We young fellows behind were all ready to spring to his aid upon a physical

---

* Arthur James Balfour, first Earl of Balfour, 1848–1930; British statesman; Prime Minister, 1902–1905.

foe; but Arthur Balfour, Leader of the House, regarded the frantic figure with no more and no less than the interest of a biologist examining through a microscope the contortions of a rare and provoked insect.

and

W.S.C.: He would very soon have put Socrates in his place, if that old fellow had played any of his dialectical tricks on him. When I go to Heaven, I shall try to arrange a chat between these two on some topic, not too recondite for me to follow.

and

W.S.C.: He passed from one Cabinet to the other, from the Prime Minister [Herbert H Asquith] who was his champion to the Prime Minister [Lloyd George] who had been his most severe critic, like a powerful graceful cat walking delicately and unsoiled across a rather muddy street.

also

EAR-WITNESS

W.S.C.: The difference between Balfour and Asquith is that Arthur [Balfour] is wicked and moral, Asquith is good and immoral.

THE AUTOBIOGRAPHY OF MARGOT ASQUITH

From a letter to Mrs Herbert H. Asquith,[*] wife of the Prime Minister.
W.S.C.: The world is not made up of heroes and heroines—luckily or where would you and I find our backgrounds!

HOUSE OF COMMONS

Of Balfour's efforts to avoid identification with any of the contending factions which were wrecking his Administration.
W.S.C.: The dignity of a Prime Minister, like a lady's virtue, is not susceptible of partial diminution.

and

---

[*] Margot Asquith, second wife of the Liberal Prime Minister.

On two brothers with quite conflicting and contradictory temperaments.

W.S.C.: In looking at the views of these two hon. Members [the brothers Sir Edgar Vincent and Col. Sir C. E. H. Vincent], I have always marvelled at the economy of nature which had contrived to grow from a single stock the nettle and the dock.

1906 — SPEECH

Seeking election at North-West Manchester in 1906.

W.S.C.: I am glad . . . that the Parliament elected in 1900 is about to be dissolved. Few Parliaments in our modern experience have been less worthy of respect. A majority elected under the spell of patriotic emotion, upon a national issue, in the stress of an anxious war, has been perverted to crude and paltry purposes of party . . . Seven more years* of dodge and dole and dawdle. Seven years of tinker, tax and trifle. Seven years of shuffle, shout and sham. Do not be taken in again.

HOUSE OF COMMONS

On the 1906 election when, after 21 years' rule, the Conservatives were defeated.

W.S.C.: (pointing to his former Conservative colleagues): Call them not the party opposite but the Party in that corner.

HOUSE OF COMMONS

On February 22, the Liberal Party was elected by an overwhelming majority at the General Election. One of its big issues was the importation of Chinese to work the Rand mines. Although their actual legal contract status was that of indentured labourers, Lloyd George had spoken of 'slavery' with much Liberal approval. Churchill evacuated the exposed position with considerable finesse:

W.S.C.: [The] contract . . . may not be a healthy or proper contract . . . but it cannot in the opinion of His Majesty's Government be classified as slavery in the extreme acceptance of the word without

* The maximum term of Parliament at that time.

49

some risk of terminological inexactitude.

and

W.S.C.: I believe that, generally speaking, given free institutions on a fair basis, the best side of men's nature will in the end surely come uppermost. But this doctrine has its limits.

and

W.S.C.: Nothing in life is as exhilarating as to be shot at without results.

WINSTON CHURCHILL, AN INTIMATE PORTRAIT

Describing to Violet Asquith, daughter of the future Prime Minister, his approach to books.

W.S.C.: . . . with a hungry, empty mind and with fairly strong jaws, and what I got I bit.

SPEECH

In Glasgow on October 11, as a Liberal declaring himself in favour of some measures of collectivism.

W.S.C.: No man can be a collectivist alone. He must be both an individualist and a collectivist. The nature of man is a dual nature. The character of the organization of human society is dual . . . For some purposes he [man] must be a collectivist, for others he is, and he will for all time remain, an individualist . . . Collectively we light our streets and supply ourselves with water. But we do not make love collectively, and the ladies do not marry us collectively and we do not eat collectively and we do not die collectively, and it is not collectively that we face the sorrows and hopes, the winnings and the losings, of this world of accident and storm.

and

Later, as a Conservative in 1946.

W.S.C.: Socialism would gather all power to the supreme party and party leaders, rising like stately pinnacles above their vast bureaucracies of civil servants no longer servants and no longer civil.

A NUMBER OF PEOPLE

After attending Sir Herbert Beerbohm Tree's* production of Antony and Cleopatra, *W.S.C. told his Secretary, Edward Marsh, that instead of speaking the line, 'Unarm Eros, the long day's task is done,' the actor misquoted it into 'Eros unarm,' which improved the metre. Edward Marsh responded that a good poet might have changed Shelley's line 'And wild roses and ivy serpentine' to 'And roses wild.'*

W.S.C.: Yes and I suppose it would have taken the greatest poet of all to write 'And wild roses and serpentine ivy'.

1907

HOUSE OF COMMONS

On the House of Lords, June 25

W.S.C.: I proceed to inquire on what principle the House of Lords deals with Liberal measures. The Right Hon. Member for Dover by an imaginative effort assures us that they occupy the position of the umpire. Are they even a sieve, a strainer, to stop legislation if it should reveal an undue or undesirable degree of Radicalism, or Socialism? . . . they will have to defend this Chamber as it is—one-sided, hereditary, unpurged, unrepresentative, irresponsible, absentee.

Two years later, in Birmingham, January 13, 1909.

W.S.C.: The powers of the House of Lords to impede, and by impeding to discredit, the House of Commons are strangely bestowed, strangely limited, and still more strangely exercised. There are little things which they can maul; there are big things they cannot touch; there are Bills which they pass, although they believe them to be wrong; there are Bills which they reject, although they know them to be right. The House of Lords can prevent the trams from running over Westminster Bridge but it cannot prevent a declaration of war.

WINSTON CHURCHILL, AN INTIMATE PORTRAIT

Sitting next to Herbert Asquith's daughter Violet and discovering she was 19.

W.S.C.: And I am already 33! Curse ruthless time! Curse our

---

* Sir Herbert Beerbohm Tree, 1853–1917; English actor-manager.

ONE STAGE
NEARER
('Privy Councillor at
21')

mortality! How cruelly short is the allotted span for all we must
cram into it! . . . We are all worms. But I do believe that I am a
glow worm.

A BIOGRAPHY OF EDWARD MARSH

*As Undersecretary for the Colonies, between November and December, 1907,
W.S.C. was accompanied to Africa by his Secretary, Edward Marsh. En
route to Aden he asked an officer for the use of a camel from the camel battery
and got No. 51, a bad-tempered kicker. Later a Somali boy reported to the
officer: 'Sahib, camel kick Churchill; Churchill, Sahib, kick camel. Him very
good camel now, Sahib.'*

W.S.C.: (*to his Secretary after a march of 107 miles in six days on this African journey*): So fari—so goodie!
also

NEW STATESMAN ('WINSTON: A MEMOIR,' LORD DALTON)

On the same tour he was informed by a Colonial Governor of the alarming spread of venereal disease among the natives.
W.S.C.: Ah, Pox Britannica!
and
Musing on the awful disparities of life between Africans and Europeans.
W.S.C.: I don't think much of God. He hasn't put enough in the pool.

EAR-WITNESS

In England, after visiting the slums of Manchester in an election campaign.
W.S.C.: (*anguished*): Fancy living in one of these streets—never seeing anything beautiful—never eating anything savoury—never saying anything clever!

1908

A NUMBER OF PEOPLE

Herbert H. Asquith, the Prime Minister who succeeded Sir Henry Campbell-Bannerman, appointed W.S.C. President of the Board of Trade in his new Cabinet instead of to the Local Government Board, as had been rumoured.
W.S.C.: I refuse to be shut up in a soup kitchen with Mrs Sidney Webb.*

A NUMBER OF PEOPLE

In a speech at Darwen on Britain's dependency on imports, he told his audience it made him think of the vulnerability of Venice, which, should the sea ever have undercut its supports would have 'perished in a moment', and Egypt, he reminded his audience, depended on the inundation of the Nile.

* Beatrice Webb, Fabian Socialist and social reformer.

W.S.C.: The Venetians are always thinking about their piles and the Egyptians about their water.

WINSTON CHURCHILL, AN INTIMATE PORTRAIT

After losing a by-election for North-West Manchester, Cabinet Ministers being required to submit themselves for re-election upon appointment W.S.C. was soon invited to stand for Dundee, did so, and won. He described one of his opponents, the man he was to lose his seat to later (in 1922).

W.S.C.: . . . a quaint and then dim figure in the shape of Mr [Edwin] Scrimgeour, the Prohibitionist, who pleaded for the kingdom of God upon earth with special references to the evils of alcohol.

A BIOGRAPHY OF EDWARD MARSH

As W.S.C. was lying in bed, working on his speech on the Land Question, the telephone rang by his side.

W.S.C.: Hullo! ullo! hullo!

(Getting no answer, he grew impatient. Suddenly a voice replied, 'Yes.')

W.S.C.: Christ damn your soul. Why do you keep me waiting?

(A soft voice answered, which he recognized as his housekeeper's)

Mrs Spender: Is that Mr Churchill?

W.S.C.: *(with magnificent presence of mind before replacing the receiver)*: No!

SPEECH

W.S.C.: The Conservative Party is not a party but a conspiracy.

SPEECH

At Kinnaird Hall, Dundee, on May 14, commenting on the reaction of the Press to the Liberal support for Irish Home Rule.

W.S.C.: *The Times* is speechless, and takes three columns to express its speechlessness.

EAR-WITNESS
On his marriage on September 12, 1908.
W.S.C.: My ability to persuade my wife to marry me [was] my most brilliant achievement. Of course it would have been impossible for any ordinary man to have got through what I had to go through in peace and war without the devoted aid of what we call in England, one's better half.
also

HOUSE OF COMMONS
Forty-two years later, in a debate in the House of Commons on housing.
W.S.C.: Where does the family start? It starts with a young man falling in love with a girl. No superior alternative has yet been found!
also

MR CHURCHILL'S SECRETARY
Later, after World War II, when his secretary, Elizabeth Nel, announced she was leaving him to marry.
W.S.C.: You must have four children. One for Mother, one for Father, one for Accidents and one for Increase!

WINSTON CHURCHILL, AN INFORMAL STUDY OF GREATNESS
De Haas, the police officer who handled W.S.C.'s escape from the Boers later became a Reuters correspondent and was asked how he fixed on the price of £25 reward for 'Churchill dead or alive.' W.S.C. was curious about it too. When he became President of the Board of Trade and married, he received a letter of congratulations from De Haas.
W.S.C.: (*in reply*): I am very much obliged to you for your courtesy and good wishes. I look back with thankfulness to my share in that long South African story. I earnestly hope that all will now be peace. I think you might have gone as high as fifty pounds without an over-estimate of the value of the prize—if living!
> Yours faithfully,
> Winston Churchill

HOUSE OF COMMONS

As President of the Board of Trade, he successfully introduced a bill creating an integrated Port of London, arguing for Government control over all docks and wharves in the port.

W.S.C.: If it was not passed, the docks, which already have become obsolescent will have to be allowed to obsolesce into obsoleteness!

1909

HOUSE OF COMMONS

W.S.C.: I am not usually accused, even by my friends, of being of a modest or retiring disposition.

HOUSE OF COMMONS

On February 19 on George Wyndham, Member of Parliament.

W.S.C.: I like the martial and commanding air with which the Right Hon. Gentleman treats facts. He stands no nonsense from them.

HOUSE OF COMMONS

On July 16 when one of the clauses of his Trade Board's bill was being criticized, he agreed to withdraw it.

W.S.C.: Under our representative institutions it is occasionally necessary to defer to the opinions of other people.

SPEECH

At Norwich, July 26, on the Budget.

W.S.C.: Lord Lansdowne* has explained, to the amusement of the nation, that he claimed no right on behalf of the House of Lords to 'mince' the Budget. All, he tells us, he has asked for, so far as he is concerned, is the right to 'wince' when swallowing it. Well, that is a much more modest claim. It is for the Conservative Party to judge whether it is a very heroic claim for one of their leaders to

---

* Lord Lansdowne, 1845–1927; a leader of the Tory Right; Governor General of Canada, 1883–1888; Viceroy of India, 1888–1893.

make. If they are satisfied with the wincing Marquis, we have no reason to protest.

SPEECH
During the Battle of the Budget.
W.S.C.: The House of Lords have only been tolerated all these years because they were thought to be in a comatose condition which preceded dissolution. That this body should claim the right to make and unmake Governments—is a spectacle which a year ago no one would have believed could happen; and which 50 years ago no peer would have dared to suggest: and which 200 years ago . . . would have been settled by charges of cavalry and the steady advance of ironclad pikemen.
and
W.S.C.: [The House of Lords] not a national institution but a party dodge.

MY DIARIES 1888–1914
On women's suffrage. On a visit to Wilfred Blunt W.S.C. discussed the violent action of Suffragettes who were chaining themselves to railings to win the vote. Mr. Blunt quoted a friend's comment, which W.S.C. reused.*
W.S.C.: I might as well chain myself to St Thomas's [Hospital] and say I would not move until I had a baby.
also

EAR-WITNESS
After a long career of opposing women's votes, as Home Secretary he softened his views when a list of suggested appointments for women for executive positions was submitted to him and he signed the order for their appointments with a flourish.
W.S.C.: Let there be women!

---

* Wilfred Scawen Blunt, 1840–1922; English poet, diarist; crusader against white exploitation of native races; supported Indian, Irish, Egyptian nationalism.

SPEECH REPORTED IN THE TIMES

Complaining that the Tory Party had few speakers who could successfully answer some of the Liberal Party charges.

W.S.C.: . . . and the small fry of the Tory Party splashing actively about in their Tory puddles . . . fall back on their Dukes. These unfortunate individuals who ought to lead quiet, delicate, sheltered lives, far from the maddening crowd's ignoble strife have been dragged into the football scrimmage, and they have got rather mauled in the process . . . Do not be too hard on them. It is poor sport—almost like teasing goldfish. These ornamental creatures blunder on every hook they see, and there is no sport whatever in trying to catch them. It would be barbarous to leave them gasping upon the bank of public ridicule upon which they have landed themselves. Let us put them back gently, tenderly in their fountains; and if a few bright gold scales have rubbed off in what the Prime Minister calls the variegated handling they have received, they will soon get over it. They have got plenty more.

1910   HOUSE OF COMMONS

Responding to a question about the punctuation used in Prayer Books.

W.S.C.: Personally, I am in full agreement with the noble Lord [Lord Hugh Cecil*] on this point, and I am glad that we have found a common ground to stand on, though it be only the breadth of a comma.

1911   AMID THESE STORMS

In the Battle of Sidney Street as Home Secretary he watched the troops he sent to protect the crowd from barricaded and armed foreign anarchists and was criticized for appearing in person, thus risking his life.

W.S.C.: No one knew how many Anarchists there were or what measures were going to be taken. In these circumstances I thought it my duty to see what was going on myself . . . I must, however, admit that convictions of duty were supported by a strong sense of curiosity which perhaps it would have been well to keep in check.

---

* Lord Hugh Cecil, 1869–1956; fifth son of third Marquis of Salisbury; Member of Parliament.

HOUSE OF COMMONS

On May 25, commenting on Old Age Pensions for those over seventy.

W.S.C.: Everyone knows that he has a prospect of getting 5s. a week when he reaches that age. It is not much, unless you have not got it.

HOUSE OF COMMONS

On May 30.

W.S.C.: Although it may be very difficult to define in law what is or what is not a trade union, most people of common sense know a trade union when they see one. It is like trying to define a rhinoceros: it is difficult enough, but if one is seen, everybody can recognize it.

HOUSE OF COMMONS

On August 7, on the House of Lords Reform.

W.S.C.: One Right Honourable Gentleman has told us that the spirit of King Henry V is surging in his breast, and the other that he stands with Clive* confronting the deadly pistol of the duellist. We may admire their courage . . . All forms of courage are praiseworthy. But there are two features about the courage of these Right Honourable Gentlemen which deserve the momentary passing notice of this House. First, it is that kind of courage which enables men to stand up unflinchingly and do a foolish thing, although they know it is unpopular. Second, it is that kind of courage which cannot only be maintained in the face of danger, but can even shine brightly in its total absence. Mr Jorrocks [celebrated sportsman character in the novels of R. S. Surtees] has described fox-hunting as providing all the glory of war with only thirty-five per cent of its danger.

Here George Wyndham MP, interrupted, calling out, 'Twenty-five per cent.'

W.S.C.: Twenty-five per cent. The Right Honourable Gentleman has arrived at a much higher economy, and I think no one has succeeded in manufacturing a greater amount of heroism with a smaller consumption of the raw material of danger than his Right

---

* Robert Clive, Baron Clive of Plassey, 1725–1774; founder of the British Empire in India.

Honourable and learned Friend [F. E. Smith, later Lord Birkenhead].

A BIOGRAPHY OF EDWARD MARSH

Attacking Bonar Law, Leader of the Conservative Opposition, with a sentence planned for delivery in the House but withdrawn.

W.S.C.: The raw and rowdy Undersecretary,* whom the nakedness of the land, and the jealousies of his betters, have promoted to the leadership of the Tory Party!

NEPTUNE'S ALLY

The First Lord of the Admiralty calls in a new element to redress the balance of the old.

---

* Bonar Law, though at that time head of his party in Opposition, had never been more than a junior minister when it was in office.

TENANTS' FIXTURES.

Mr. Winston Churchill. "CONGRATULATIONS, MY DEAR BOY. YOU CAN TAKE OVER THE STRIKE PROBLEM."

Mr. McKenna. "THANKS SO MUCH; AND YOU CAN HAVE BERESFORD."

EAR-WITNESS

As First Lord of the Admiralty, he analysed the 'four most memorable years of my life.'

W.S.C.: That is because I can now lay eggs instead of scratching around in the dust and clucking. It is a far more satisfactory occupation. I am at present in process of laying a great number of eggs—'good eggs', every one of them. And there will be many more clutches to follow . . . New appointments to be made. Admirals to be 'poached', 'scrambled' and 'buttered'. A fresh egg from a fruitful hen.

HOUSE OF COMMONS

Responding, on December 20, to Lord Charles Beresford's* criticism of him as First Lord of the Admiralty.

W.S.C.: He can best be described as one of those orators who, before they get up, do not know what they are going to say; when they are speaking, do not know what they are saying; and when they have sat down, do not know what they have said.

1912

MY DIARIES (1888–1914)

Discussing with Wilfred Blunt the Turko-Italian War.

W.S.C.: The Italians remind me of the story of the giant who went to cleave an oak in two with his sword, and who caught his hand in the cleft and was held by it, till he was eaten alive by the wild beasts in the forest.

BATTLE

As First Lord of the Admiralty he began plans for an intensive, large-scale, stepped-up ship building programme involving new shipyards.

W.S.C.: Megalomania is the only form of sanity.

---

* Lord Charles William de la Poer Beresford, later first Baron Beresford, 1846–1919; famous, popular, noisy British Admiral; sometime MP; advocate of large Navy programme.

WINSTON CHURCHILL, AN INTIMATE PORTRAIT

As First Lord, playing over-adventurous bridge on the Admiralty's yacht, 'Enchantress.'

W.S.C.'s partner, Masterton-Smith:* But, First Lord, you discarded the knave.

**INNOVATOR
W.S.C. CONVERTS
ROYAL NAVY FROM
COAL TO OIL**

W.S.C.: The cards I throw away are not worthy of observation or I should not discard them. It is the cards I play on which you should concentrate your attention.

and

Playing with his Secretary, Edward Marsh, he led up, then sacrificed his king.

W.S.C.: Nothing is here for tears. The king cannot fall unworthily if he falls to the sword of the ace.

1913   HOUSE OF COMMONS

Responding to the charge of 'contemptible' during the Home Rule debate, by Captain James Craig,[†] an Ulster Member.

W.S.C.: If I valued the honourable Gentleman's opinion I might get angry.

---

[*] J. E. Masterton-Smith, W.S.C.'s joint Private Secretary.
[†] Later Lord Craigavon, Prime Minister of Northern Ireland.

EAR-WITNESS

As First Lord of the Admiralty, he was having trouble with some of his admirals at a strategy meeting. The arguments intensified until one of them accused him of having impugned the traditions of the Royal Navy.

W.S.C.: (*rising*): And what are they? They are rum, sodomy and the lash—Good morning, Gentlemen!

1914

HOUSE OF COMMONS

March 17 speech on Navy estimates.

W.S.C.: The offensive power of modern battleships is out of all proportion to their defensive power. Never was the disproportion so marked. If you want to make a true picture in your mind of a battle between great modern ironclad ships you must not think of it as if it were two men in armour striking at each other with heavy swords. It is more like a battle between two egg-shells striking each other with hammers . . . The importance of hitting first, and hitting hardest and keeping on hitting . . . really needs no clearer proof.

THE WORLD CRISIS, 1911–1914

Evaluating the Zeppelin as an instrument of war.

W.S.C.: I rated the Zeppelin much lower as a weapon of war than almost any one else. I believed that this enormous bladder of combustible and explosive gas would prove to be easily destructible.

EAR-WITNESS

Description of naval strategy in 1914 when his prime job in World War I was to transport the British Expeditionary Force to France. But he wanted also to raid German ships at Heligoland Bight. In this he was successful. British cruisers and destroyers sank three cruisers and put five others out of action.

W.S.C.: The nose of the bulldog has been slanted backward so that he can breathe without letting go!

UNDER HIS MASTER'S EYE.

SCENE—*Mediterranean, on board the Admiralty yacht "Enchantress."*

MR. WINSTON CHURCHILL. "ANY HOME NEWS?"

MR. ASQUITH. "HOW CAN THERE BE WITH YOU HERE?"

A SEA-CHANGE.

Tory Chorus (*to Winston*). "YOU'VE MADE ME LOVE YOU; I DIDN'T WANT TO DO IT."

WORLD WAR I | 1914-1918

1ST AUGUST 1914	Germany declared war on Russia.
2ND AUGUST 1914	German troops entered France.
4TH AUGUST 1914	German troops crossed the Belgian frontier.
4TH AUGUST 1914	Britain declared war on Germany.
2ND OCTOBER 1914	When Belgian front disintegrated, W.S.C. organized and accompanied expedition to Antwerp, then asked Prime Minister Asquith for a military command which was refused.
7TH OCTOBER 1914	Second daughter, Sarah, born.
30TH OCTOBER 1914	Recalled Admiral Lord Fisher* into Service as First Sea Lord.
3RD JANUARY 1915	Proposed a joint naval and military attack on the Dardanelles at a meeting of the War Council (Combined Operations). Plan was to relieve pressure on Russia, take Turkey out of the war, and bring the Balkans in as allies. W.S.C. believed success of plan would have prevented Russia from falling to Bolshevism and would have shortened the war two or three years. The plan, which Clement Attlee, Labour's Prime Minister, later called 'the only imaginative strategic concept of the war' and in which he fought, failed for lack of unity.
26TH MAY 1915	*New Government, Asquith Coalition, Herbert H. Asquith, Liberal Prime Minister.*
28TH MAY 1915	Under Conservative pressure W.S.C. resigned from the Admiralty and was appointed Chancellor of the Duchy of Lancaster, which he labelled, 'Four thousand pounds a year for doing nothing.' Experimented with painting.
11TH NOVEMBER 1915	Resigned from the Cabinet, returned to the Army.
19TH NOVEMBER 1915	Left for France to join a Brigade of Guards, soon promoted to Sixth Battalion, Royal Scots Fusiliers.
1916	Six months in trenches as a Major in Grenadier Guards. Returned to political life.
7TH DECEMBER 1916	*New Government, David Lloyd George, Liberal Prime Minister.* Liberal Party fatally split, with Asquith as Leader of the Opposition.
16TH JULY 1917	Became Minister of Munitions in Lloyd George's Government. Pressed for new 'Big Wolves' tanks.

* Admiral Lord Fisher, first Baron Fisher of Kilverstone, 1841–1920.

20ᵀᴴ NOVEMBER 1917	Cambrai, 378 tanks attacked, took 10,000 German prisoners. Given credit for his 'general idea of the use of such an instrument of warfare.'
11ᵀᴴ NOVEMBER 1918	Armistice signed.
DECEMBER 1918	Re-elected Coalition Liberal Member* for Dundee at General Election.

1914

THE WORLD CRISIS, 1911–1914

W.S.C., as a Lieutenant in the 4th Queen's Own Hussars, tried by wire-pulling to join the army Lord Kitchener was leading against the Mahdi in Africa, but Lord Kitchener remained disapproving of W.S.C.

W.S.C.: My relations with Lord Kitchener had been limited. Our first meeting had been on the field of Omdurman . . . He had disapproved of me severely in my youth, had endeavoured to prevent me from coming to the Soudan Campaign, and was indignant that I had succeeded in getting there. It was a case of dislike before first sight.

EAR-WITNESS

In Antwerp to confer with a Belgian Minister on ways of holding Antwerp, an official of the Ministry staff pointed to the glittering uniform of an Elder Brother of Trinity House.

W.S.C.: *Moi, je suis un frère aîné de la Trinité.*†

(*The confused Belgians believed he thought himself divine and treated him with awe!*)

and

THE WORLD CRISIS, 1911–1914

Responding to Lord Esher, diarist and historian, who had criticized his plan to defend Antwerp.

W.S.C.: It is remarkable that Lord Esher should be so much astray

---

* Coalition—i.e. separate from Mr Asquith and the main line Liberals.
† I am an Elder Brother of the Trinity.

. . . We must conclude that an uncontrollable fondness for fiction forbade him to forsake it for fact. Such constancy is a defect in an historian.

EAR-WITNESS

Humbert Wolfe, British poet of Austrian descent, called on him at the Admiralty to offer his services to the Navy. So passionate was the anti-German fever and Hun-hunting then that W.S.C. was forced to accept the resignation of Prince Louis of Battenberg (father of Lord Mountbatten) from his post as First Sea Lord. For the same reason—German ancestry—he had to refuse Humbert Wolfe.

W.S.C.: Ah Humbert! Hun-wept, Hun-honoured and Hung-sung.[*]

EAR-WITNESS

After the Dardanelles disaster.

W.S.C.: Perhaps it is better to be irresponsible and right than responsible and wrong.

1915   WINSTON CHURCHILL, AN INTIMATE PORTRAIT

During the Coalition period Lady Violet Bonham Carter asked W.S.C. if coalition between his then Liberal Party and the Conservatives wasn't what he had worked for.

W.S.C.: Ah . . . I wanted it in a different way. I wanted us to go to the Tories when we were strong . . . not in misfortune to be made an honest woman of.

THE AMAZING MR CHURCHILL

As Major of the Sixth Royal Scots Fusiliers, his first words to his men at the front line in France.

W.S.C.: War is declared, gentlemen—on the lice!

Dewar Gibbs, one of the officers, wrote, 'With these words was inaugurated such a discourse on pulex Europeaus, its origin, growth, and nature, its

---

[*] Parody of Sir Walter Scott's *Lay of the Last Minstrel*, 'Unwept, unhonoured and unsung.'

*habitat and its importance as a factor in wars ancient and modern, as left one
agape with wonder at the force of its author.*

AMID THESE STORMS
As Major under command of Lord Cavan of the Guards Division he
suggested to his Colonel that he live with his company in the line instead of
at battalion headquarters.*

W.S.C.: Battalion Headquarters when in the line was strictly 'dry'.
Nothing but strong tea with condensed milk, a very unpleasant
beverage . . . The companies' messes in the trenches were . . .
allowed more latitude. As I have always believed in the moderate
and regular use of alcohol, especially under conditions of winter
war, I gladly moved my handful of belongings from Ebenezer Farm
to a Company in the line.

EAR-WITNESS
*After taking up painting he compared his delight in it to the boredom of a
game of golf.*

W.S.C.: Like chasing a quinine pill around a cow pasture.

1916   THE AMAZING MR CHURCHILL
*His farewell to the Sixth Royal Scots Fusiliers near the town of Béthune
before becoming Minister of Munitions.*

W.S.C.: Whatever else they may say of me as a soldier, at least
nobody can say that I have ever failed to display a meet and proper
appreciation of the virtues of alcohol.

A LETTER
*In a letter to Prime Minister Lloyd George who was proposing to visit
Russia.*

W.S.C.: Don't get torpedoed[†] for if I am left alone your colleagues
will eat me.

---

* The 10th Earl of Cavan, 1865–1946, served with distinction in France and Italy in World Wars I and
II; Chief of Imperial General Staff, 1922–1926; Field Marshal, 1932.

A NUMBER OF PEOPLE

*Retort to the War Office request for the 'combing out' (conscription) of
manpower in industries and Departments other than the War Office.*
W.S.C.: Physician, comb thyself.

1917   THE WORLD CRISIS, 1916–1918

*Becoming Minister of Munitions in 1917 he reorganized his staff of
12,000 into a dozen groups under a Council of businessmen.*
W.S.C.: Once the whole organization was in motion it never
required change. Instead of struggling through the jungle on foot
I rode comfortably on an elephant, whose trunk could pick up a
pin or uproot a tree with equal ease, and from whose back a wide
scene lay open.

EAR-WITNESS

On Bolshevism. His earliest definition.
W.S.C.: A ghoul descending from a pile of skulls.
also

THE AFTERMATH, 1918–1928

W.S.C.: . . . they [the Germans] turned upon Russia the most grisly
of all weapons. They transported Lenin[†] in a sealed truck like a
plague bacillus from Switzerland into Russia.
W.S.C.: The Supreme Committee [Bolsheviks]—sub-human or
super-human which you will—crocodiles with master minds,
entered upon their responsibilities upon November 8.
and

[†] Lord Kitchener had been drowned while on his way to Russia a year earlier, when his ship was torpedoed or struck a mine.
[†] Lenin (Vladimir Illich Ulyanov), 1870–1924; Marxist leader; became first Premier of Soviet Union.

On Lenin.

W.S.C.: He alone could have led Russia into the enchanted quagmire; he alone could have found the way back to the causeway. He saw; he turned; he perished. The strong illuminant that guided him was cut off at the moment when he had turned resolutely for home. The Russian people were left floundering in the bog. Their worst misfortune was his birth: their next worse—his death.

and

W.S.C.: Meanwhile, the German hammer broke down the front and Lenin blew up the rear . . . Could any men . . . have made head at once against the double assault? . . .All broke, all collapsed, all liquefied in universal babble and approaching cannonade, and out of the anarchy emerged the one coherent, frightful entity and fact—the Bolshevik punch.

HOUSE OF COMMONS

Later, on November 5, 1919

W.S.C.: Lenin was sent into Russia by the Germans in the same way that you might send a phial containing a culture of typhoid or of cholera to be poured into the water supply of a great city, and it worked with amazing accuracy.

and

W.S.C.: In Russia a man is called a reactionary if he objects to having his property stolen and his wife and children murdered.

also

EAR-WITNESS

Russian children were taught to repeat a poem:

I love Lenin

Lenin was poor, therefore I love poverty.

Lenin went hungry, therefore I can go hungry.

Lenin was often cold, therefore I shall not ask for warmth.

W.S.C.: Christianity with a tomahawk!

and

Of the Hungarian Communist Béla Kun.

W.S.C.: An offshoot of the Moscow fungus.

also

HOUSE OF COMMONS
W.S.C.: Bolshevism is not a policy; it is a disease. It is not a creed; it is a pestilence.

and

W.S.C.: There is not one single social or economic principle or concept in the philosophy of the Russian Bolshevik which has not been realized, carried into action, and enshrined in immutable laws a million years ago by the white ant.

1918

THE DECLINE AND FALL OF LLOYD GEORGE
Asked why Sir Philip Sassoon, affluent, generous Parliamentary Private Secretary to Prime Minister David Lloyd George, had been so lucky in his jobs.

W.S.C.: When you are leaving for an unknown destination, it is a good plan to attach a restaurant car at the tail of the train.

THE AFTERMATH, 1918–1928
On the demand for hanging Kaiser Wilhelm II in 1918.

W.S.C.: It was evident however that the lawyers would have to have their say . . . This opened up a vista both lengthy and obscure.

THE WORLD CRISIS, VOL. I, ENGLISH EDITION
On World War I.

W.S.C.: When all was over, Torture and Cannibalism were the only two expedients that civilized scientific Christian States had been able to deny themselves and these were of doubtful utility.

and

THE AFTERMATH, 1918–1928
On war after World War I.

W.S.C.: Healing and surgery . . . returned them [war's victims] again and again to the shambles. Nothing was wasted that could contribute to the process of waste.

EAR-WITNESS

After the Allied victory W.S.C. was awarded the American Distinguished Service Cross for servicing Americans with munitions. He was the only Englishman to receive the D.S.C., presented to him by General John J. Pershing. *

W.S.C.: (*to a friend*): The award designates, . . . for distinguished service and gallantry in the face of the enemy. The latter qualification was waived in my case.

---

* General John J. Pershing, 1860–1948; Commander in Chief, American Expeditionary Force, 1917–1919; chief of Staff, US Army, 1921–1924.

LIBERAL BACK TO
CONSERVATIVE
1918–1929

15TH NOVEMBER 1918	Third daughter, Marigold Frances, born (died August 23, 1921)
DECEMBER 1918	Became Secretary of State for War and Minister for Air.
1919	Escaped unhurt from an aircraft crash at Croydon Aerodrome. Exhibited painting at Royal Society of Portrait Painters exhibition.
28TH JUNE 1919	Peace Treaty with Germany signed at Versailles.
1920	Involved in the massive demobilization plans.
MARCH 1921	Succeeded Lord Milner as Colonial Secretary and attended a Middle Eastern Conference at Cairo. Obtained settlement following fall of Turkish Empire. Used T. E. Lawrence as top adviser. After rebellion, put Emir Feisal on throne of Iraq, and Feisal's brother, Emir Abdullah, on throne of Transjordan. Generals Anton Denikin and Peter Wrangel and Admiral Aleksandr Kolchak organized White Russian counter-revolution from outer provinces of Russia with 25,000 Allied (British, American, French, Italian, Czech and Japanese) troops. They fought against Lenin, the Bolsheviks and the Germans in Moscow and central regions. W.S.C., though for continuing support, was defeated by Labour votes and British postwar exhaustion. Assisted David Lloyd George in negotiations with *Sinn Fein* leaders. Appealed to the Dominions for support against threatened Turkish invasion of Thrace under Kemal Atatürk. Helped pilot through the House of Commons a treaty establishing the Irish Free State with its own Government under Arthur Griffith and Michael Collins. W.S.C.'s mother died.
1922	Resigned post of Colonial Secretary upon fall of Lloyd George Coalition; defeated at Dundee when during the campaign his appendix had to be removed. Made a Companion of Honour.
15TH SEPTEMBER 1922	Fourth daughter, Mary, born.
23RD OCTOBER 1922	*New Government, Andrew Bonar Law, Conservative Prime Minister.*
APRIL 1923	Published *The World Crisis*, Vol. I (six volumes 1923–1931). Arthur Balfour called it, 'Winston's brilliant autobiography, disguised as a

history of the universe.'

22ND MAY 1923	*New Government, Stanley Baldwin, Conservative Prime Minister.*
	Contested by-election at West Leicester as National Liberal Free Trader; defeated.
22ND JANUARY 1924	*New Government, Ramsay MacDonald, Labour Prime Minister.*
20TH MARCH 1924	Broke with the Liberal Party (February) on its lack of firmness against Communists and Labour Party. Stood as a Constitutionalist for the Abbey Division of Westminster in a by-election, but defeated by the Conservative candidate. Won a criminal libel case against the poet Lord Alfred Douglas.
OCTOBER 1924	In a General Election was elected Member of Parliament for Epping as a Constitutionalist and Anti-Socialist, supported by Conservatives.
4TH NOVEMBER 1924	*New Government, Stanley Baldwin, Conservative Prime Minister.*
	Rejoined Conservative Government as Chancellor of the Exchequer.
28TH APRIL 1925	First Budget: counselled by orthodox bankers (notably Montagu Norman, Governor of the Bank of England) to return to Gold Standard to strengthen the pound. Raised death duties on all but largest estates; reduced super income tax in lower ranges. Reimposed protective duties on imported cars to encourage productive enterprise. The passionate Free Trader needed money to finance widows' and orphans' pensions.
MAY 1926	Organized and edited *The British Gazette* (published by Government during General Strike), with a circulation reaching over two million on its eighth and last day.
1927	On a trip to Greece and Egypt visited Benito Mussolini in Rome.
1928	Joined Amalgamated Union of Building Trades Workers as bricklayer.
8TH JUNE 1929	*New Government, Ramsay MacDonald, Labour Prime Minister.*
	Re-elected Constitutionalist Conservative Member for Epping Division, Essex. Visited Canada with his son Randolph, his brother Jack and Jack's son John.

1919   THE AFTERMATH, 1918–1928

*On President Woodrow Wilson.**

W.S.C.: The spacious philanthropy which he exhaled upon Europe stopped quite sharply at the coasts of his own country . . .

---

* Thomas Woodrow Wilson, 1856–1924; 28th US President, 1913–1921.

Peace and goodwill among all nations abroad, but no truck with the Republican Party at home . . . It is difficult for a man to do great things if he tries to combine a lambent charity embracing the whole world with the sharper forms of populist party strife.

EAR-WITNESS

After World War I speaking in Paris before French notables, W.S.C. pronounced French as if it were English. He was advised to turn his speech over to an interpreter, who prepared a flowery translation, delivered with such effect that the interpreter seemed to have stolen the show and received thunderous applause, leaving W.S.C. out in the cold. But not for long.
W.S.C.: (*in French*): Until I heard your splendid version, Monsieur, I did not realize what a magnificent, indeed, epoch-making speech I had made. Allow me to embrace you, Monsieur.
(As he kissed the interpreter on both cheeks, the applause redoubled.)

EAR-WITNESS

American-born Nancy, Lady Astor entered Parliament as its first woman member.
W.S.C.: Nancy, when you entered the House, I felt you had come upon me in my bath and I had nothing to protect me but my sponge.
also

THE GLITTER AND THE GOLD

Later in 1935, during the appeasement period, both were weekend guests at Blenheim and exchanged barbs perhaps not original with either.
Lady Astor: Winston, if I were your wife I'd put poison in your coffee.
W.S.C.: If I were your husband, Nancy, I'd take it.

A NUMBER OF PEOPLE

During a drought the Duke of Rutland urged a manifesto for Prayers for Rain in the prayer book. This caught W.S.C.'s eye, and he replied.

Sir—

Observing reports in various newspapers that prayers are about to be offered up for rain in order that the present serious drought may be terminated, I venture to suggest that great care should be taken in framing the appeal.

On the last occasion when this extreme step was resorted to, the Duke of Rutland took the leading part with so much well meaning enthusiasm that the resulting downpour was not only sufficient for all immediate needs, but was considerably in excess of what was actually required, with the consequence that the agricultural community had no sooner been delivered from the drought than they were clamouring for a special interposition to relieve them from deluge. Profiting by this experience, we ought surely on this occasion to be extremely careful to state exactly what we want in precise terms, so as to obviate the possibility of any mis-understanding, and to economize so far as possible the need for these special appeals. After so many days of drought, it certainly does not seem unreasonable to ask for a change in the weather, and faith in a favourable response may well be fortified by actuarial probabilities.

While therefore welcoming the suggestion that His Grace should once again come forward, I cannot help feeling that the Board of Agriculture should first of all be consulted. They should draw up a schedule of the exact amount of rainfall required in the interests of this year's harvest in different parts of the country. This schedule could be placarded in the various places of worship at the time when the appeal is made. It would no doubt be unnecessary to read out the whole schedule during the service, so long as it was made clear at the time that this is what we have in our minds, and what we actually want at the present serious juncture.

I feel sure that this would be a much more businesslike manner of dealing with the emergency than mere vague appeals for rain. But after all, even this scheme, though greatly preferable to the haphazard methods previously employed, is in itself only a partial makeshift. What we really require to pray for is the general amelioration of the British climate. What is the use of having these piece-meal interpositions—now asking for sunshine, and now for rain? Would it not be far better to ascertain by scientific investigation, conducted under the auspices of a Royal Commission, what is the proportion of sunshine and rain best suited to the ripening of the crops? It would no doubt be necessary that other interests beside agriculture should be represented, but there must be certain broad general reforms in the British weather upon which an overwhelming consensus of opinion could be found. The proper proportion of rain to sunshine during each period of the year: the regulation of the rain largely to the hours of darkness: the apportionment of rain and sunshine as between different months, with proper reference not only to crops but to holidays: all these could receive due consideration. A really scientific basis of climatic reform would be achieved. These reforms, when duly embodied in an official volume, could be made the object of the sustained appeals of the nation over many years, and embodied in general prayers of a permanent and not of an exceptional character. We should not then be forced from time to time to have recourse to such appeals at particular periods, which, since they are unrelated to any general plan, must run the risk of deranging the whole economy of nature, and involve the interruption and deflection of universal processes, causing reactions of the utmost complexity in many directions which it is impossible for us with our limited knowledge to foresee.

I urge you, Sir, to lend the weight of your powerful organ to the systematization of our appeals for the reform of the British climate.

Yours very faithfully,
Scorpio [W.S.C.]

THE AFTERMATH, 1918–1928

On the Versailles Peace Conference after Germany's defeat.

W.S.C.: What would democracy do with diplomacy? On the one hand, one hundred million strong, stood the young American democracy. On the other cowered furtively, but at the same time obstinately, and even truculently, the old European diplomacy. Here young, healthy, hearty, ardent millions, advancing so hopefully to reform mankind. There, shrinking from the limelights, cameras and cinemas, huddled the crafty, cunning, intriguing, high-collared, gold-laced diplomatists. Tableau! Curtain! Slow music! Sobs: and afterwards chocolates!

GREAT CONTEMPORARIES

*On Georges Clemenceau.**

W.S.C.: The Clemenceau of the Peace was a great statesman. He was confronted with enormous difficulties. He made for France the best bargain that the Allies, who were also the world, would tolerate. France was disappointed; Foch[†] was disappointed, and also offended by personal frictions. Clemenceau, unrepentant to the end, continued to bay at the church. The Presidency passed to an amiable nonentity [Paul Deschanel],[‡] who soon tumbled out of a railway carriage.

THE AFTERMATH, 1918–1928

Referring to the Greek expedition in Ionia that, two years later, led to the defeat of the Greek Army by Mustapha Kemal,[§] which destroyed the first (Sèvres) peace treaty with Turkey and ended Venizelos'[**] dreams of a more powerful Greece.

W.S.C.: Venizelos is entitled to plead that in going to Smyrna he acted as mandatory for the four greatest Powers. But he went as readily as a duck will swim.

1920

HOUSE OF COMMONS

Criticizing the action of General Dyer[††] in shooting into an unarmed crowd at Amritsar.

W.S.C.: Frightfulness is not a remedy known to the British pharmacopoeia.

---

* Georges Clemenceau, 1841–1929; French statesman; Premier of France, 1906–1909; 1917–1920; called 'the Tiger'.

† Marshal Ferdinand Foch, 1851–1929; French Commander in Chief of Allied Armies, 1918.

‡ Paul Deschanel, President of France from February 18 to September 21, 1920, became insane in office; died in 1922, from the effects of the fall referred to by W.S.C.

§ Mustapha Kemal, later styled Atatürk 1881–1938; Turkish general; President of Turkish Republic, 1923–1938.

** Eleutherios Venizelos, 1864–1936; Greek statesman and champion of Allied cause; Premier, 1917, upon abdication of King Constantine; fought for Greek interests at Paris Peace Conference.

†† General Reginald E. H. Dyer, 1864–1927; British soldier in command in Punjab during the infamous Amritsar massacre.

CHURCHILL BY HIS CONTEMPORARIES

Inspector Walter H. Thompson, his private bodyguard from 1920–1932 and 1939–1945, accompanied him to Egypt and Palestine when he was Colonial Secretary. As the party rode camels across the desert W.S.C.'s saddle slipped round and he fell into the sand. Bedouins dashed up and each offered the Colonial Secretary his horse.

W.S.C.: I started on a camel and I will finish on a camel.

HOUSE OF COMMONS

After World War I, as Colonial Secretary he backed Palestine as a Homeland for the Jews.

W.S.C.: It is hard enough in all conscience to make a new Zion, but if over the portals of the new Jerusalem you are going to inscribe the legend 'no Israelites need apply', I hope the House will permit me in future to confine my attention exclusively to Irish matters.

SPEECH

A staunch defender of the Zionists, he was speaking to a Jewish audience in New York in March 1949, after Israel defeated the Arabs in its war of independence, and was asked what he thought about it.

W.S.C.: Remember, I was for a free and independent Israel all through the dark years when many of my most distinguished countrymen took a different view. So do not imagine for a moment that I have the slightest idea of deserting you now in your hour of glory.[*]

AMID THESE STORMS

On the Irish Treaty, which he piloted through Parliament, setting up the Irish Free State with their own Government under Arthur Griffith and Michael Collins.[†]

W.S.C.: I remember one night Mr Griffith and Mr Collins came to

---

[*] February 24, 1949, first armistice between Israel and Egypt; March 23, with Lebanon; April 3, with Jordan.
[†] Irish Republican Leaders.

HATS THAT HAVE HELPED ME.

MR. WINSTON CHURCHILL (*trying on Colonial headgear*). "VERY BECOMING—BUT ON THE SMALL SIDE, AS USUAL."

my house to meet the Prime Minister [Lloyd George]. It was a crisis, and the negotiations seemed to hang only by a thread. Griffith went upstairs to parley with Mr Lloyd George alone. Lord Birkenhead and I were left with Michael Collins meanwhile. He was in his most difficult mood, full of reproaches and defiances, and it was very easy for everyone to lose his temper.

Michael Collins: You hunted me night and day. You put a price on my head.

W.S.C.: Wait a minute. You are not the only one. And I took from my wall the framed copy of the reward offered for my recapture by the Boers. At any rate it was a good price—5,000 pounds.* Look at me—25 pounds dead or alive. How would you like that?

THE AFTERMATH, 1918–1928

On the role of Britain, France and America during the Russian Civil War, 1918–1922.

W.S.C.: Were they at war with Soviet Russia? Certainly not; but they shot Soviet Russians at sight. They stood as invaders on Russian soil. They armed the enemies of the Soviet Government . . . But war—shocking! Interference—shame! It was, they repeated, a matter of indifference to them how Russians settled their own internal affairs. They were impartial—Bang!

and

Irritated with what he deemed to be the United States' small commitment to White Russian resistance to the Bolsheviks.

W.S.C.: . . . They also proposed to send a detachment of Young Men's Christian Association to offer moral guidance to the Russian people.

also

EAR-WITNESS

As Secretary for War, he had been held responsible for intervention in the Russian counter-revolution.

W.S.C.: I am accustomed to being blamed for everything

---

* W.S.C. later remarked that actually no such reward had ever been offered for Michael Collins by the British Government but he did not know it at the time.

[Dardanelles, etc.]. Why, when I was First Lord of the Admiralty, whenever a ship was sunk, I'd sunk it—unless it was an enemy ship. *also*

SPEECH

At Mansion House.

W.S.C.: . . . these Russian armies who . . . are now engaged in fighting against the foul Baboonery of Bolshevism.

also

GREAT CONTEMPORARIES

On the Russian Revolutionary Boris Savinkov, Vice Minister of War in the 1917 Kerensky* Government and agent of Kolchak† during the White Russian counter-revolution.

W.S.C.: He was that extraordinary product—a Terrorist for moderate aims. A reasonable and enlightened policy—the Parliamentary system of England . . . freedom, toleration and good will—to be achieved wherever necessary by dynamite at the risk of death.

also

THE AFTERMATH, 1918–1928

W.S.C.: He was the essence of practicality and good sense expressed in terms of nitroglycerin.

1922

EAR-WITNESS

In October, just before the contest for a Parliamentary seat in Dundee opened, W.S.C. was operated on for appendicitis. Though shaky, he made an appearance before the polling day. The returns announced his defeat.

W.S.C.: In the twinkling of an eye I found myself without an office, without a seat, without a party and even without an appendix.

also

---

* Aleksandr Kerensky succeeded Prince Lvov, July–October, 1917, as Premier of Provisional Government.

† Aleksandr V. Kolchak, 1874–1920; Russian admiral and counter-revolutionist; captured and shot by Bolsheviks.

THE DECLINE AND FALL OF LLOYD GEORGE

Prime Minister Andrew Bonar Law was ill at the same time under the care of the same doctor, Sir Thomas Horder.

W.S.C.: How is our ambitious invalid? What about our gilded tradesman?

EAR-WITNESS

After his 1922 defeat, while vacationing in the South of France.

Paul Maze, the painter, to W.S.C.: Well, Winston, I'm painting hard, trying to forget all about the war. What are you doing?

W.S.C.: I'm writing a book on the war.

Paul Maze: . . . it's like digging up a cemetery.

W.S.C.: Yes, but with a resurrection.

THE DECLINE AND FALL OF LLOYD GEORGE

On farming at Chartwell.

W.S.C.: (*to Mr. Lloyd George*): I'm going to make it pay, whatever it costs.

EAR-WITNESS

After Andrew Bonar Law was made Prime Minister in 1922, following upon the Coalition Government of David Lloyd George.

W.S.C.: If the character and composition of the Government reminds us of the days of King George III rather than of George V, the policy that has been announced by the new Prime Minister carries us back to the Middle Ages.[*]

and

On Prime Minister Law's appealing to a mandate of tranquillity.

W.S.C.: Tranquillity[†] indeed! There is nothing more tranquil than the grave. I will never stifle myself in such a moral and intellectual sepulchre.

---

[*] He added that an inscription over the door of 10 Downing Street should read: 'Abandon hope all ye who enter here.'

[†] Lady Violet Bonham Carter told an audience: 'We have to choose between one man suffering from St Vitus' dance [Lloyd George] and another [Bonar Law] from sleeping sickness.'

and

W.S.C. to Prime Minister Law.

W.S.C.: I am resisting all temptation to say, I told you so.

THE SECOND WORLD WAR, VOL. I

To fight Germany, Britain sold a thousand million pounds of investments built up in America by the efforts of preceding generations, and contracted a debt of a similar size. Her Allies had incurred a comparable debt to Britain. As Chancellor of the Exchequer W.S.C. insisted on linking the two. Later, a delegation met in Washington to discuss war debts, and it was decided Britain would pay the whole debt to the United States at interest reduced from 5 to 3 ½ per cent.

W.S.C.: It imposed upon Great Britain, much impoverished by the war, in which . . . she had fought from the first day to the last, the payment of thirty-five millions sterling a year for sixty-two years. The basis of this agreement was considered . . . a severe and improvident condition for both borrower and lender.

President Coolidge's view that 'They hired the money, didn't they?'*

W.S.C.: This laconic statement was true, but not exhaustive.

EAR-WITNESS

On Sir William Joynson-Hicks, MP., Postmaster General, Minister of Health and later Home Secretary.

W.S.C.: The worst that can be said of him is that he runs the risk of being most humorous when he wishes to be most serious.

also

HOUSE OF COMMONS

After Sir William Joynson-Hicks made a statement in the House of Commons with which W.S.C. seemed to disagree.

Joynson-Hicks: I see my Right Honourable Friend shakes his head, but I am only expressing my own opinion.

W.S.C.: And I am only shaking my own head.

---

* President Calvin Coolidge, 1872–1933; 30th President of the United States, 1923–1929.

1923   SPEECH

After his election, speaking in the Free Trade Hall, Manchester, on the assassination of Free Trade.

W.S.C.: Mr Baldwin is a very honest man; he tells us so himself . . . It is a fine thing to be honest, but it is very important for a Prime Minister to be right.

1924   THE WORLD CRISIS, VOL. 5, ENGLISH EDITION

Comparing the British and French Prime Ministers in 1924.

W.S.C.: The breach of sentiment and understanding between Lloyd George and Poincaré was complete. Every form of mutual repulsion operated between them.

EAR-WITNESS

A passion for the game of mahjong coincided with one of the first performances of the play St Joan, *by George Bernard Shaw,* which W.S.C. attended. In Act I, Scene III, Dunois, waiting on the banks of the Loire for good portents for the battle, invoked, 'West Wind, West Wind, West Wind.'*

W.S.C.: Pong!

(This outburst stopped the show as the mahjong-conscious audience knew that 'West Wind' was a mahjong title and that 'Pong' meant the player held three of a kind.)

also

RICHARD BURTON, ON A JACK PAAR SHOW

Years later, the Director of London's Old Vic Theatre advised actor Richard Burton before a performance of Hamlet, *'Do be good tonight because the Old Man's out there in the front row.'*

Richard Burton: In Britain the Old Man is only one person and that's Churchill. I panicked. But I went onstage and started to play Hamlet. I heard a dull rumble from the front row of the stalls. It was Churchill speaking the lines with me, and I could not shake him off. I tried going fast; I tried going slow; we did cuts. Every

---

* George Bernard Shaw, 1856–1950; Irish playwright, novelist and critic.

time there was a cut, an explosion occurred. He knew the play absolutely backward; he knows perhaps a dozen of Shakespeare's plays intimately. Generally you can't keep him for more than one act. When the first curtain came down I looked through the spyhole. He got up from his seat and I thought: That's it, we've lost him.

(A few minutes later W.S.C. appeared in Richard Burton's dressing room.)

W.S.C.: My Lord Hamlet, may I use your lavatory?

Richard Burton: And he did.

EAR-WITNESS

Just after completing a head of dictator Benito Mussolini, Clare Sheridan, the sculptor, did a portrait-head of her cousin W.S.C., portraying him with an exaggerated, jutting jaw. After the first few sittings he looked hard at what she had done of him.*

W.S.C.: Remember, Clare, *I* am a servant of the House of Commons.

EAR-WITNESS

Mr. Herbert H. Asquith (Liberal, created 1st Earl of Oxford and Asquith in 1925) referred to the new Chancellor of the Exchequer (W.S.C.) as 'a Chimborazo or Everest among the sand hills of the Baldwin Cabinet.' On taking office W.S.C. doubtingly returned Britain to the Gold Standard at the advice of the bankers, which resulted in pricing British exports out of world markets.

W.S.C.: Are we to be at the mercy of a lot of Negro women scrabbling with their toes in the mud of the Zambesi?

EAR-WITNESS

During Prime Minister Stanley Baldwin's 'muddling-through' period.

W.S.C.: History will deal severely with the Prime Minister. I know, because I shall write it.

---

* Benito Mussolini, 1883–1945; Italian Fascist; summoned by King Victor Emmanuel III to form Ministry, 1922; established dictatorship; overthrown 1943; executed 1945.

and

To his colleagues on Stanley Baldwin.*

W.S.C.: The greatest Party Leader of them all.

(Asked why.)

W.S.C.: Making me Chancellor of the Exchequer.

THE TOPPER
NOW, THAT'S
SOMETHING LIKE
A HAT

SPEECH

At the London School of Economics.

W.S.C.: Too often the strong, silent man is silent because he does not know what to say.

---

* Prime Minister Baldwin showed skill putting W.S.C. in the Cabinet as it ensured that Lloyd George would be unable to bring W.S.C. into any anti-governmental intrigue.

EAR-WITNESS

Preparing for a Budget he asked his experts what certain figures meant. They could not give him an answer.

W.S.C.: They sent for a little man from the basement, who in words of one syllable told me exactly what those figures meant. I thanked him. He went back to his basement and was never seen again.

and

W.S.C.: The higher mind has no need to concern itself with the meticulous regimentation of figures.

DAILY TELEGRAPH

Years later, in the House of Lords on August 4, 1965, Lord Boothby referred back to unjust criticisms levelled at W.S.C. when he was Chancellor of the Exchequer (1924–1929) and returned Britain to the Gold Standard at the prewar parity of exchange. Mr Robert Boothby, then W.S.C.'s Parliamentary Private Secretary, later declared that the gold policy that led to the General Strike was made on the advice of Montagu Norman, Governor of the Bank of England, and Philip Snowden, the Labour ex-Chancellor of the Exchequer.

W.S.C.: (*to Boothby*): I wish they [Montagu Norman, Philip Snowden and the experts] were admirals or generals. I can sink them if necessary. But when I am talking to bankers and economists, after a while they begin to talk Persian, and then they sink me instead.

1925 HOUSE OF COMMONS

Presenting his first Budget, a lengthy business, to the House of Commons on April 28, he paused and filled a glass beside the despatch box before him with some spirits.

W.S.C.: It is imperative that I should fortify the revenue, and this I shall now, with the permission of the Commons, proceed to do.

also

GREAT CONTEMPORARIES

*On Philip Snowden.**

W.S.C.: We must imagine with what joy Mr Snowden was welcomed at the Treasury by the permanent officials. All British Chancellors of the Exchequer have yielded themselves, some spontaneously, some unconsciously, some reluctantly to that compulsive intellectual atmosphere. But here was the High Priest entering the sanctuary. The Treasury mind and the Snowden mind embraced each other with the fervour of two long-separated kindred lizards.

and

HOUSE OF COMMONS

W.S.C.: A perverse destiny has seemed to brood over the Right Hon. Gentleman's career; all his life has been one long struggle to overcome the natural amiability of his character.

and

Snowden criticized W.S.C. as Chancellor of the Exchequer, for changing his mind in taxing silk imports as 'the worst rich man's budget of recent times,' accusing the Chancellor of shifting his views on free trade.

W.S.C.: There is nothing wrong with change, if it is in the right direction.

Philip Snowden: You are an authority on that.

W.S.C.: To improve is to change; to be perfect is to change often.

HOUSE OF COMMONS

W.S.C.: As I said the other night in the small hours of the morning [laughter]—that is an Irishism; I mean the other day in the small hours of the morning.

A NUMBER OF PEOPLE

Inspired by his private secretary, Edward Marsh, he once sent to the Press the following corruption of the line beginning with 'Heard Melodies' in Keats's

---

* Philip Snowden, Labour MP who preceded and succeeded W.S.C. as Chancellor of the Exchequer.

Ode on a Grecian Urn, *concerning one of his Budgets as Chancellor of the Exchequer.*

W.S.C.: Earned increments are sweet, but those unearned are sweeter.

1926   CHURCHILL BY HIS CONTEMPORARIES

During the General Strike of May 4–13, all newspapers but The Times *and the* Daily Worker *closed. W.S.C., though Chancellor of the Exchequer, took over the* Morning Post, *his bitterest right-wing critic, gathered a skeleton staff and produced the* British Gazette—*with a huge circulation. He was criticized in the House by the Labour Party for partiality in its editing.*

W.S.C.: The State cannot be impartial as between itself and that section of its subjects with whom it is contending.

also

THE NEW
BRITANNIA,
BY LOW

HOUSE OF COMMONS

W.S.C.: I decline utterly to be impartial as between the Fire Brigade and the fire.

(After the strike the Labour Opposition in the House was in a savage mood. W.S.C. rose, wagging his finger at them.)

W.S.C.: I warn you [catcalls], I warn you—(Order! Keep quiet!)— If there is another general strike, we will let loose on you [ominous pause] another *British Gazette!*

(The House went into peals of laughter.)

EAR-WITNESS

In a Cabinet meeting Neville Chamberlain passed a note to him saying, 'I'm 100 per cent with you.'

W.S.C.: I'm not sure I'm with myself.

Stanley Baldwin: I know what you mean.

EAR-WITNESS

Asked for embarrassing statistics in the House of Commons, W.S.C., like his father before him, also a Chancellor of the Exchequer, 'did not take to those damned dots,' but gave assurances he would have the figures the following day. True to his word he poured forth a dazzling array to the House. His amazed staff confessed it would have taken them six months to produce them.

W.S.C.: And it will take the Opposition six months to prove I am in error!

1927   HOUSE OF COMMONS

On April 13, after his proposal for Widows' Pensions was described as inhuman.*

W.S.C.: It only shows the British public, and the great nation which inherits this somewhat foggy island, are less likely to be grateful for benefits received than they are for evils averted.

and

---

* In 1915, W.S.C. had advocated the highest pensions to war widows, opposing the rest of the Cabinet, in an unlikely triumvirate with King George V and George Bernard Shaw.

Describing Lloyd George's criticism of him.
W.S.C.: A certain vein of amiable malice.

HOUSE OF COMMONS
On April 26, during the Budget debate.
W.S.C.: It is absolutely necessary to invoke the great name of Mr Gladstone, a name which is received with reverence below the Gangway* on the Opposition side, and with a certain amount of respect by some Hon. Members who sit opposite.
Hon. Members: What about yourself?
W.S.C.: I occupy the impartial position of historian.
and
In the same debate two days later.
W.S.C.: There is nothing that gives greater pleasure to a speaker than seeing his great points go home. It is like the bullet that strikes the body of the victim.
and
W.S.C.: I am not going to follow the Right Hon. Member for Ross and Cromarty in the arguments he has used as to whether the money raised by the Motor Licence Duties was for all time finally assigned to the upkeep of the roads. I went through all that last year. At that time the argument was used that it belonged to the motorists and that it was 'Government of the motorists, by the motorists, for the motorists' . . . I am not fighting that battle this year. I am merely pursuing, and collecting some of the baggage which they left behind.

HOUSE OF COMMONS
W.S.C.: (*to American-born Nancy Lady Astor, a Prohibitionist*): I have a great regard and respect for the noble lady, but I do not think we are likely to learn much from the liquor legislation of the United States.

---

* Gangway—cross passage halfway down the House of Commons, giving access to back benches, where the remnant of the old-fashioned, economical Liberals sat, at some distance from both the high-rolling Lloyd George faction and the Socialist mass of the Labour Party.

HOUSE OF COMMONS
On May 19.

W.S.C.: Mr Lowe* seems to have been walking over my footsteps before I have trodden them, because he said, trying to explain what had occurred for the satisfaction of a very strict House in those days: 'And so each year will take money from its successor, and this process may go on till the end of time, although how it will be settled when the world comes to an end I am at a loss to know.' It was unconscious anticipatory plagiarism.

EAR-WITNESS

The late Lord Melchett told the story of a small dinner that took place at Pratt's Club in London. In addition to Lord Melchett, the richest guest and only non-member of the Club, the guests were Mr Leopold Amery, Lord Birkenhead, the Duke of Devonshire, Harold Macmillan,† and W.S.C. At the close of the feast, Lord Birkenhead rose and, in his highest oratorical style, toasted 'the richest of them all, Lord Melchett, who, because of his skill and wisdom, has much of this world's goods and thus will meet the bill of this modest repast.'

W.S.C.: My dear Freddie [Lord Birkenhead], surely you would not deprive me of the pride and pleasure of giving a crust to Croesus?

1928   HOUSE OF COMMONS
Third Budget Speech, April 24.

W.S.C.: It would be easy to give an epitome of the financial year which has closed. The road has lain continually uphill, the weather has been wet and cheerless, and the Lords Commissioners of His Majesty's Treasury have been increasingly uncheered by alcoholic stimulants. Death has been their frequent companion and almost their only friend.

---

* Robert Lowe, later Lord Sherbrooke; Chancellor of the Exchequer, 1868–1873.
† Harold Macmillan, MP, later Prime Minister.

95

HOUSE OF COMMONS

On April 28, commenting on the £860,000 Lloyd George had allocated to roadbuilding in 1910.

W.S.C.: That was the value of his generosity. My stinginess, what is left over after my rapacity . . . amounts to £20,000,000.

HOUSE OF COMMONS

On May 1, during the Budget debate, referring to Lloyd George's very radical 1909 speeches at Limehouse.

W.S.C.: He [Mr Lloyd George] has distinguished himself upon this subject in a manner which deserves the widest public notice. He said on Saturday: 'You are blessed, for you will not receive, you will give. Every time the lamp illuminates your cottage, and perfumes it, as it used to do in my own days, you will have the feeling that the wick is oozing wealth for Sir Alfred Mond [Imperial Chemicals] and Mr [Samuel] Courtauld [silk industry].' That is the contribution to an important public controversy of a man who has been nine years Chancellor of the Exchequer and five years Prime Minister, who, after having held the greatest situation in Europe, looks forward with the utmost gusto to another series of 'Limehouse Nights'.*

EAR-WITNESS

In 1928 he joined the Amalgamated Union of Building Trade Workers as an adult apprentice. But he had earned the enmity of the Trades Union Council after the General Strike because of his leading role for the Government as Chancellor of the Exchequer. The Builder's Union denounced his membership. Later, in 1935, when Britain was again in mortal peril, he resumed building one of his cottages as an antidote against the rage he felt at Baldwin's seeming indifference to the danger in German rearmament.

W.S.C.: (*to F. William Deakin, his personal assistant*): I suppose these bricks will be excavated in 500 years as a relic of Stanley Baldwin's England.

---

* Limehouse, poor district in London.

SPEECH

In Epping Division on October 25; his disarmament fable.

W.S.C.: Once upon a time all the animals in the Zoo decided that they would disarm, and they arranged to have a conference to arrange the matter. So, the Rhinoceros said when he opened the proceedings that the use of teeth was barbarous and horrible and ought to be strictly prohibited by general consent. Horns, which were mainly defensive weapons, would of course, have to be allowed. The Buffalo, the Stag, the Porcupine, and even the little Hedgehog all said they would vote with the Rhino, but the Lion and the Tiger took a different view. They defended teeth and even claws, which they described as honourable weapons of immemorial antiquity. The Panther, the Leopard, the Puma, and the whole tribe of small cats all supported the Lion and the Tiger. Then the Bear spoke. He proposed that both teeth and horns should be banned and never used again for fighting by any animal. It would be quite enough if animals were allowed to give each other a good hug when they quarrelled. No one could object to that. It was so fraternal, and that would be a great step towards peace. However, all the other animals were very offended with the Bear, and the Turkey fell into a perfect panic.

The discussion got so hot and angry, and all those animals began thinking so much about horns and teeth and hugging when they argued about the peaceful intentions that had brought them together that they began to look at one another in a very nasty way. Luckily the keepers were able to calm them down and persuade them to go back quietly to their cages, and they began to feel quite friendly with one another again.

1929

SPEECH

In London, on the Labour Government.

W.S.C.: One can quite easily see that if they have their way they will reduce this powerful country to one vast soup kitchen.

HOUSE OF COMMONS

Budget Speech of April 15.

W.S.C.: The Right Hon. Member for Carnarvon Boroughs [Mr

David Lloyd George] is going to borrow 200 million pounds and to spend it upon paying the unemployed to make racing tracks for well-to-do motorists to make the ordinary pedestrian skip; and we are assured that the mere prospect of this has entirely revivified the Liberal Party. At any rate, it has brought one notable recruit. Lord Rothermere [a Press Lord], chief author of the anti-waste campaign, has enlisted under the Happy Warrior of Squandermania [Mr Lloyd George].

The detailed methods of spending the money has not yet been fully thought out, but we are assured on the highest authority that if only enough resource and energy is used there will be no difficulty in getting rid of the stuff. This is the policy which used to be stigmatized by the late Mr Thomas Gibson Bowles as the policy of buying a biscuit early in the morning and walking about all day looking for a dog to give it to. At any rate, after this, no one will ever accuse the Right Hon. Gentleman of cheap electioneering.

and

Comparing the budget of 1929 with that of the previous year. Referring to beer taxes and death duties.

W.S.C.: Again, the failure of beer was repaired by the harvest of death.

and

Introducing tax changes.

W.S.C.: I never had much sympathy with the consumer of luxuries, and particularly of foreign luxuries.

THE 'PROPHET OF EVILS'
1930–1939

Isolated from Conservative Party councils, comfortably settled into Chartwell, W.S.C. became a one-man intelligence centre on rising Nazi power and intentions. He was already multi-careered as soldier, war correspondent, novelist, biographer, essayist, journalist, orator, statesman, lover of poetry, tunester, reviewer, horse racer, polo player, fencer, flyer and huntsman (which included shooting a white rhinoceros in Africa, pig sticking in India and hunting wild boar in Normandy). He was painter, sculptor (on rare occasions), bricklayer, innovator, seer, lecturer, newspaper publisher and occasional violinist. He collected dogs, cats, white and black swans, tropical fish, race horses and butterflies, especially an imported white-veined species, extinct in Britain, which he raised in his Butterfly House and then liberated. He fondly cherished his collection of hats, especially a blood-stained American Indian chieftain's feathered war bonnet hung with enemy scalps. Among his Homburgs, hussar, polo and pith helmets and Russian fur hat he was most attached to his broad-brimmed Stetsons as they shaded him from the sun which poisoned his skin. He disliked draughts, dial telephones, aesthetes, whistling, loud voices, the radio, ticking clocks, the sun, people pronouncing foreign names in an un-English way and the word 'can't'. He wrote, 'My tastes are simple, I like only the best.' To him this meant the best food and wines, incense, toilet waters, games of bezique and backgammon, hot-rod speeding, Gilbert and Sullivan music, two hot baths a day, an after-lunch nap in bed with a black silk scarf covering his eyes, Wild West films, English actress Vivien Leigh in *That Hamilton Woman*, open-throated white silk shirts, polka-dot bow ties and his gold-headed cane, a wedding gift from Edward VII 'to my youngest minister.'

The maxim, Nothing avails but perfection may be spelled, Paralysis.

—Winston S. Churchill

1930	Breach with Stanley Baldwin's Conservative 'Shadow Cabinet'* over India policy.
APRIL 1930	Resigned from the chairmanship of the Conservative Finance Committee.
OCTOBER 1930	Published *My Early Life* (*A Roving Commission*, American edition).
JANUARY 1931	Resigned from Conservative 'Shadow Cabinet' on India issue. Took a stand against early independent rule for India, putting him outside Conservative councils when most needed.
MAY 1931	Published *India*.
25TH AUGUST 1931	*New Government, under Ramsay MacDonald (as Prime Minister) and Stanley Baldwin, leader of the predominant Conservatives*. Government was a coalition of Conservatives, Liberals, and a splinter Labour group, created to cope with crisis resulting from the financial crash in the United States. W.S.C. re-elected Conservative member for Epping Division, Essex. Lecture tour in the United States.
13TH DECEMBER 1931	Knocked down by a taxi on Fifth Avenue. Watched Ramsay MacDonald disarm in face of German remilitarization. While Stanley Baldwin proceeded on business as usual, W.S.C. became almost a one-man opposition to Nazi aims.
NOVEMBER 1932	Published *Thoughts and Adventures* (American title: *Amid These Storms*).
AUGUST 1933	Speech warning of danger of German rearmament.
OCTOBER 1933	Published *Marlborough, His Life and Times*, Vol. I.
NOVEMBER 1933	Criticized an attempt to revive Disarmament Conference.
MARCH 1934	Urged stronger air defences.
OCTOBER 1934	Published *Marlborough, His Life and Times*, Vol. II.
NOVEMBER 1934	Warned Commons Germans would reach parity in the air in 1935.
1935	Assisted in production of film, *The Conquest of the Air*.
7TH JUNE 1935	*New Government, Stanley Baldwin coalition*.
JULY 1935	Joined Committee of Imperial Defence on Air Defence Research on which he served four years. Re-elected Conservative member for Epping Division, Essex.
NOVEMBER 1935	Germany protested at critical article by W.S.C. in *Strand* magazine warning of Hitler's plans.
DECEMBER 1935	Painting holiday in Morocco.
OCTOBER 1936	Published *Marlborough, His Life and Times*, Vol. III.
NOVEMBER 1936	Demanded Parliamentary inquiry on state of defences.

* 'Shadow Cabinet': unofficial group of leading members and/or ex-ministers of the Opposition Party seeking to succeed the incumbent Party.

DECEMBER 1936	Advised King Edward VIII through abdication crisis.
1937	Exclusion from office continued when Neville Chamberlain succeeded Stanley Baldwin.
28TH MAY 1937	*New Government, Neville Chamberlain Coalition.*
	Warned German Ambassador Joachim von Ribbentrop on under-rating England. Though basically loyal to Neville Chamberlain, kept attacking his unpreparedness.
OCTOBER 1937	Published *Great Contemporaries*.
MARCH 1938	Attended series of meetings with French military and political leaders in Paris.
MAY 1938	Protested at renunciation of naval base rights in the ports of the Irish Free State.
JUNE 1938	Published *Arms and the Covenant* (American edition titled *While England Slept*).
SEPTEMBER 1938	Published *Marlborough, His Life and Times*, Vol. IV.
OCTOBER 1938	Attacked Munich Agreement.
MARCH 1939	Czechoslovakia over-run by Nazis.
APRIL 1939	Benito Mussolini invaded Albania.
JUNE 1939	Published *Step by Step*.
JULY 1939	Visited the French Rhine Front.

1930   A ROVING COMMISSION

W.S.C.: I adopted quite early in life a system of believing what I wanted to believe, while at the same time leaving reason to pursue unfettered whatever paths she was capable of treading.

A NUMBER OF PEOPLE

Snubbing Sir Oswald Mosley,* then a rising young Labour MP who had just abandoned the Tories. Mosley liked nothing better than talking.

W.S.C.: I can well understand the Honourable Member speaking for practice—which he badly needs.

---

* Sir Oswald E. Mosley, successively Conservative, Independent and Labour member; leader of British Fascists. He and his followers 'grovelled to Nazi dictatorship . . . that they could make people . . . grovel to them', as W.S.C. put it. Interned by wartime authorities, 1940; released for health reasons, largely at W.S.C.'s urging, 1943.

WINSTON CHURCHILL, AN INTIMATE PORTRAIT

At a birthday party given him by Mrs Edwin Montague,* he revelled in the gathering of worldly divorcées she had seated around him.

W.S.C.: Yes—this is the sort of company I should like to find in heaven. Stained perhaps—stained but positive. Not those flaccid sea anemones of virtue who can hardly woggle an antenna in the turgid waters of negativity.

HOUSE OF COMMONS

On April 15, commenting on the Budget Proposals of the Labour Government.

W.S.C.: I said that if I could have foreseen the General Strike and the coal stoppage I should not have felt justified in making an addition to taxation.

Mr Frederick Pethick-Lawrence: I do not deny that. The Right Hon. Gentleman, like a bad bridge player, blames his cards.

W.S.C.: I blame the crooked deal.

GREAT CONTEMPORARIES

On Trotsky.[†]

W.S.C.: All his scheming, all his daring, all his writing, all his harangues, all his atrocities, all his achievements, have led only to this—that another 'comrade', his subordinate in revolutionary rank, his inferior wit, though not perhaps in crime, rules in his stead, while he, the once triumphant Trotsky, whose frown meted death to thousands, sits disconsolate, a skin of malice stranded on the shores of the Black Sea. [Later he added] . . . and now washed up on the Gulf of Mexico.

and

W.S.C.: He possessed in his nature all the qualities requisite for the art of civic destruction—the organizing command of a Carnot,[‡]

---

* Venetia Montagu, cousin of Mrs Churchill, brilliant hostess, widow of Edwin Montagu (1879–1924), Secretary of State for India, who drafted the Report on Indian Constitutional Reforms.

[†] Leon Trotsky (born Lev Davidovich Bronstein), 1879–1940; Russian revolutionary and Communist Leader; defeated by Stalin, 1924, for control of the Communist Party.

[‡] Lazare Nicolas Marguerite Carnot, 1753–1823, French revolutionist known as 'the organizer of victory,' the military genius of the revolution; exiled by Louis XVIII.

the cold detached intelligence of a Machiavelli, the mob oratory of a Cleon, the ferocity of a Jack the Ripper, the toughness of a Titus Oates.

and

W.S.C.: But the dull, squalid figures of the Russian Bolsheviks are not redeemed in interest even by the magnitude of their crimes. All form and emphasis is lost in a vast process of Asiatic liquefaction.

and

ANEURIN BEVAN, BY MICHAEL FOOT

While the Labour Party was riven with disputes, Prime Minister Ramsay MacDonald tried to devise a policy to discourage Sir Oswald Mosley's rebellion and to appeal to the two Opposition parties. After a Parliamentary debate, Aneurin Bevan, accompanied by a fellow conspirator, W. J. Brown, met W.S.C. in the Smoking Room of the House of Commons.

W.S.C.: Well, you young members of the Suicide Club, what have you been up to?

Aneurin Bevan: Well, for that matter, what have *you* been up to? We haven't seen much of you in the fight lately.

W.S.C.: Fight? I can't see any fight. All I can see in this Parliament is a lot of people leaning against each other.

1931 SPEECH

At Winchestesr House, February 23.

W.S.C.: It is alarming and also nauseating to see Mr Gandhi,[*] a seditious Middle Temple lawyer now posing as a fakir of a type well-known in the East, striding half naked up the steps of the Viceregal Palace, while he is still organizing and conducting a defiant campaign of civil disobedience, to parley on equal terms with the representative of the King-Emperor.

---

[*] Mahatma Gandhi, 1869–1948; Indian National leader; waged campaign of civil disobedience, 1929–30, causing rioting and his imprisonment for second time.

HOUSE OF COMMONS

W.S.C.: The Government . . . are defeated by thirty votes and then the Prime Minister [Ramsay MacDonald] rises in his place utterly unabashed, the greatest living master of falling without hurting himself, and airily assures us that nothing has happened.

HOUSE OF COMMONS

On January 26, opposing the swift development of self-government for India—to which both Labour and Conservatives were pledged.

W.S.C.: How will the British nation feel about all this? I am told that they do not care. I am told that from one quarter to another. They are all worried by unemployment or taxation or absorbed in sport and crime. The great liner is sinking in a calm sea. One bulkhead after another gives way; one compartment after another is bilged; the list increases; she is sinking; but the captain and the officers and the crew are all in the saloon dancing to the jazz band. But wait till the passengers find out what is their position!

HOUSE OF COMMONS

On the Trade Disputes Act. The Labour Party wanted to repeal the measure which the Tories had introduced after the General Strike to reduce the power of the Trades Unionists. Prime Minister MacDonald did not strongly support his Party on their stand.

W.S.C.: What is the Prime Minister going to do? I spoke the other day, after he had been defeated in an important division about his wonderful skill in falling without hurting himself. He falls, but up he comes again, smiling, a little dishevelled but still smiling. But this is a juncture, a situation, which will try to the fullest the peculiar arts in which he excels. I remember when I was a child, being taken to the celebrated Barnum's Circus which contained an exhibition of freaks and monstrosities, but the exhibit on the programme which I most desired to see was the one described as 'The Boneless Wonder'. My parents judged that that spectacle would be too revolting and demoralizing for my youthful eyes, and I have waited fifty years to see the boneless wonder sitting on the Treasury Bench. *and*

An imaginary conversation dreamed by W.S.C. between Ramsay MacDonald and David Lloyd George. It was directed at Mr MacDonald because of the debate on the Trade Disputes Act.

W.S.C.: We have never been colleagues, we have never been friends—at least not what you would call holiday friends—but we have both been Prime Minister, and dog don't eat dog. Just look at the monstrous Bill the trade unions and our wild fellows have foisted on me. Do me a service and I will never forget it. Take it upstairs and cut its dirty throat.

SPEECH

On March 5, at Liverpool.

W.S.C.: The British lion, so fierce and valiant in bygone days, so dauntless and unconquerable through all the agony of Armageddon, can now be chased by rabbits from the fields and forests of his former glory.

SPEECH

On March 11, at the Constitutional Club.

W.S.C.: It makes me sick when I hear the Secretary of State saying of India 'she will do this and she will do that'. India is an abstraction . . . India is no more a political personality than Europe. India is a geographical term. It is no more a united nation than the Equator.

HOUSE OF COMMONS

On April 29.

W.S.C.: We have all heard of how Dr [Joseph] Guillotine was executed by the instrument that he invented.

Sir Herbert Samuel (*Secretary of State for India*): He was not.

W.S.C.: Well, he ought to have been.

HOUSE OF COMMONS

Referring to Miss Margaret Bondfield, Minister of Labour in the Labour Government of 1929–1931, and her failure to check the rising tide of unemployment.

W.S.C.: I used to be much affected by a popular drama called *The Girl Who Took the Wrong Turning*.

HOUSE OF COMMONS
Answering a persistent interrupter.
W.S.C.: The Hon. Gentleman . . . has arrogated to himself a function which did not belong to him, namely to make my speech instead of letting me make it.

GREAT CONTEMPORARIES
On Bernard Shaw.
W.S.C.: Mr Bernard Shaw was one of my earliest antipathies . . . This bright, nimble, fierce, and comprehending being . . . Jack Frost dancing bespangled in the sunshine which I should be very sorry to lose . . . He is at once an acquisitive Capitalist and a sincere Communist. He makes his characters talk blithely about killing men for the sake of an idea; but would take great trouble not to hurt a fly . . .

If the truth must be told, our British island has not had much help in its troubles from Mr Bernard Shaw. When nations are fighting for life, when the palace in which the jester dwells not uncomfortably is itself assailed, and everyone from prince to groom is fighting on the battlements, the jester's jokes echo only through deserted halls, and his witticisms and condemnations, distributed evenly between friend and foe, jar the ear of hurrying messengers, of mourning women and wounded men. The titter ill accords with the tocsin, or the motley with the bandages . . .
and
On Nancy, Lady Astor's trip to Russia with Bernard Shaw.
W.S.C.: The choice [Bernard Shaw's selection of Lady Astor as his companion on the trip] was happy and appropriate. Lady Astor, like Bernard Shaw, enjoys the best of both worlds . . . She denounces the vice of gambling in unmeasured terms, and is closely associated with an almost unrivalled racing stable. She accepts Communist hospitality and flattery, and remains the Conservative member for Plymouth . . . The Russians have always been fond of circuses and travelling shows . . . here was the world's

most famous intellectual Clown and Pantaloon in one, and the charming Columbine of the capitalist pantomime.*

also

EAR-WITNESS

George Bernard Shaw is said to have told W.S.C.: Am reserving two tickets for you for my premiere. Come and bring a friend—if you have one.

W.S.C. to G.B.S.: Impossible to be present for the first performance. Will attend the second—if there is one.

THE SECOND WORLD WAR, VOL. I

Almost alone in his opposition to self-government for India, he felt it would bring 'measureless disaster upon the Indian people.'

W.S.C.: A portentous conference [first London Round Table Conference] was held in London of which Mr Gandhi, lately released from commodious internment, was the central figure.

HOUSE OF COMMONS

About Socialist William Graham on the revised Budget proposals.

W.S.C.: He spoke without a note and almost without a point.

HOUSE OF COMMONS

On the formation of the National Government.

W.S.C.: Is this Coalition to be above party government or below party government?

---

* Bernard Shaw told his biographer, Hesketh Pearson, that on that visit to Russia he asked Stalin if W.S.C. would be more welcome than Lloyd George in Moscow. Stalin said yes, that in 1921, as Secretary of State for War, W.S.C. had inadvertently equipped the Red Army by handing over £100,000,000-worth of equipment voted by Parliament for the war against Germany, to help the Russian counter-revolution. As the Bolsheviks won they armed and clothed themselves, thanks to W.S.C.'s generosity.

EAR-WITNESS

Referring to the Coalition team of Stanley Baldwin and Ramsay MacDonald.

W.S.C.: Two nurses fit to keep silence around a darkened room.

EAR-WITNESS

In New York City preparing for a lecture tour his agent, Louis Albers, informed him that Scotland Yard had learned that his life was threatened.

W.S.C.: Please fetch me a bottle of champagne.

Mr Albers: I had better go ahead first and make plans against these plots.

W.S.C.: First things first. Get the champagne.

(It was part of his contract that he be provided with a bottle of champagne before each lecture.)

COLLIER'S

On being run down by a cab in New York.

W.S.C.: There was a moment of a world aglare, of a man aghast . . . I do not understand why I was not broken like an eggshell, or squashed like a gooseberry.

1932   SPEECH

Responding to questions after a speech in New York City.

Q: Would you become an American citizen if we could make you President of the United States? I know our Constitution disqualifies you but we can amend that, as we did in the case of Prohibition.

W.S.C.: There are various little difficulties in the way. However, I have been treated so splendidly in the United States that I should be disposed, if you can amend the Constitution, seriously to consider the matter.

EAR-WITNESS

W.S.C. was a lover of cats, fish, dogs—all animals. At one Sunday lunch, a goose raised at Chartwell was brought in and put before him to be carved.

W.S.C.: You carve him, Clemmie, he was my friend.

and

Planning to feed some baby swans just hatched on his Chartwell ponds he discovered they had vanished. Only the mother swan, forlornly alone, sat in the middle of the pond.

W.S.C.: The bloody toads have had 'em.

(An elaborate strategic plan followed, involving the construction of a brick wall around the pond to block off the toads. Whereupon the mother swan lifted her wings, disclosing all her babies snuggled close to her body.)

HOUSE OF COMMONS

It is said that after a new member had finished his maiden speech W.S.C. inquired of a colleague the speaker's name and was told it was Alfred Blossom.*

W.S.C.: Blossom, Blossom, that's an odd name! Neither one thing nor the other.

THE DAILY MAIL

In a May 2 speech at the Royal Academy Banquet at Burlington House, Piccadilly, in saluting the Royal Academy of Arts W.S.C. remarked it was characteristic of the chivalry of the Royal Academy that they should have picked out among all the politicians open to their choice for the places of honour at their gathering, the Home Secretary Sir Herbert Samuel and himself.

W.S.C.: I think we are two of the least understood politicians outside this festal scene.

The National Government has a great deal in common with the Royal Academy. It is not so ancient, and it may not live so long, but it meets an indubitable public need and it embraces—I am not quite sure the word embraces is well chosen—every style and shade of political artistry.

I must tell you of some of our leading political painters. First of all there is the Prime Minister [Ramsay MacDonald]; how glad we are all to learn that his health is so much better. His works are well known; we all regret they are not more frequently visible at home.

---

* Alfred Blossom, successful modern architect who entertained lavishly at his house at Carlton House Gardens.

He has been exhibiting so much in foreign galleries lately that we rather miss his productions here.

We believe that on the Continent he has several most important masterpieces still unhappily in an unfinished condition, and we look forward hopefully to their arrival and to his return.

I have watched for many years the Prime Minister's style and methods. For a long time I thought there was a great deal too much vermilion in his pictures. All those lurid sunsets of capitalist civilization began rather to pall upon me, and I am very glad to see he has altered his style so fundamentally.

In all his new pictures we see the use of cobalt, of French ultramarine, of Prussian blue, and all the other blues not excluding, I am glad to say, British true blue, and also we see that cerulean, that heavenly colour we all admire so much.

But I think the Prime Minister in his picture uses blue very much like the late John Sargent. He uses it not only for atmosphere but for foundation.

We like his modern style very much better than the earlier methods.

Then there is the Lord President of the Council [Mr Baldwin], who is still quite a distinguished painter in our academy. If I were to criticize him at all I would say his work lacked a little in colour, and also was a little lacking in the precise definition of objects in the foreground. He too has changed not only his style but also his subjects.

We all miss very much the jolly old English pictures which he used to paint—'The Worcestershire Farm', 'Pigs in Clover',* 'Broccoli in Autumn', and, above all, we have missed just now that subject which no pencil could have done more justice to than Mr Baldwin's, 'Brewing the Audit Ale'.

Making a fair criticism, I must admit there is something very reposeful about the half-tones of his twilight studies.

We have in our Academy the Dominions Secretary [Mr J. H. Thomas†], who represents a very fruity kind of Cubism. Some people find it shocking; others say it lacks conviction. That is a very

---

* Mr Baldwin popularized his image as a pig breeder.
† Mr Thomas, a genial Labour alcoholic with a taste for fast society and a great fund of off-colour stories.

serious criticism, isn't it? But, nevertheless, it is a most interesting contribution to our national show.

I could go on all night about these political painters, but we all want to get out into the galleries. But you will want to ask me how it is I am not exhibiting this season. Why is it I have not got a row of important pictures on the line at my Academy.

I will be perfectly frank. I make no concealment. I had some differences with the committee—with the hanging committee. Luckily in our case their powers are limited as far as I am concerned, and I am not submitting any of my works for their approval this year.

I have joined the teaching profession. We have a sort of Slade School at Westminster, a very fine lot of young students, most ardent and with much before them—to learn.

I am endeavouring to assist them in acquiring a knowledge of parliamentary technique, so I have a few things on my easel which I hope one day to present to the public.

COLLIER'S

The Shattered Cause of Temperance.

W.S.C.: It is possible that the dry, bracing electrical atmosphere of North America makes the use of alcohol necessary and more potent than does the humid climate of Britain . . .

I must confess that on one occasion I was taken to a speakeasy. I went of course in my capacity as a Social Investigator.

THE SECOND WORLD WAR, VOL. I

W.S.C.: In the summer of 1932 for the purposes of my life of Marlborough I visited his old battlefields in the Low Countries and Germany . . . At the Regina Hotel (in Munich) a gentleman introduced himself . . . He was Herr Hanfstaengl,* and spoke a great

---

* Ernst ('Putzi') Hanfstaengl, of wealthy Munich family; Harvard graduate; early friend of Adolf Hitler; chief of Foreign Press Department of the Nazi Party until forced to flee for his life to U.S., where he became an 'adviser' to U.S. on Nazi Germany.

deal about 'the Fuehrer', with whom he appeared to be intimate . . . He said I ought to meet him . . . However, in the course of conversation with Hanfstaengl I happened to say, 'Why is your chief so violent about the Jews? I can quite understand being angry with Jews who have done wrong or are against the country, and I understand resisting them if they try to monopolize power in any walk of life; but what is the sense of being against a man simply because of his birth? How can any man help how he is born?'

He must have repeated this to Hitler,[*] because about noon the next day he came around with a rather serious air and said that the appointment he had made for me to meet Hitler could not take place . . . Thus Hitler lost his only chance of meeting me. Later on when he was all-powerful, I was to receive several invitations from him. But by that time a lot had happened, and I excused myself.

HOUSE OF COMMONS

Even before Adolf Hitler became Chancellor, W.S.C. warned against Germany's cry for equal status.

W.S.C.: All these bands of sturdy Teutonic youths, marching along the streets and roads of Germany, with the light of desire in their eyes to suffer for their Fatherland are not looking for status—they are looking for weapons!

SPEECH

At a party conference in England at the time of apathy, appeasement and undergraduate resolutions not to fight for King and Country.

W.S.C.: Is it for this you propose to fling away the ancient heritage bequeathed to us by the architects of our magnitude and renown?

and

Asked by the writer Harold Nicolson if he had improvised this final phrase extemporaneously.

W.S.C.: Improvised be damned! I thought of it this morning in my bath and I wish now I hadn't wasted it on this crowd.

[*] Adolf Hitler, 1889–1945; named German Chancellor by President Paul von Hindenburg, 1933; combined office of President and Chancellor to become Dictator-Führer, August 1934; suicide, April 1945.

AMID THESE STORMS

On cartooning politicians.

W.S.C.: Just as eels are supposed to get used to skinning, so politicians get used to being caricatured . . . If we must confess it, they are quite offended and down cast when the cartoons stop . . . They fear old age and obsolescence are creeping upon them. They murmur: 'We are not mauled and maltreated as we used to be. The great days are ended.'

EAR-WITNESS

Picasso* said of W.S.C.'s painting, 'If that man were a painter by profession he would have no trouble in earning a good living.'

A friend to W.S.C.: Why do you paint only landscapes and never portraits?

W.S.C.: Because a tree doesn't complain that I haven't done it justice.

and

AMID THESE STORMS

W.S.C.: I agree with Ruskin[†] in his denunciation of the school of painting who 'eat slate, pencil and chalk and assure everybody that they are nicer and purer than strawberries and plums'. I cannot pretend to feel impartial about the colours. I rejoice with the brilliant ones, and am genuinely sorry for the poor browns.

1933

EAR-WITNESS

Asked to speak at Oxford after the Oxford Union (debating society) had voted 'that this house will in no circumstances fight for King and Country,' and remembering that Cambridge defeated Oxford each year in rowing.

W.S.C.: A curious set of young gentlemen. They will not fight and they cannot row.

---

[*] Pablo Picasso, Spanish painter and sculptor.
[†] John Ruskin, 1819–1900; English art critic and writer.

A CHURCHILL CANVAS

He commissioned his nephew John Spencer Churchill to paint murals in his garden loggia at Chartwell commemorating the great battles of their ancestor John, the first Duke of Marlborough. Every morning at eleven, W.S.C. inspected the progress of the work.

W.S.C.: (*pointing with his cigar to a lower part of the ceiling*): Can't we get rid of this vast white space?

John Churchill: My method is to start at the top and work downwards, thus avoiding any danger of messing up the bottom part.

W.S.C.: I always survey the whole scene with greater clarity if I attack the white areas first and afterwards concentrate on the pockets of resistance.

also

EAR-WITNESS

Later, in 1954, as Prime Minister at the age of eighty, he came upon a painting of Aesop's fabled Lion and the Mouse attributed to Peter Paul Rubens hanging high up in the Great Hall at Chequers.* The drawing and colours of the lion were still clear but the mouse had faded almost into oblivion. This inspired him to call for his oil paints and brushes.

W.S.C.: What! A Lion without a Mouse?

The painting was then placed on an easel and he proceeded to paint in the mouse.†

also

F.D.R.: HIS PERSONAL LETTERS

F.D.R. to W.S.C.

The White House Feb. 11, 1942

Dear Winston [W.S.C. was then painting under the alias, Charles Marin]:

---

* Official country residence of British Prime Ministers presented to the nation by Lord and Lady Lee of Fareham in 1921.

† Julius S. Held, Professor of Art History, Columbia University, who had recently studied the paintings at Chequers, wrote me: 'To my surprise I found the picture was not by Rubens. It is fully signed by Franz Snyders who was a specialist in painting animals . . . The mouse painted in by Churchill is indeed there and is,' he added, 'I hope you will forgive me, a most disagreeable coloristic element.'

These people who go around under assumed names render themselves open to all kinds of indignity and suspicion . . . Ned Bruce [Chief of the Section of Fine Arts, District of Columbia] . . . sent a letter to a man named 'Marin' in my care.

The British Embassy has asked for verification and I suppose the matter has been to Scotland Yard and back again.

Someday I want to see a painting by this alias fellow—and someday I hope you will get enough time to resume the painting and that I will be able to return to making ship models and collecting stamps! As ever yours.

HOUSE OF COMMONS

On March 14, opposing a reduction in the size of the Royal Air Force.
W.S.C.: We must not allow our insular pride to blind us to the fact that some of these foreigners are quite intelligent, that they have an extraordinary knack, on occasion, of rising fully up to the level of British comprehension.

HOUSE OF COMMONS

On Ramsay MacDonald's oratory.
W.S.C.: Here I say very little of the Prime Minister's [Mr Ramsay MacDonald] oratorical style. We are familiar with it here. We know that he has, more than any other man, the gift of compressing the largest number of words into the smallest amount of thought.
and
W.S.C.: I associate myself with my Right Hon. Friend in welcoming the Prime Minister [Ramsay MacDonald] back [from his visit to Rome]. We have got our modern Don Quixote home again, with Sancho Panza [Sir John Simon]* at his tail, bearing with them these somewhat dubious trophies which they have collected amid the nervous titterings of Europe. Let us hope that now the Right Hon. Gentleman is safely back among us he will, first of all, take a good rest.[†]

---

* Sir John Simon, first Viscount, 1873–1954; British statesman and jurist; Foreign Secretary, 1931–1935; Chancellor of the Exchequer, 1937–1940; Lord Chancellor, 1940–1945.
[†] Ramsay MacDonald's intellect, undermined by overwork and stress, was beginning noticeably to disintegrate.

SPEECH

On April 24, to the Royal Society of St George.

W.S.C.: I am a great admirer of the Scots. I am quite friendly with the Welsh, especially one of them [Lloyd George]. I must confess to some sentiment about Old Ireland, in spite of the ugly mask she tries to wear. But this is not their night. On this one night in the whole year we are allowed to use a forgotten, almost a forbidden word. We are allowed to mention the name of our own country, to speak of ourselves as 'Englishmen', and we may even raise the slogan 'St George for Merrie England'.

We must be careful, however. You see these microphones? They have been placed on our tables by the British Broadcasting Corporation. Think of the risk these eminent men are running. We can almost see them in our mind's eye, gathered together in that very expensive building with the questionable statues on its front. We can picture Sir John Reith,* with the perspiration mantling on his lofty brow, with his hand on the control switch, wondering, as I utter every word, whether it will not be his duty to protect his innocent subscribers from some irreverent thing I might say about our peripatetic Prime Minister. But let me reassure him. I have much more serious topics to discuss. I have to speak to you about St George and the Dragon. I have been wondering what would happen if that legend were repeated under modern conditions.

St George would arrive in Cappadocia, accompanied not by a horse, but by a secretariat. He would be armed not with a lance, but with several flexible formulas. He would, of course, be welcomed by the local branch of the League of Nations Union. He would propose a conference with the dragon—a Round Table Conference, no doubt—that would be more convenient for the dragon's tail. He would make a trade agreement with the dragon. He would lend the dragon a lot of money of the Cappadocian taxpayers. The maiden's release would be referred to Geneva, the dragon reserving all his rights meanwhile. Finally St George would be photographed with the dragon (inset—the maiden).

---

* The Director General of the British Broadcasting Corporation, overbearing, stiff and puritanical engineer and public servant.

COLLIER'S

In a November 4 article titled, 'The Bond Between Us.'

W.S.C.: The American chicken is a small bird compared with the standard of English fowl. Attractively served with rice and auxiliaries of all kinds, he makes an excellent dish. Still I am on the side of the big chicken as regularly as Providence is on the side of the big battalions. Indeed it seems strange in so large a country to find such small chickens. Conscious, perhaps, of their inferiority, the inhabitants call them 'Squabs'. What an insulting title for a capon.

HOUSE OF COMMONS

W.S.C.: [Mr Lansbury]* said just now that he and the Socialist Party would never consent to the re-arming of Germany . . . But is the Right Hon. Gentleman quite sure that the Germans will come and ask him for his consent before they re-arm? Does he not think they might omit that formality and go ahead without even taking a card vote of the Trades Union Congress?

HOUSE OF COMMONS

On Britain's unpreparedness.

W.S.C.: It is much better to be frightened now than to be killed hereafter.

1934   HOUSE OF COMMONS

W.S.C.: Eight years ago we were told that disarmament had been discussed at Geneva. For two and a half years the actual conference has been proceeding. The leader of the Liberal Opposition [Sir Herbert Samuel] has, therefore, had a good run for his experiment. His hope has been abounding. It has preserved him at every stage from seeing the facts.

---

* George Lansbury, Leader of the Labour Party, 1931–1935; deposed for confused pacifism.

THE SECOND WORLD WAR, VOL. I

On July 30, quoting one of his own speeches urging rearmament of Britain in the face of Germany's growing superiority of arms.

W.S.C.: We are a rich and easy prey. No country is so vulnerable, and no country would better repay pillage than our own . . . With our enormous Metropolis here, the greatest target in the world, a kind of tremendous, fat, valuable cow tied up to attract the beast of prey . . .

THE LIGHT
OF EPPING
GOES OUT

1935

HOUSE OF COMMONS

W.S.C.: The flying peril is not a peril from which one can fly . . . We cannot possibly retreat. We cannot move London.

HOUSE OF COMMONS

On rearmament.

W.S.C.: It is only a little while ago that I heard ministers say . . . 'Whatever happens, we cannot have that. Rearmament is unthinkable.' Now all our hope is to regulate the unthinkable. Regulated unthinkability—that is the proposal now; and very soon it will be a question of making up our minds to unregulated unthinkability.

THE SECOND WORLD WAR, VOL. I

On the May trip of Premier Pierre Laval to Moscow to discuss the Franco-Soviet mutual assistance pact.

W.S.C.: Stalin and Molotov* were, of course, anxious to know above all else what was to be the strength of the French Army on the Western Front; how many divisions? What period of service? After this field had been explored, Laval said, 'Can't you do something to encourage religion and the Catholics in Russia? It would help me so much with the Pope [Pius XII].' 'Oho!' said Stalin. 'The Pope! How many divisions has he got?' Laval's answer was not reported to me; but he might certainly have mentioned a number of legions not always visible on parade.

HOUSE OF COMMONS

Clement Attlee, then Lord Privy Seal, made a mis-step and crashed over in his seat landing in a heap on the floor of the House of Commons.

W.S.C.: Get up, get up, Lord Privy Seal! This is no time for levity.

HOUSE OF COMMONS

W.S.C.: All the years that I have been in the House of Commons I have always said to myself one thing: 'Do not interrupt', and I have never been able to keep to that resolution.

EAR-WITNESS

On December 1 in the House of Commons Smoking Room, W.S.C. to A. P. Herbert, witty Independent Member, after Herbert had made his Maiden Speech.

W.S.C.: Call that a maiden speech? It was a brazen hussy of a speech. Never did such a painted lady of a speech parade itself before a modest Parliament!

also

---

* Vyacheslav Mikhailovich Molotov, Soviet statesman; President of Communist Party, 1930–1941, and member of Politburo; Minister of Foreign Affairs, 1939–1949, 1953–1956.

CHURCHILL BY HIS CONTEMPORARIES

The first public speech of the son of a noted though unloved Conservative Minister was reported in the newspapers.

W.S.C.: Isn't it enough to have this parent volcano continually erupting in our midst? And now we are to have these subsidiary craters spouting forth the same unhealthy fumes . . .!

WINSTON CHURCHILL, THE ERA AND THE MAN

On a trip to North Africa with Lloyd George and his daughter Megan, a native Prince honoured them with a feast. According to custom, no forks and knives were served. All eyes were on W.S.C., as 'any deviation from comfort arranged in the name of pleasure fills him with gloom.'

W.S.C.: (*rolling up his sleeves and plunging his fingers into the pot*): Come on, Megan, to hell with civilization.*

EAR-WITNESS

During the Abyssinian Crisis.

Questioner: Don't you think that it is high time that the British lion showed its teeth?

W.S.C.: It must go to the dentist first.

1936   A ROVING COMMISSION

On education.

W.S.C.: When I am in a Socratic mood and planning *my* Republic, I make drastic changes in the education of the sons of well-to-do citizens. When they are sixteen or seventeen they begin to learn a craft and to do healthy manual labour, with plenty of poetry, songs, dancing, drill and gymnastics in their spare time. They can thus let off their steam on something useful. It is only when they are really thirsty for knowledge, longing to hear about things, that I would let them go to a university. It would be a favour, a coveted privilege, only to be given to those who had either proved their worth in

---

* On this trip W.S.C. was eager to accompany his wife and Megan Lloyd George on a visit to the Pasha's harem, but was told that only women might go. Ruffling his hair, and winding a scarf turban-wise around his head, he suggested he might go as his own mother-in-law.

factory or field or whose qualities and zeal were pre-eminent. However, this would upset a lot of things; it would cause commotion and bring me perhaps in the end a hemlock draught.

EAR-WITNESS
In the presence of an off-colour joke.
W.S.C.: Young man, what you are saying is a lot of——. I predict you will go far—in the wrong direction.

HOUSE OF COMMONS
On the national Coalition Government led by Stanley Baldwin and Ramsay MacDonald.
W.S.C.: Their ideal of government appears to be well expressed by the noble lord in the Gilbert and Sullivan opera who did nothing in particular, but did it very well. No wonder they agree so happily when, instead of throwing the ball to one another across the Parliamentary table, they settle down as colleagues side by side.

EAR-WITNESS
Fighting many political battles with Prime Minister Stanley Baldwin for the soul of the Conservative Party.
W.S.C.: [He is] no better than an epileptic corpse.
later
After one of the heaviest air raids over Britain in World War II he was awakened at 10 Downing Street with the news that a bomb had fallen on Lord Baldwin's house.
W.S.C.: What base ingratitude!

HOUSE OF COMMONS
As Colonial Secretary during the Middle East Crisis.
W.S.C.: I have no hostility for the Arabs. I think I made most of the settlements over fourteen years ago governing the Palestine situation. The Emir Abdullah is in Transjordania, where I put him one Sunday afternoon in Jerusalem.

EAR-WITNESS

A nonconformist traditionalist, during the Constitutional crisis over abdication, his advice to King Edward VIII was to defy his adversaries of Church and State and put himself in Windsor Castle.

W.S.C.: Raise the drawbridge, lower the portcullis, and tell them to come and get us.

also

On a June weekend in 1942 at Hyde Park, a discussion with President and Mrs Franklin Roosevelt centred on what small but significant gestures might be made to strengthen Anglo-American understanding. W.S.C., the traditionalist, listened gravely to a suggestion from Richard Miles of the British Embassy staff in Washington that the British might make a start by changing from their right-hand steering wheel to the American custom of left-hand driving as a small gesture of international goodwill.

W.S.C.: No! No!—It *won't* do. If a band of ruffians should set upon you, your sword arm wouldn't be free!

A HORNET'S NEST, POOR WINNIE-THE-POOH.

HOUSE OF COMMONS

After Hitler had militarized the Rhineland, British leaders and the Press counselled cool heads. Only W.S.C. attacked Stanley Baldwin's unpreparedness in the face of clear and present danger.

W.S.C.: The First Lord of the Admiralty [Sir Samuel Hoare] said ... Everything is fluid. The Government simply cannot make up their minds, or they cannot get the Prime Minister to make up his mind. So they go on in strange paradox, decided only to be undecided, resolved to be irresolute, adamant for drift, solid for fluidity, all powerful to be impotent. So we go on preparing more months and years—precious perhaps vital to the greatness of Britain—for the locusts to eat.

EAR-WITNESS
On Stanley Baldwin.
W.S.C.: Occasionally he stumbled over the truth, but hastily picked himself up and hurried on as if nothing had happened.

1937   HOUSE OF COMMONS
On the Spanish Civil War.
W.S.C.: I have tried very sincerely to adopt a neutral attitude of mind in the Spanish quarrel; I refuse to become the partisan of either side. I will not pretend that, if I had to choose between Communism and Nazi-ism, I would choose Communism. I hope not to be called upon to survive in the world under a Government of either of those dispensations.
and
On the Civil War in Spain and need for Defensive Alliances.
W.S.C.: The man who mocks at the existence of the non-Intervention Committee ... mocks at the hopes of Geneva and the League of Nations ... Hypocrisy, it is said, is the tribute which vice pays to virtue ... I say frankly I would rather have a peace-keeping hypocrisy than straight-forward, brazen vice, taking the form of unlimited war.
and
On supporting non-intervention in Spain.
W.S.C.: It is no use leading other nations up the garden and then running away when the dog growls.

THE SECOND WORLD WAR, VOL. I.

On Neville Chamberlain.

W.S.C.: [He] was alert, business-like, opinionated, and self-confident in a very high degree . . . His all-pervading hope was to go down in history as the Great Peacemaker; and for this he was prepared to strive continually in the teeth of facts, and face great risks for himself and his country . . . In these closing years before the war, I should have found it easier to work with Baldwin, as I knew him, than with Chamberlain; but neither of them had any wish to work with me except in the last resort.

THE LIVES OF WINSTON CHURCHILL

Someone remarked that one never hears of Baldwin nowadays—he might as well be dead.

W.S.C.: The candle in that great turnip has gone out.

HOUSE OF COMMONS

On June 21, on the National Defence Contribution proposed by Neville Chamberlain, W.S.C. was for its withdrawal, quoting his own experience as Chancellor of the Exchequer.

W.S.C.: I acted with great promptitude. In the nick of time just as Mr Snowden was rising with overwhelming fury, I got up and withdrew the tax on kerosene. Was I humiliated? Was I accused of running away? No! Everyone said: 'How clever! How quick! How right!' Pardon me for referring to it. It was one of my best days.

STEP BY STEP

Comparing Great Britain and France.

W.S.C.: In Great Britain, governments often change their policies without changing their men. In France, they usually change their men without changing their policy. In Great Britain, a Minister enters a department expecting to stay there three or four years. In France, he makes a bow of greeting or farewell here today and gone tomorrow—to the permanent official who keeps the whole thing going . . . France has always been prodigal of the blood of her sons, but she has a reluctance to pay taxes. The British are good at paying taxes but detest drill. The French do not mind drill but avoid taxes. Both nations can still fight . . . but in such a case France would have a small surplus and Britain a small army . . . This Government [Camille Chautemps*-Leon Blum†] is one of transition. I am very careful not to prophesy. 'Never prophesy unless you know.'

STEP BY STEP
Summing up the Far Eastern situation.
W.S.C.: Not only the British empire and the United States, but the greater part of Europe, have a lively interest in . . . China. China as the years pass, is being eaten by Japan like an artichoke—leaf by leaf.
later
W.S.C.: Japan's policy is to make Hell while the sun shines.

STEP BY STEP
W.S.C.: Dictators ride to and fro upon tigers from which they dare not dismount. And the tigers are getting hungry.

HOUSE OF COMMONS
W.S.C.: Moral force is, unhappily, no substitute for armed force, but it is a very great reinforcement.

1938

On the new French Government of Édouard Daladier.‡
W.S.C.: In both English speaking democracies when a man's in he's in; and when he's out he's out for a good long time. But the accomplished players at the French musical chairs monopolize with

---

* Camille Chautemps, French politician; Premier 1930, 1937–1938; Minister of State of Blum government, 1936–1937.
† Leon Blum, 1872–1950; leader of French Socialist Party; Premier, 1936–1937; Provisional President, 1946.
‡ Édouard Daladier, French statesman; Premier, 1934, 1938–40; arrested after French defeat, 1940; liberated. 1945.

their own fads and prejudices, their own airs and graces, their own personal egotisms or partyisms, an altogether undue part of the life of France, and thus of the life of the free democracies . . . How they strut and pose. Here is a good man capable of giving the necessary directions, but if he moves one inch this way he loses the Left, or one inch that way he loses the Right. Shuffle the cards again; shake the kaleidoscope . . . Ministers of State pass through their departments like week-end guests at Le Touquet.

EAR-WITNESS

As an opponent of peace-at-any-price.
W.S.C.: Look at the Swiss! They have enjoyed peace for centuries. And what have they produced? The cuckoo clock!

STEP BY STEP

Prime Minister Eamon de Valera of Eire urged recognition of the Italian conquest of Abyssinia.
W.S.C.: Mr de Valera, oblivious to the claims of conquered peoples has also given his croak in this sense. No sooner had he clambered from the arena into the Imperial box than he hastened to turn his thumb down upon the first prostrate gladiator he saw.

HOUSE OF COMMONS

Responding to critics of collective security in the debate following the seizure of Austria by Adolf Hitler.
W.S.C.: . . .I urge His Majesty's Government to proclaim a renewed, revivified, unflinching adherence to the Covenant of the League of Nations. What is there ridiculous about collective security? The only thing that is ridiculous about it is that we have not got it.

STEP BY STEP

On manufacture of British aircraft.
W.S.C.: We have never been likely to get into trouble by having an extra thousand or two of up-to-date aeroplanes at our disposal . . .

As the man whose mother-in-law had died in Brazil replied, when asked how the remains should be disposed of, 'Embalm, cremate, and bury. Take no risks!'

HOUSE OF COMMONS

On Britain's air defences and emergency preparations which Prime Minister Neville Chamberlain appeared to be resisting.

W.S.C.: I will avail myself of the avuncular relationship which I hope I may still possess in respect of the Government to put it to the Prime Minister personally and even intimately. Has he ever heard of Saint Anthony the Hermit? Saint Anthony the Hermit was much condemned by the Fathers of the Church because he refused to do right when the Devil told him to. My Right Hon. Friend should free himself from this irrational inhibition for we are only at the beginning of our anxieties.

and

W.S.C.: We are told that 'All is ready for a Ministry of Munitions on the outbreak of war.' Lord Zetland* tells us that all that happens is that he or some other noble personage has to press a button. I hope that it is not a button like the last gaiter button which was talked of before the war of 1870.† He has only to press this button and a Ministry of Munitions will leap into being fully armed like Minerva from the head of the Minister for the Co-ordination of Defence. Do not let the House believe that, I beg of it.

STEP BY STEP

Describing Japan's position in the Far East, between a neutral Russia and a China resisting all efforts at conquest.

W.S.C.: On the one side, a great bear growling low; on the other, an enormous jelly-fish stinging poisonously.

---

* Governor of Bengal, 1917–1922; Secretary of State for India and Burma.
† In 1870 it was said that France was ready for war with Prussia down to the last gaiter button. But the war was not fought with gaiter buttons, and France was forced to capitulate six months later.

STEP BY STEP

On Adolf Hitler's rape of Austria.

W.S.C.: Two months ago I reminded the House of Commons that after a boa-constrictor had devoured a goat or a deer it usually slept the sleep of repletion for several months. It may, however, happen that this agreeable process is disturbed by indigestion. If the prey has not been sufficiently crushed or covered with slime beforehand, especially if it has been swallowed horns and all, very violent spasms . . . retchings and gaspings are suffered by the great snake. These purely general zoological observations . . . suggest a parallel . . . to what has happened since Austria was incorporated in the German Reich.

also

EAR-WITNESS

Referring to Adolf Hitler's aggressions.

W.S.C.: . . . when like a snake he wants to eat his victims he first covers them with saliva.

also

STEP BY STEP

W.S.C.: Thus, by every device from the stick to the carrot, the emaciated Austrian donkey is made to pull the Nazi barrow up an ever steepening hill.

EAR-WITNESS

As Neville Chamberlain alighted from his plane upon returning from the Munich Conference with Adolf Hitler, he waved before the waiting crowd the piece of paper signed by Hitler.

W.S.C.: See that old town clerk[*] looking at European affairs through the wrong end of a municipal drainpipe.

and

In the House of Commons on November 24, 1938, after the Munich

---

[*] Chamberlain had been Lord Mayor of Birmingham, the only Prime Minister to base his career on municipal government.

Agreement of September 29–30, Prime Minister Neville Chamberlain, a son of Birmingham, was being hailed as the architect of peace-in-our-time.

Malcolm MacDonald, Secretary for the Colonies, in a debate in the House on early negotiations between the Jews, Arabs and the Government, concluded with emotion that he could not remember a time when he was not told stories of Jerusalem and Bethlehem, the birthplace of the Prince of Peace.

W.S.C.: (*in an aside*): I always thought he was born in Birmingham.

and

W.S.C.: You [Prime Minister Neville Chamberlain] were given the choice between war and dishonour. You chose dishonour and you will have war.

and

A friend, referring to Mr Chamberlain's effort to make Mr Attlee swallow the Munich appeasement, compared Chamberlain and Attlee to a snake dominating a rabbit.

W.S.C.: It's more like a rabbit dominating a lettuce!

also

HOUSE OF COMMONS

Later, attacking the Munich Agreement.

W.S.C.: We have sustained a defeat without a war.

but later

In a memorial to ex-Prime Minister Neville Chamberlain in the House of Commons, November 12, 1940, he said, 'Whatever else history may or may not say about these terrible . . . years, we can be sure that Neville Chamberlain acted with perfect sincerity according to his lights and strove to the utmost of his capacity and authority, which were powerful, to save the world from the awful, devastating struggle in which we are now engaged.'

EAR-WITNESS

On Britain after Munich.

W.S.C.: Britain is like a Laocoön* strangled by old school ties.

(*Sometimes the 'old school ties' moved him to repeat, 'The English Public School system is like feeding sham pearls to real swine.'*)

---

* Laocoön, in Greek mythology, the priest of Apollo at Troy who, with his two sons, was strangled by huge sea serpents as punishment for having warned against the Wooden Horse.

HOUSE OF COMMONS

On dictatorship.

W.S.C.: The Dictator . . . is held in the grip of his Party machine. He can go forward; he cannot go back. He must blood his hounds and show them sport, or else like Actaeon* of old, be devoured by them. All strong without he is weak within. As Byron[†] wrote a hundred years ago: 'These Pagod things of sabre sway, with fronts of brass and feet of clay.' . . .

You see these dictators on their pedestals, surrounded by the bayonets of their soldiers and the truncheons of their police . . .— they boast and vaunt themselves before the world, yet in their hearts there is unspoken fear. They are afraid of words and thoughts: words spoken abroad, thoughts stirring at home—all the more powerful because forbidden—terrify them. A little mouse, a tiny little mouse of thought appears in the room, and even the mightiest potentates are thrown into panic.

STEP BY STEP

On Japan's war upon China.

W.S.C.: These Communist guerrillas are fierce, clever and elusive. They appear; they strike, they vanish. The Japanese army holds the railway lines, the blockhouses, the bridgeheads, the fortified posts and the walled towns they have taken. They have not enough troops to go outside these: . . . The guerrillas who capture . . . or trap . . . and destroy some unwary reconnoitring Japanese party cannot be found. It is quite easy to massacre Chinese villagers in reprisal. But what is the good of that? As 'Mr Dooley'[‡] said long ago: 'Flogging China is like flogging a jellyfish.'

and

W.S.C.: Yet sometimes the comfortable feather heads in their feather beds in New York, Paris and London might give a passing thought to the tremendous drama and tragedy [of China].

---

* Actaeon, hero-hunter; changed by Artemis into a stag, then was pursued and killed by fifty hounds.
† George Gordon, Lord Byron, 1788–1824; English poet.
‡ Irish saloonkeeper-philosopher character created by Finley Peter Dunne (1867–1936), American humorist.

HOUSE OF COMMONS

W.S.C.: My Right Hon. Friend the Air Minister [Sir Kingsley Wood] has not been long enough in the office to grow a guilty conscience.

I WAS WINSTON CHURCHILL'S PRIVATE SECRETARY

In the course of a lively argument, Lord Londonderry asked his cousin
*W.S.C. if he had read his latest book (*Ourselves and Germany*).*
W.S.C.: No, I only read for pleasure or for profit.

MARLBOROUGH, HIS LIFE AND TIMES

On the choice of Lord Townshend to represent the Captain General,
Marlborough, as a peace negotiator.
W.S.C.: Lord Townshend . . . was an amiable and well-informed politician . . . He was a student of foreign affairs, and had much personal charm. 'Everybody who knew Townshend loved him.' This last must always be considered a dubious qualification.

STEP BY STEP

On Nazi aggression.
W.S.C.: . . . are the Western democracies to sit by with folded hands and watch resignedly . . .? We remember the sardonic joke about the optimist and the pessimist. The optimist was the man who did not mind what happened, so long as it did not happen to him. The pessimist was the man who lived with the optimist. Is this, then, to describe our joint or respective futures?

EAR-WITNESS

On being invited by the Chamberlain Cabinet to meet Joachim von
Ribbentrop, German Ambassador to Britain.
W.S.C.: I suppose they asked me to show him that, if they couldn't bark themselves, they kept a dog which could bark and might bite.

A FAMILY VISIT

HOUSE OF COMMONS

On his failure to convince the Admiralty to reinstate the reserves and his belief that, in spite of added expense, it was right to do so.

W.S.C.: All that I could say, after having made four or five attempts to persuade them [Admiralty] was, 'Never force little dogs to eat mutton: Now they are eating their mutton.'

EAR-WITNESS

On March 16, the day Prague was seized by the Nazis, he was hurrying to complete a 300,000-word history of the English-speaking peoples.

W.S.C.: (*to a dinner guest*): It's hard to take one's attention off the events of today and concentrate on the reign of James II, but I am going to do it.

EAR-WITNESS

When the Germans swallowed Czechoslovakia, following the Munich Agreement, Mr Chamberlain complained that he could not imagine anyone lying to him, declaring he had been wretchedly betrayed by Hitler.

W.S.C.: This high belief in the perfection of man is appropriate in a man of the cloth, but not in a Prime Minister.

THE SECOND WORLD WAR, VOL. I

Of the man Stalin put at the head of Soviet foreign policy.

W.S.C.: Vyacheslav Molotov was a man of outstanding ability and cold-blooded ruthlessness . . . His cannon-ball head, black moustache, and comprehending eyes, his slab face, his verbal adroitness and imperturbable demeanour, were appropriate manifestations of his qualities and skill . . . I have never seen a human being who more perfectly represented the modern conception of a robot . . . In the conduct of foreign affairs, Mazarin,* Talleyrand,† Metternich‡ would welcome him to their company, if there be another world to which Bolsheviks allow themselves to go.

---

* Jules Mazarin, originally Giuilo Mazarini, of Italian descent, 1602–1661. Became a Cardinal and statesman in France; Richelieu's successor.
† Charles Maurice de Tallyrand-Périgord, 1754–1838.
‡ Prince Klemens von Metternich, 1773–1859; Austrian statesman and diplomat.

SPEECH

At the Cambridge Union. Cambridge graduates in June 1939 were commissioned into the British Army without having to serve in the ranks. After June 1939, they were subject to conscription. W.S.C. visited the Cambridge Union after this date.

W.S.C.: (*sang to them*):
Onward Cambridge soldiers,
Onward as to war,
You would not be conscripts
Had you gone before.[*]

SPEECH

On June 28, at the Carlton Club.

W.S.C.: I see that Herr Goebbels[†] and his Italian counterpart Signor Gayda[‡] have been jeering at us because we have not gone to war with Japan on account of the insults to which Englishmen and New Zealanders have been subjected at Tientsin. They say this shows we are effete . . . But perhaps thinking men in these dictator countries . . . will feel that we may be keeping what strength we have for someone else.

EAR-WITNESS

In Paris on July 14, the French national holiday—the 150th Bastille Day—W.S.C. was a guest of honour at a large military review and admired the large tanks that shook the Champs Élysées as they rolled by.

W.S.C.: The Government had to show the French that their economies had been transferred from the idleness of their stockings to the safety of the tank.

---

[*] W.S.C. remembered *War Birds—Diary of an Unknown Aviator*, which described a shipload of American volunteers on the 'Carmania' in the harbour of Halifax off to Italy being serenaded by a shipload of New Zealanders off to France, under the misapprehension they were conscripts, with:
Onward conscript soldiers,
Marching as to war,
You would not be conscripts,
Had you gone before.
[†] Joseph Paul Goebbels, 1897–1945; Nazi Party propaganda leader, 1929; member of Hitler's cabinet council; murdered his six children and committed suicide.
[‡] Virginia Gayda, 1885–1944; Italian propaganda chief; director of newspaper.

WORLD WAR II |
1939–1945

1ST SEPTEMBER 1939	Hitler invaded Poland.
3RD SEPTEMBER 1939	Britain and France declared war on Germany. W.S.C. joined Chamberlain's Cabinet as First Lord of the Admiralty, his second time in that office, and set the convoy system in operation. A signal was flashed to all British ships—'Winston is Back.'
1ST OCTOBER 1939	In his first war broadcast he urged the creation of an all-party Government.
30TH NOVEMBER 1939	Russia attacked Finland.
APRIL 1940	Appointed President of the Military Co-ordination Committee of Service Ministers.
9TH APRIL 1940	Germany fell upon neutral Norway and Denmark.
11TH APRIL 1940	Made a statement on naval operations after the first battle of Narvik.
10TH MAY 1940	Germany invaded Netherlands, Belgium, and Luxembourg as preliminary to grand offensive. Battle of France began. Supported Chamberlain in a debate that brought the fall of Chamberlain as Prime Minister. Called by King George VI to form Coalition Government to include Labour and Liberal Parties. Commented writer Hilaire Belloc, 'Are we going to be ruled by that "Yankee careerist"?'
11TH MAY 1940	*New Government, Churchill Coalition, Winston Churchill Prime Minister.*
13TH MAY 1940	In first speech as Prime Minister offered the House of Commons nothing but 'blood, toil, tears and sweat.'
15TH MAY 1940	Sought, and obtained by vote of Congress, the loan of fifty US destroyers.
19TH MAY 1940	In first broadcast as Prime Minister warned nation of the coming 'battle for our Island.'
4TH JUNE 1940	Reported to the House of Commons news of Dunkirk and determination not to surrender.
16TH JUNE 1940	On fourth visit invited France to join Great Britain in a Federal Union. Offer rejected.
18TH JUNE 1940	Made a statement on the possibilities of invasion.
4TH JULY 1940	Forced to order bombardment of French fleet at Oran after it refused to

	join the British fleet to avert its falling to the Germans.
20TH AUGUST 1940	In the House of Commons paid tribute to the gallantry of fighter pilots.
17TH SEPTEMBER 1940	Made a statement on German invasion preparations to the House of Commons and asked for organization of Commando units.
9TH OCTOBER 1940	Accepted leadership of the Conservative Party.
21ST OCTOBER 1940	Made a broadcast appeal to French nation.
1ST DECEMBER 1940	Attended the christening of his son Randolph's son Winston.
DECEMBER 1940	Rejoiced in American Lend-Lease Bill.
7TH MARCH 1941	Sent troops to Greece in vain attempt to halt German advance.
10TH MAY 1941	House of Commons bombed: left a smoking ruin.
10TH JUNE 1941	Answered House of Commons critics of campaign in Crete.
22ND JUNE 1941	When Russia invaded by Germans, W.S.C. broadcast immediate assurance of help.
10TH AUGUST 1941	Atlantic meeting with President Roosevelt on board *Prince of Wales*.
12TH AUGUST 1941	Atlantic Charter signed.
17TH AUGUST 1941	Visited Iceland.
22ND SEPTEMBER 1941	The Beaverbrook-Harriman Mission left for Moscow to negotiate supplies for Russia.
2ND DECEMBER 1941	Introduced new National Service Bill including provisions to conscript women.
12TH DECEMBER 1941	Left for Washington.
22ND DECEMBER 1941	Arrived in Washington for Arcadia Conference.
26TH DECEMBER 1941	Addressed joint meeting of both Houses of Congress in Washington.
30TH DECEMBER 1941	Addressed Canadian Legislature at Ottawa. Made Lord Warden of Cinque Ports.*
1ST JANUARY 1942	Signed United Nations Pact in Washington.
14TH JANUARY 1942	Left Washington for London.
27TH JANUARY 1942	Asked Commons for Vote of Confidence: granted 464 to 1.
FEBRUARY 1942	Appointed Clement Attlee Deputy Prime Minister, Stafford Cripps Lord Privy Seal and Leader of the House.
MARCH 1942	Sent Stafford Cripps to New Delhi with offer of Dominion status for India after the war.
22ND MAY 1942	Saw Vyacheslav Molotov in London.
17TH JUNE 1942	Flew to Washington to discuss invasion of North Africa.

---

* The Cinque Ports: an association centred on five South-East English seaports—Hastings, Romney, Hythe, Sandwich and Dover—dating from William the Conqueror's Norman invasion of England. Its duty, to ward off invasions by supplying men and ships for the King's service. The Lord Warden, its highest officer, is constable of Dover Castle, its headquarters. Once powerful, the Lord Warden is now an honorary office.

21ST JUNE 1942	First meeting with General Dwight D. Eisenhower; discussed cross-Channel invasions.
2ND JULY 1942	On return to England faced Motion of No Confidence; motion defeated 475 to 25.
	Took decision to occupy French North Africa.
2ND AUGUST 1942	Flew to Cairo. General Montgomery* commanding Eighth Army; General Alexander Commander in Chief, Middle East.
12TH AUGUST 1942	Arrived Moscow for first meeting with Josef Stalin.
12TH JANUARY 1943	Flew to Casablanca to confer with President Roosevelt.
29TH JANUARY 1943	Mutual Agreement on Unconditional Surrender of enemy.
30TH JANUARY 1943	Held discussions with President Ismet Inönü† of Turkey at Adana.
16TH FEBRUARY 1943	Contracted pneumonia.
5TH MAY 1943	Embarked for Washington.
19TH MAY 1943	Addressed US Congress. Received news Tunisian campaign was over.
22ND MAY 1943	Discussed postwar settlements; suggested Supreme World Council.
30TH MAY 1943	Visited North Africa to consult with Generals de Gaulle‡ and Giraud.
30TH JUNE 1943	In speech at London's Guildhall pledged to crush Japan after Germany.
10TH AUGUST 1943	Arrived in Canada for Quebec Conference with President Roosevelt.
1ST SEPTEMBER 1943	Visited Washington.
6TH SEPTEMBER 1943	In speech at Harvard, advocated world-wide instruction in Basic English. Sent Brigadier Fitzroy Maclean on mission to Marshal Tito§ in Yugoslavia. Corresponded with Stalin about Arctic convoys; sent Anthony Eden to Moscow.
NOVEMBER 1943	Attended conference of Allied leaders in Cairo, followed by another in Teheran with President Roosevelt and Marshal Stalin. Returned to Cairo for discussions with President Inönü of Turkey.
17TH NOVEMBER 1943	Conferred with Generals Eisenhower and Alexander in Malta.
23RD NOVEMBER 1943	Cairo Conference with President Roosevelt and Generalissimo Chiang Kai-shek.
28TH NOVEMBER 1943	Teheran Conference opened with President Roosevelt and Marshal Stalin. Threat of assassination.

* Bernard Law Montgomery, first Viscount Montgomery of Alamein, British soldier; Commander, 8th Army in Egypt, 1942; drove Rommel out of Egypt, Libya, Tripolitania; commanded Allied armies in northern France, 1944.
† Ismet Inönü, President of Turkey, 1938–1950.
‡ Charles de Gaulle, French soldier who advocated mechanization of French Army; head of Provisional Free French National committee in England after France fell to Nazis; Prime Minister, Fifth Republic, June 2, 1958; President, 1959.
§ Marshal Tito (Josip Broz), Marshal of the People's Army; President and Premier of National Liberation Council of Yugoslavia, 1943.

3RD DECEMBER 1943	Visited Sphinx with President Roosevelt.
11TH DECEMBER 1943	Flew to Tunis. Attacked by pneumonia in Carthage.
27TH DECEMBER 1943	Flew to Marrakesh to convalesce. Visited by Eduard Benes, President-in-exile of Czechoslovakia.
1ST MAY 1944	Conference of Commonwealth Prime Ministers in London.
15TH MAY 1944	Final conference before D-Day. King George VI presided.
10TH JUNE 1944	Visited Normandy beaches four days after D-Day.
20TH JULY 1944	Flew to Cherbourg to visit General Montgomery's Headquarters.
11TH AUGUST 1944	Flew to Naples for talks with Marshal Tito.
17TH AUGUST 1944	Visited Italian Front.
20TH AUGUST 1944	Appealed to President Roosevelt and Marshal Stalin to assist Warsaw insurrection.
21ST AUGUST 1944	Met Premier George Papandreou in Rome.
23RD AUGUST 1944	Received by Pope Pius XII in audience.
24TH AUGUST 1944	Liberation of Paris.
5TH SEPTEMBER 1944	Sailed for second Quebec Conference with President Roosevelt.
9TH OCTOBER 1944	Arrived Moscow; met Marshal Stalin in Kremlin.
10TH NOVEMBER 1944	Flew to Paris to meet General de Gaulle.
5TH DECEMBER 1944	Instructed British troops to intervene in Greece.
24TH DECEMBER 1944	Flew to Athens.
2ND FEBRUARY 1945	Met President Roosevelt at Malta.
4TH FEBRUARY 1945	Joined by Marshal Stalin at Yalta. Visited Balaklava.
16TH FEBRUARY 1945	Conferred with rulers of Middle Eastern states in Cairo.
17TH FEBRUARY 1945	Met Saudi Arabian King Ibn Saud at Fayoum.
25TH MARCH 1945	Crossed Rhine two days after Allied armies.
12TH APRIL 1945	Received news of death of President Roosevelt.
8TH MAY 1945	V-E Day. Unconditional surrender of all German fighting forces. W.S.C. broadcast event.
23RD MAY 1945	Coalition Government broke up. Resigned his Premiership and invited to form 'Caretaker Government' until General Election results were declared (July 26).
17TH JULY 1945	In Berlin for three-power Potsdam Conference. Met President Truman. Joint decision taken to use atomic bomb against Japan.
26TH JULY 1945	Conservatives heavily defeated in General Election; resigned Premiership, but remained Leader of the Conservative Party. *New Government, Clement Attlee, Labour Prime Minister.* Elected Conservative Member for Woodford.
6TH AUGUST 1945	Atom bomb dropped on Hiroshima: 200,000 dead.
9TH AUGUST 1945	Atom bomb dropped on Nagasaki: 39,000 dead.

14TH AUGUST 1945	V-J Day. Japan surrendered.
2ND SEPTEMBER 1945	Formal surrender.

1939

EAR-WITNESS

Before World War II, Fitzroy Maclean, a member of the Foreign Office, discovered that the only way he could resign and join the Army was by standing for Parliament. Once elected member for Lancaster, then seated, he enlisted in the Army, turning over the administrations of his constituency to Jim Thomas. As Brigadier Fitzroy Maclean, Chief of a British Special Mission to Marshal Tito in Yugoslavia, he met W.S.C. in a conference in Cairo who introduced him to General Smuts.

W.S.C.: (*grinning*): Here is the young man who has used the Mother of Parliaments as a public convenience.

THE SECOND WORLD WAR, VOL. I

September; on the eve of war.

W.S.C.: It is a curious fact about the British Islanders, who hate drill and have not been invaded for nearly a thousand years, that as danger comes nearer and grows, they become progressively less nervous; when it is imminent, they are fierce; when it is mortal, they are fearless. These habits have led them into some very narrow escapes.

THE SECOND WORLD WAR, VOL. I

On September 3, after the first [mistaken] wailing signal of air-raid sirens.

W.S.C.: We [W.S.C. and Mrs Churchill] gave the Government a good mark for this evident sign of preparation [the immediate launching of barrage balloons] and . . . made our way to the shelter assigned to us, armed with a bottle of brandy and other appropriate medical comforts.

EAR-WITNESS

Descended from Sir Francis Drake, Master Mariner and privateer, who *smashed the Spanish Armada, W.S.C. became First Lord of the Admiralty for a second time. Admiral Sir Dudley Pound,* impersonal and remote, was made his chief naval adviser.*

W.S.C.: Dudley Pound's a funny old boy. People think he's always asleep, but you've only got to suggest reducing the naval estimates by a million and he's awake in a flash.

and

As First Lord he used green and red stylo pens for appropriate comments on departmental documents.

W.S.C.: Must have port and starboard.

and

A marginal note marked at the bottom of a report from Admiral Pound.

W.S.C.: Pennywise.

BRIGADIER CHARLES LINDEMANN

During the Phoney War[†] W.S.C. arrived in Paris at the Gare du Nord from London with all the brass waiting to greet him. Furiously he pushed his way past welcoming officials, made for his car and asked to be driven to the British Embassy. His manner suggested that he had received tidings of disaster, until he explained later at dinner.

W.S.C.: You may have observed this morning when you came to greet me I was not my usual merry self. I should like you to know what had happened. I had decided that as there was a war on and I was visiting France it would be appropriate for me to strike a blow for equality and fraternity. In other words to travel without my valet, a thing I had not done for twenty years. To my surprise I found I was quite able to walk down the red carpet; to get into the train, to call for a drink, to light a cigar and to collect my evening papers. In due course I was able to find my way to my bedroom— to put on my pyjamas, get into bed and after a most comfortable night I was wakened the next morning with a nice cup of tea. I had no difficulty at all in shaving, brushing my hair—what is left of it—tying my tie, putting on my coat. It was only when I attempted

* Sir Dudley Pound, 1877–1943; First Sea Lord, Chief of Naval Staff, 1939–1943.
† The Phoney War was that period between the fall of Poland (September 1939) and the invasion of Norway and Denmark (April 1940), during which virtually no fighting took place. It was also called the Sitzkrieg.

to respond to your friendly reception I discovered that I had left my teeth in the train!*

EAR-WITNESS

During the Phoney War, General Sikorski, the Polish war leader who later met his death in an airplane crash, asked W.S.C. what he thought of the Russians who were occupying part of Poland. After the Russians became allies of Britain and the United States following the German attack on Russia, General Sikorski, by then leader of the exiled Polish Government on London, asked W.S.C. what he thought of the Russians now.

W.S.C.: Mon Général, the baboon in his natural setting is an object of interest; the baboon in his cage is an object of curiosity. But I admit that the baboon in bed with one's wife is an object of grave suspicion.

BBC BROADCAST

On October 1, in the first month of the war, he gave his first broadcast as First Lord of the Admiralty.

W.S.C.: But the Royal Navy has immediately attacked the U-boats, and is hunting them night and day—I will not say without mercy, because God forbid we should ever part company with that—but at any rate with zeal and not altogether without relish.

and

On the Russians.

W.S.C.: I cannot forecast to you the action of Russia. It is a riddle wrapped in a mystery inside an enigma; but perhaps there is a key. That key is Russian national interest.

ASSIGNMENT: CHURCHILL

W.S.C., inspecting the harbour at Scapa Flow,† pointed to a fake ship on one end of the Northern Group where the fleet was hiding.

---

* Edward Marsh, W.S.C.'s Private Secretary, once waited with Mrs Churchill at a railroad station for W.S.C. who was overdue. Marsh remarked to Mrs Churchill, 'Winston is such a sportsman he always gives the train a chance to get away!'

† A channel in the Orkney Islands, northern Scotland; British naval base.

Warrant Officer (to W.S.C.): But she's not even been spotted by our own reconnaissance, Sir.

W.S.C.: Then they need spectacles.

Warrant Officer: How so, sir?

W.S.C.: No gulls about her . . .bow and stern, of all the dummies. Feed the gulls and fool the Germans!

And they did.

THE SECOND WORLD WAR, VOL. I

A Minute, dated October 7; First Lord, to Second Sea Lord, Parliamentary Secretary and Secretary.

W.S.C.: Will you kindly explain to me the reasons which debar individuals in certain branches from rising by merit to commissioned rank? If a cook may rise, or a steward, why not an electrical artificer or an ordnance rating or a shipwright? If a telegraphist may rise, why not a painter? Apparently there is no difficulty about painters rising in Germany!

THE SECOND WORLD WAR, VOL. I

On Soviet absorption of the independent Baltic States of Estonia, Latvia and Lithuania.

W.S.C.: A ferocious liquidation of all anti-Communist and anti-Russian elements was carried through by the usual methods. Great numbers of people who for twenty years had lived in freedom in their native land and had represented the dominant majority of its people disappeared. A large proportion of these were transported to Siberia. The rest went farther. This process was described as 'Mutual Assistance Pacts'.

EAR-WITNESS

Sir Roy Harrod tells the story that British shipping losses at this period were particularly heavy and alarmed all but W.S.C. The news of the losses was heavily accented in the press and over radio.

W.S.C.: *(to his Admiralty staff)*: Must we have this lugubrious ingemination of the news of our shipping losses?

(His staff, thinking W.S.C.'s secretary had mistyped 'insemination,' scurried to

the Oxford English Dictionary where they found 'ingemination' meant saying the same thing twice over.)

HOUSE OF COMMONS
On December 6.

W.S.C.: When I see statements, as I have done lately, that the Germans during 1940 will have as many as 400 U-Boats in commission, and that they are producing these vessels by what is called 'the chain belt system', I wonder if they are producing the U-boat captains and crews by a similar method. If so, it seems likely that our rate of destruction might well undergo a similar expansion.

BBC BROADCAST
When the enemy was bombing and machine-gunning merchant vessels and fishing boats in December 1939.

W.S.C.: I am glad to tell you . . . that the heat of their fury has far exceeded the accuracy of their aim.

THE FIRST LORD SPENT
HIS BIRTHDAY WITH
WORK AS USUAL

1940

At the beginning of World War II, the BBC used to play the national anthems of all the Allies at the conclusion of their Sunday programmes. In 1940 the number of countries overrun by the Nazis, making them Britain's allies, increased with almost breathtaking rapidity. Dining at the Savoy Hotel and growing impatient listening to the long sequence of anthems, W.S.C. called a waiter.

W.S.C.: Pray turn off the wireless. Enough of that Beggar's Opera!

THE SECOND WORLD WAR, VOL. II

Theme for the second volume of his World War II Memoirs.

W.S.C.:   How the British people
held the fort
alone
till those who
hitherto had been half blind
were half ready

EAR-WITNESS

W.S.C.: In war you do not have to be nice—you only have to be right.

ALL
BEHIND
YOU,
WINSTON

BBC BROADCAST
On January 20, warning the neutrals of their dire fate if they did not stand up to Hitler.
W.S.C.: They bow humbly and in fear to German threats of violence, comforting themselves meanwhile with the thought that the Allies will win . . . Each one hopes that if he feeds the crocodile enough, the crocodile will eat him last. All of them hope that the storm will pass before their turn comes to be devoured.

BBC BROADCAST
On March 30.
W.S.C.: Although the fate of Poland stares them in the face there are thoughtless, dilettante or purblind worldlings who sometimes ask us: 'What is it that Britain and France are fighting for?' To this I answer: 'If we left off fighting you would soon find out.'
also

EAR-WITNESS
At a later date.
W.S.C.: There is only one thing worse than fighting with allies, and that is fighting without them.

THE SECOND WORLD WAR, VOL. I
On May 9, Prime Minister Neville Chamberlain, no longer commanding the confidence of the House of Commons, was about to suggest that King George VI appoint a new Prime Minister.
W.S.C.: . . . by the afternoon, I became aware that I might well be called upon to take the lead. The prospect neither excited nor alarmed me. I thought it would be by far the best plan.

THE SECOND WORLD WAR, VOL. II
On assuming the Prime Ministership in the World War II Coalition Government.
W.S.C.: At the top there are great simplifications. An accepted leader has only to be sure of what it is best to do, or at least to have

made up his mind about it. The loyalties which centre upon number one are enormous. If he trips he must be sustained. If he makes mistakes they must be covered. If he sleeps he must not be wantonly disturbed. If he is no good he must be pole-axed. But this last extreme process cannot be carried out every day; and certainly not in the days just after he has been chosen.

EAR-WITNESS

In the spring, when he was being piteously entreated by the French Government during the Battle of France for RAF planes desperately needed to defend Britain.

W.S.C.: Snowballs into hell! Snowballs into hell!

EAR-WITNESS

During the beginning of World War II, in April and May of 1940, accompanied by Major General Lord Ismay, his Chief of Staff whom he called 'Pug', he shuttled between Britain and France devising every possible plan to buck up the French into continued resistance, even offering them common citizenship with Britain. Their Premier, Paul Reynaud, kept blowing hot and cold to the persuasive offers. But it became obvious to General Ismay that Premier Reynaud's mistress, Madame de Portes, held a powerful and decisive influence over the French leader.

W.S.C.: We MUST face up to it, Pug, she has certain advantages that we have not.

EAR-WITNESS

After a row and the dismissal of his very tall, rather pompous Minister of Transport, Lord Reith.

W.S.C.: (*to an aide*): Thank God we have seen the last of the Wuthering Height.

HOUSE OF COMMONS

Comparing 1920, when Stanley Baldwin was a Junior Minister, with 1935, when he was Prime Minister.

W.S.C.: In those days the Lord President was wiser than he is now;

he used frequently to take my advice.

SPEECH
His pronunciation of foreign place-names was pure British.
W.S.C.: I must say, even from the point of view of the ordinary uses of English that it is not customary to quote a term in a foreign language, a capital town, a geographic place, where there exists a perfectly well-known English equivalent. It is usual to say 'Paris'—not 'Paree'.
also

THE WAR AND COLONEL WARDEN
When someone was rash enough to render Walshavn as 'Vals-havern', the Prime Minister looked at him resentfully.
W.S.C.: Don't be so BBC [British Broadcasting Corporation], the place is WALLS-HAVEN.
also

CHURCHILL BY HIS CONTEMPORARIES
To his great friend, Jack Seely (later Lord Mottistone).
W.S.C.: Jack, when you cross Europe you land at Marsai, spend a night in Lee-on and another in Par-ee, and, crossing by Callay, eventually reach Londres. I land at Mar-sales, spend a night in Lions, and another in Paris, and come home to London!
and

THE SECOND WORLD WAR, VOL. III
Hating any change that upset a sense of continuity, he sent a Minute to Cabinet Secretary Sir Edward Bridges and Major General Ismay.
W.S.C.: In all correspondence, it would be more convenient to use the word 'Persia' instead of 'Iran', as otherwise dangerous mistakes may easily occur through the similarity of Iran and Iraq . . . Formal correspondence with the Persian Government should of course be conducted in the form they like.
also

HOUSE OF COMMONS
On May 7, 1941.
W.S.C.: I always thought it was a most unfortunate and most tiresome thing when both Persia and Mesopotamia changed their names at about the same time to two names which were so much alike—Iran and Iraq. I have endeavoured myself in the domestic sphere to avoid such risks [in naming Ministers].
also

EAR-WITNESS
Visiting Russia on February 13, 1945, he was told by a Russian-speaking RAF officer that arrangements had been made to fly him homewards via 'Sevastopol.'
W.S.C.: Sebastopol's good enough for me, young man.

THE SECOND WORLD WAR, VOL. IV
A Minute dated April 23, 1945, fifteen days before V-E Day.
W.S.C.: (*to Foreign Office*): I do not consider that names that have been familiar for generations in England should be altered to study the whims of foreigners living in those parts. Where the name has not particular significance the local custom should be followed. However, Constantinople should never be abandoned, though for stupid people Istanbul may be written in brackets after it. As for Angora, long familiar with us through the Angora cats, I will resist to the utmost of my power its degradation to Ankara.
and
W.S.C.: You should note, by the way, the bad luck which always pursues people who change the names of their cities. Fortune is rightly malignant to those who break with the traditions and customs of the past. As long as I have a word to say in the matter Ankara is banned, unless in brackets afterwards. If we do not make a stand we shall be in a few weeks be asked to call Leghorn, Livorno, and the BBC will be pronouncing Paris 'Paree'. Foreign names were made for Englishmen, not Englishmen for foreign names. I date this minute from St George's Day.
also
He would pronounce Montevideo in its bluntest Anglicized form, 'Monte

Viddyoh,' and refer to the German pocket battleship of River Plate fame as the 'Graf Speeeee.'
also

SPEECH

Later, on receiving the Charlemagne Prize on May 10, 1956, in the city of Aachen.

W.S.C.: . . . It is for me a high honour to receive today the Charlemagne Prize in this famous German and European city of Aachen, which some call Aix-la-Chapelle.
also

THE SECOND WORLD WAR, VOL. II

A May 27 Minute, Prime Minister to Secretary of State for Air.

W.S.C.: . . . you distinguish in several cases between enemy aircraft 'put out of action' or 'destroyed'. Is there any real difference between the two, or is it simply to avoid tautology? If so, this is not in accordance with the best authorities on English. Sense should not be sacrificed to sound.

HOUSE OF COMMONS

In his great rallying speech to the House of Commons on June 4, after the miracle of Dunkirk.

W.S.C.: We shall fight on the beaches, we shall fight on the landing grounds, we shall fight in the fields and in the streets, we shall fight in the hills: we shall never surrender. And [in an aside to a colleague, as the House thundered with cheers] . . . we will fight them with the butt end of broken bottles because that's bloody well all we've got.*

and

W.S.C.: We are told that Herr Hitler has a plan for invading the British Isles. This has often been thought of before. When

---

* A British Planning Group was asked to imagine it was the German High Command and draw up plans designed to demolish the enemy. The Report began, 'The elimination of Churchill must be an essential feature of any attack on British morale. There is no other statesman who could possibly take his place.'

Napoleon lay at Boulogne for a year with his flat-bottomed boats and his Grand Army, he was told by someone: 'There are bitter weeds in England.' There are certainly a great many more of them since the British Expeditionary Force returned.

BBC BROADCAST

On France. In a broadcast to the French people on October 21.

W.S.C.: Here in London, which Herr Hitler says he will reduce to ashes, and which his aeroplanes are now bombarding, our people are bearing up unflinchingly. Our Air Force has more than held its own. We are waiting for the long promised invasion. So are the fishes. [These words were translated over the BBC into French by Michel Saint Denis, Inspector General of the French theatre, then of the BBC team of French broadcasters.]

W.S.C.: (*to Mr Saint Denis before the broadcast*): What I want is to be understood as I am, not as you are, not even as the French language is. Don't make it sound too correct.

also

EAR-WITNESS

Meeting with Turkish leaders, W.S.C. spoke to them in French, with Anthony Eden volunteering to assist.

W.S.C.: (*to Anthony Eden*): Will you *please* stop translating my French into French!

also

As First Lord of the Admiralty, complaining to a French guest on lack of unity in the French Government.

W.S.C.: *Nous allons perdre l'omnibus.**

and

Explaining to a group of French parliamentarians his position as Leader of the National Coalition Government (composed of Conservatives and Labourites, each with equal voice).

W.S.C.: *Quand je considère mon derrière, je constate qu'il est divisé en deux parties égales.*†

---

* 'We are going to miss the bus.'

† 'When I consider my behind [he meant 'what is behind me'], I perceive that it is divided into two equal parts.'

and

Speaking of the French Navy he correctly referred to it in the feminine gender,
'la Marine Française'. But he switched to 'I mean, le Marine Français', for
to him such a gallant group had *to be masculine!*
and

Shocking a Free-French General by his explanation of the British Women's
Voluntary Services.
W.S.C.: *Les femmes qu'on ne paie pas!**
also

SPEECH
Later, in the speech at Hotel de Ville on November 12, 1944, acknowledging
the welcome of the Paris Liberation Committee.
W.S.C.: . . . I am going to give you a warning: be on your guard,
because I am going to speak in French, a formidable undertaking
and one which will put great demands on your friendship with
Great Britain.

EAR-WITNESS
Once, in a burst of temper, he frightened his poodle Rufus into loud barking.
W.S.C.: (*to his Secretary*): Take that dog away. We cannot both be
barking at once!

EAR-WITNESS
Feeding his swans at Chartwell, W.S.C. lost his balance and pitched
headlong into the pond, to be fished out by his bodyguard, Inspector Davis.
Worried that his charge might develop pneumonia, Davis attempted to order
him into a car.
W.S.C.: Shut your bloody mouth.
Then, dripping, he turned on his soggy heel and trudged up the hill with the
chastened detective at his rear. Arriving in the hall of Chartwell, he suddenly put
his arm around Davis's shoulders.
W.S.C.: You know, Davis, your mouth isn't really bloody.

---

* 'The women whom one does not pay!'

HOUSE OF COMMONS

In June, when air raids became heavy, he scribbled a marginal note on a speech delivered in Secret Session.

W.S.C.: Learn to get used to it [bombing]. Eels get used to skinning.

also

EAR-WITNESS

During one heavy raid, instead of remaining down in his Annex Air Raid Shelter at Storey's Gate, he watched the Blitz from the roof, until an air raid warden shyly begged him to move.

W.S.C.: Why?

Air Raid Warden: Well, Sir, you're sitting on the smoke vent and the building's full of smoke!

and

Again on the roof, during another bad raid.

Staff member (to W.S.C.): Sir, it is tempting Providence to remain here.

W.S.C.: My time will come when it comes.

MEMOIRS OF FIELD MARSHAL MONTGOMERY

At the close of an inspection tour with General Montgomery at 3rd Divisional Headquarters near Steynsing, they dined in the Royal Albion Hotel in Brighton.

General Montgomery (refusing drink in favour of water): I neither drink nor smoke and I'm 100% fit.

W.S.C.: I both drink and smoke and I'm 200% fit.

THE MEMOIRS OF ANTHONY EDEN

After digesting a secret paper by Lord Halifax and anticipating opposition from the Ministry of Economic Warfare to a Foreign Office policy, W.S.C. indiscreetly sent the secret paper on to the Ministry, causing Hugh Dalton, Minister of Economic Warfare, marked displeasure.

W.S.C.: I only marked the paper 'MEW', it seems he has mewed.

THE TIMES

On August 21. To Government Heads of Departments in Civil Service on brevity of official papers.

W.S.C.: Let us have an end of such phrases as these: 'It is also of importance to bear in mind the following considerations . . .' or 'Consideration should be given to the possibility of carrying into effect . . .' Most of these woolly phrases are mere padding, which can be left out altogether or replaced by a single word. Let us not shrink from using the short expressive phrase, even if it is conversational.

also

EAR-WITNESS

After receiving a Minute issued by a priggish civil servant, objecting to the ending of a sentence with a preposition and the use of a dangling participle in official documents.

W.S.C.: (*red pencilled on margin*): This is the sort of pedantry up with which I will not put.

and

W.S.C.: Pray remember that the British people is no longer able to tolerate such lush disorganization.

also

MY DEAR MR CHURCHILL

W.S.C.: Splitting an infinitive isn't so bad—not nearly so bad— humph, as splitting a party; that is always regarded as the greatest sin.

EAR-WITNESS

During the London Blitz he motored to Canterbury to see what precautions had been taken to protect the famous Cathedral. After his experts had worked out a plan to bolster the edifice and approaches with sandbags, he opened a conversation with Archbishop Lang, whom he disliked because of Lang's behaviour during the Abdication Crisis.

W.S.C.: What, my Lord Primate, are you doing to protect your sacred person against the bombs of our heathen foe?

Archbishop: No more than other people, Prime Minister. When the warning siren sounds I go to my shelter.

W.S.C.: But an ordinary shelter is by no means adequate in your case, Archbishop. You owe it to the Established church to take refuge in the Cathedral crypt. There you would be quite safe. Unless of course there was a direct hit. Then I fear [with relish], my Lord Primate, you would have to regard that as a summons!

THE SECOND WORLD WAR, VOL. II

On the English territorial defence.

W.S.C. I have often wondered . . . what would have happened if two hundred thousand German storm troops had actually established themselves ashore. The massacre would have been on both sides grim and great . . . They would have used terror, and we were prepared to go all lengths. I intended to use the slogan, 'You can always take one with you.' This was a time when it was equally good to live or die.

EAR-WITNESS

It was a tradition that night fighter pilots leave the top button of their tunics open to distinguish them from bomber pilots. One morning in September W.S.C. visited a fighter base that had been experiencing a heavy fighting schedule. His early morning visit caused the pilots to pile hurriedly out of bed for inspection. Passing down the line in review he noticed that one pilot had not had time to button up his trousers.

W.S.C.: Night fighters, I presume!

EAR-WITNESS

During the London Blitz, in an attempt to divert him from its horrors, his faithful aide Brendan Bracken placed before him a newspaper account of a man over seventy-five years arrested in Hyde Park for making improper advances to a very young girl in sub-zero weather.

W.S.C.: Over 75 and below zero! Makes you *proud* to be an Englishman.

EAR-WITNESS

Mrs Churchill and the Cabinet forever tried to dissuade him from running risks during the London Blitz.

W.S.C.: I will have you know that as a child my nurse maid could never prevent me from taking a walk in the park if I wanted to do so. And as a man, Adolf Hitler certainly won't.

EAR-WITNESS

At the height of the Battle of Britain he sent the last fully-equipped armoured division to Egypt, reasoning that if the RAF and Navy could not stop the Germans, one armoured division could not save England. It might save Suez and Middle East oil fields.

W.S.C.: (*to War Cabinet*): We are at home on the sea and we know the desert. And there is of course the added attraction of being able to kill a lot of Germans before we settle down to the main course.

HOUSE OF COMMONS

On September 5.

W.S.C.: There is really no good sense in having these prolonged banshee howlings from sirens two or three times a day over wide areas, simply because hostile aircraft are flying to or from some target which no one can possibly know or even guess. All our precaution regulations have hitherto been based on this siren call, and I must say that one must admire the ingenuity of those who devised it as a means of spreading alarm. Indeed, most people now see how very wise Ulysses [Homeric hero] was when he stopped the ears of his sailors from all siren song and had himself tied up firmly to the mast of duty.

HOUSE OF COMMONS

During the war, a Conservative MP, Mr Oswald Lewis, asked him whether the German bombing would bring about reprisals.

W.S.C.: If the answer were in the negative it would remove a deterrent for the enemy. If it were in the affirmative, it would spur him on to increase his preparations and add to the difficulties of our airmen. If it were non-committal, it would not add to the enlightenment of the Honourable Member.

THE SECOND WORLD WAR, VOL. II

On September 23.

W.S.C.: . . . by subtlety and trickery [Dictator Francisco] Franco succeeded . . . in keeping Spain out of the war to . . . the advantage of Britain when she was all alone . . . It is fashionable at the present time to dwell on the vices of General Franco, and I am therefore glad to place on record this testimony to the duplicity and ingratitude of his dealings with Hitler and Mussolini. I shall presently record even greater services which these evil qualities in General Franco rendered to the Allied cause.

THE SECOND WORLD WAR, VOL. II

On the magnificent work of bomb disposal squads during the London Blitz.

W.S.C.: One squad . . . consisted of three people—the Earl of Suffolk, his lady private secretary, and his rather aged chauffeur. They called themselves 'The Holy Trinity'. Their prowess and continued existence got around among all who knew. Thirty-four unexploded bombs did they tackle with urbane and smiling efficiency. But the thirty-fifth claimed its forfeit. Up went the Earl of Suffolk in his Holy Trinity. But we may be sure that, as for Greatheart, 'all the trumpets sounded for them on the other side.'

and

One of his footnotes.

W.S.C.: It seems incongruous to record a joke in such sombre scenes. But in war the soldier's harsh laugh is often a measure of inward compressed emotions. The party were digging out a bomb, and their prize man had gone down the pit to perform the delicate act of disconnection. Suddenly he shouted to be drawn up. Forward went his mates and pulled him out. They seized him by the shoulders and, dragging him along, all rushed off together for the fifty or sixty yards which were supposed to give a chance. They flung themselves on the ground. But nothing happened. The prize man was seriously upset. He was blanched and breathless. They looked at him inquiringly. 'My God,' he said, 'there was a bloody great rat!'

and

At the climax of the Battle of Britain, on the heroism of the pilots.

W.S.C.: There is such a thing as sheer exhaustion, both of the spirit and the animal. I thought of Wellington's[*] mood in the afternoon of the Battle of Waterloo: 'Would God that night or Blücher[†] would come.' This time we did not want Blücher.

also

HOUSE OF COMMONS

Referring to the particular night of September 23, 1940.

W.S.C.: On that particular Thursday night 180 persons were killed in London as a result of 251 tons of bombs. That is to say, it took one ton of bombs to kill three-quarters of a person.

and

W.S.C.: Statisticians may amuse themselves by calculating that after making allowance for the working law of diminishing returns, through the same house being struck twice or three times over, it would take ten years at the present rate, for half the houses of London to be demolished. After that, of course, progress would be much slower.

also

THE SECOND WORLD WAR, VOL. II

Rejoicing that his fears that epidemics would stem from Londoners' being driven underground by the bombings proved groundless.

W.S.C.: Man is a gregarious animal, and apparently the mischievous microbes he exhales fight and neutralize each other. They go out and devour each other, and Man walks off unharmed. If this is not scientifically correct, it ought to be . . .

[*] Arthur Wellesley, first Duke of Wellington, 1769–1852; soldier; the 'Iron Duke'; crushed Napoleon at Waterloo, 1815.
[†] Marshal Gebhard Leberecht von Blücher, famous soldier; Prussian Field Marshal who aided Wellington in victory at Waterloo.

WINSTON IS BACK

HOUSE OF COMMONS

In October, on an attempt to thwart three French destroyers carrying Vichy partisans from entering Dakar harbour.

W.S.C.: Orders were instantly given to stop them at Casablanca, or if that failed, to prevent them entering Dakar. If we could not cork them in, we could at least, we hoped, have corked them out.

THE SECOND WORLD WAR, VOL II

After viewing the grim wreckage from the London Blitz and the indomitable spirit of the British people.

W.S.C.: When we got back into the car, a harsher mood swept over this haggard crowd. 'Give it 'em back,' they cried, and, 'Let *them* have it too.' I undertook forthwith to see that their wishes were carried out; and this promise was certainly kept.

THE CENTRAL BLUE

Relaxing in the First Lord's Room in the Admiralty after dinner, he was tinkering with a model bomb which he thought could be used to mine the Rhine against river traffic. The model was built and tested in a fire bucket. He commented upon it to Sir John Slessor, Director of Plans at the Air Ministry.

W.S.C.: This is one of those rare and happy occasions when respectable people like you and me can enjoy pleasures normally reserved to the Irish Republican Army.

and

Sir John Slessor and W.S.C. were walking together one evening in the gardens of Chequers, commenting on how few good songs World War II had produced compared to World War I. They could view London aglow with fires from the bombings.

W.S.C.: I must write to [Ivor] Novello[*] and tell him to produce a good war song . . . but this time it will have to be *Stop the Home Fires Burning.*

EAR-WITNESS

At a time when the war news was particularly bad, he sighed to his Chief of Staff, General Ismay.

W.S.C.: Pug, this is a world of vice and woe—of vice and woe. But I'll take the vice and you can have the woe!

and

W.S.C.: We shall forgo our luxuries. But not our pleasures.

FROM MY LEVEL

W.S.C.: You are afraid to eat your words. There is no need to be. I have eaten a great many of mine in my time and on the whole I have found them a most wholesome diet.

THE SECOND WORLD WAR, VOL. II

On the Battle of Britain.

W.S.C.: The next target was Birmingham and three successive raids from the 19th to the 22nd of November inflicted much damage and loss of life. When I visited the city . . . it was the dinner hour and a very pretty girl ran up to the car and threw a box of cigars into it . . . She said, 'I won the prize this week for the highest output.' This gift must have cost her two or three pounds. I was very glad [in my official capacity] to give her a kiss.

[*] Ivor Novello composed *Keep the Home Fires Burning* for World War I.

THE SECOND WORLD WAR, VOL. II

Four years on the Air Defence Research Committee and searching questions and briefings from his scientific adviser Professor Lindemann (Lord Cherwell) made him almost an expert though he had nothing but honorary college degrees.

W.S.C.: I knew nothing about science, but I knew something of scientists, and had had much practice as a Minister in handling things I did not understand. I had, at any rate, an acute military perception of what would help and what would hurt, of what would cure and of what would kill.

THE SECOND WORLD WAR, VOL. II

On Mussolini's receiving reports of the pulverization of five Italian divisions.
W.S.C.: On Dec. 13 a 'catastrophic telegram' came from Graziani.*
He contemplated retiring as far as Tripoli . . . He was indignant that he should have been forced into so hazardous an advance upon Egypt by Rommel's† undue influence on Mussolini. He complained that he had been forced into a struggle between 'a flea and an elephant'. Apparently the flea had devoured a large portion of the elephant.

SPEECH

On December 18, at his old school, Harrow.
W.S.C.: Hitler in one of his recent discourses declared that the fight was between those who have been through the Adolf Hitler schools and those who have been to Eton. Hitler has forgotten Harrow!

HOUSE OF COMMONS

W.S.C.: I certainly deprecate any comparison between Herr Hitler and Napoleon; I do not wish to insult the dead.

---

* Rodolfo Graziani, Italian administrator and soldier, then Governor of Libya.
† Erwin Rommel, 1891–1944, German Field Marshal in World War II; Commander of Afrika Korps, defeated by British at El Alamein.

THE SECOND WORLD WAR, VOL. II

On December 31.

W.S.C.: As the end of the year approached . . . we were alive. We had beaten the German air force . . . London had stood triumphant through all her ordeals . . . The smear of Communists who obeyed their Moscow orders gibbered about a capitalist-imperialist war.

1941

THE SECOND WORLD WAR, VOL. III

A Minute of January 6: Prime Minister to Minister of Public Works and Buildings.

W.S.C.: Do not let plans for a new world divert your energies from saving what is left of the old.

THE SECOND WORLD WAR, VOL. I

A Minute, dated February 2, to First Lord (Mr A. V. Alexander), Controller and others. Reclassification of smaller war vessels.

W.S.C.: I agree with the First Sea Lord about the needlessness of repeating the word 'vessel', and his wish to simplify all titles to one word. I should like the word 'destroyer' to cover ships formerly described as 'fast escort vessels' . . . I do not like the word 'whaler', which is an entire misnomer, as they are not going to catch whales . . . what is, in fact, the distinction between an 'escorter', 'patroller' and a 'whaler' as now specified? It seems most important to arrive at simple conclusions quickly on this subject . . .

HOUSE OF COMMONS

On the logistics of war.

W.S.C.: I must say a word about the function of the Minister charged with the study of post-war problems and reconstruction. It is not his task to make a new world, comprising a new Heaven, a new earth, and no doubt a new hell (as I am sure that would be necessary in any balanced system).

and

W.S.C.: I am, of course, aware that a mechanized army makes an enormous additional drain . . . I have thought nevertheless for some time that the Army and Air Force—the Navy not so much—have a great need to comb their tails in order to magnify their teeth.[*]

HOUSE OF COMMONS

A January 22 letter to The Times *stating that public school boys made the best officers offended the Labour Party and coincided with W.S.C.'s reference to a Chairman of a newly formed committee in the House.*

W.S.C.: *(an old Harrovian)*

As to the chairman of this Committee, he is not *facile princeps*, but *primus inter pares* which, for the benefit of any—[he stopped, noticing Labour members rising in protest to the slur on their classical education]—*old Etonians* present, I should, if very severely pressed, venture to translate.

THE SECOND WORLD WAR, VOL. III

A Minute of February 4, to Secretary of State for War (Captain H. D. R. Margesson).

W.S.C.: Please see *The Times* of February 4. Is it really true that a seven-mile cross-country run is enforced upon all in this division, from generals to privates? Does the Army Council think this is a good idea? It looks to me rather excessive. A colonel or a general ought not to exhaust himself in trying to compete with young boys running across country seven miles at a time. The duty of officers is no doubt to keep themselves fit, but still more to think for their men, and to take decisions affecting their safety or comfort. Who is the general of this division, and does he run the seven miles himself? If so, he may be more useful for football than war. Could Napoleon have run seven miles across country at Austerlitz? Perhaps it was the other fellow he made run. In my experience based on many years' observation, officers with high athletic qualifications are not usually successful in the higher ranks.

EAR-WITNESS

From early experience with Commandos in the Boer War—'Butcher and

---

[*] He was referring to the need to re-deploy technical and administrative staff into the fighting line.

Run', as he called their tactic—he had studied the uses of unorthodox warfare. During World War II he made effective use of hush-hush operations and issued orders that no stone be left unturned to receive and equip such groups. The nature of covert work always attracted unusual personnel. On one round of visits he inspected a Group's Installation.

W.S.C.: (to their Chief): I told you to leave no stone unturned to get the people you needed, but I didn't think you were going to take me so literally.

HOUSE OF COMMONS

Introducing a Bill to allow MPs to remain MPs while holding appointments abroad, he explained that the House had already abandoned its practice of having by-elections every time a ministerial appointment was made.

W.S.C.: Now that I have shown Hon. Members the camel they have already swallowed, I hope they will address themselves with renewed sense of proportion to this somewhat inconsiderable gnat.

HOUSE OF COMMONS

In March, on Government powers over broadcasting.

W.S.C.: I think we should have to retain a certain amount of power in the selection of the music. Very spirited renderings of 'Deutschland Über Alles' would hardly be permissible.*
(Asked whether a pacifist should be excluded from an orchestra.)

W.S.C.: I see no reason to suppose that the holding of pacifist views would make him play flat.

THE SECOND WORLD WAR. VOL. III

W.S.C. saw a party of middle-aged men in civilian clothes wearing armlets marked 'LDV' (Local Defence Volunteers). He had already proposed '. . . this title should be changed to "Home Guard" . . .' On learning that Communal Feeding Centres were about to be established, on March 21 he addressed a Minute to the Minister of Food.

W.S.C.: I hope the term 'Communal Feeding Centres' is not going

---

* Probably a reference to the fact that the music of 'Deutschland' is identical with that of the great Olney hymn, 'Glorious things of thee are spoken, Zion, city of our God.'

163

to be adopted. It is an odious expression, suggestive of Communism and the workhouse. I suggest you call them 'British Restaurants'. Everybody associates the word 'restaurant' with a good meal and they may as well have the name if they cannot get anything else.

HOUSE OF COMMONS
Referring to World War I.
W.S.C.: I remember at the Ministry of Munitions being told we were running short of . . . bauxite and steel, and so forth; but we went on, and in the end the only thing we ran short of was Huns. One fine morning we went down to our offices . . . and found they had all surrendered.

EAR-WITNESS
In a meeting with officers of the three services, anxiously discussing Rashid Ali's rebellion in Iraq that was threatening Britain's oil supplies, tempers grew edgy. W.S.C. became so fascinated by the Iraqi names that he parodied a line in Hamlet.
W.S.C.: What's Bakuba to him, or he to Bakuba?*

EAR-WITNESS
During the World War II Coalition Government, Hugh Dalton, Labour MP, served for two years as Minister of Economic Warfare and Special Operations. He was often referred to by W.S.C. as the 'Minister of Ungentlemanly Warfare'. Towards his Military Chiefs he was cosier.
W.S.C.: I and my Three Teddy Bears.

THE SECOND WORLD WAR VOL. VI
A Minute of April 8, to Foreign Office.
W.S.C.: This war would never have come unless, under American and modernizing pressure, we had driven the Hapsburgs out of Austria and Hungary and the Hohenzollerns out of Germany. By

---

* *Hamlet*, II, ii, 554: 'What's Hecuba to him, or he to Hecuba?'

making these vacuums we gave the opening for the Hitlerite monster to crawl out of its sewer on to the vacant thrones. No doubt these views are very unfashionable . . .

HOUSE OF COMMONS

On March 27, a revolution in Yugoslavia overthrew the pro-Axis Government. As that government had dispersed the Yugoslav Army, it proved impossible to concentrate significant forces to make a fight against the German invasion.

W.S.C.: A boa constrictor, who had already covered his prey with his foul saliva and then had it suddenly wrested from his coils, would be in an amiable mood compared with Hitler, Goering, Ribbentrop and the rest of the Nazi gang when they experienced this bitter disappointment.

BBC BROADCAST

On April 27, on the Italian dictator Mussolini.

W.S.C.: I turn aside from the stony path we have to tread, to indulge a moment of lighter relief. I daresay you have read in the newspapers that by a special proclamation, the Italian dictator had congratulated the Italian army in Albania on the glorious laurels they have gained by their victory over the Greeks. Here surely is the world's record in the domain of the ridiculous and the contemptible. This whipped jackal, Mussolini, who to save his own skin has made all Italy a vassal state of Hitler's Empire, comes frisking up at the side of a German tiger with yelpings not only of appetite—that can be understood—but even of triumph.

HOUSE OF COMMONS

On May 7.

W.S.C.: My Right Hon. Friend the Member for Devonport [Mr Leslie Hore-Belisha, former war secretary] and some others have spoken of the importance in war of full and accurate Intelligence of the movements and intentions of the enemy. That is one of those glimpses of the obvious and of the obsolete with which his powerful speech abounded.

EAR-WITNESS
During the German rocket attacks in May he invited his Cabinet colleagues to dine at 10 Downing Street. Mr Herbert Morrison (Minister for Supply) asked if it might be dangerous to have them all together in case of a direct hit.

W.S.C.: I have consulted Lord Cherwell. He tells me the odds against meeting our Maker are not more than one in 600,000. *(All his colleagues came.)*

THE MEMOIRS OF ANTHONY EDEN
On June 6, on the complicated problems of a Foreign Secretary (Anthony Eden) not being a free agent in many matters.

W.S.C.: He has to conceal what he would most wish to make public, and make public what he would most wish to conceal.

EAR-WITNESS
On the eve of Hitler's attack on Russia, of which he had advance knowledge, his principal private Secretary, Jock (John R) Colville, asked him how, as a longtime anti-Communist, he would address the House.

W.S.C.: I have only one purpose, the destruction of Hitler, and my life is simplified thereby. If Hitler invaded Hell, I would make at least a favourable mention of the Devil in the House of Commons.

HOUSE OF COMMONS
In June, to Leslie Hore-Belisha who, having been dismissed by Chamberlain, had hope for reinstatement by W.S.C. and, when disappointed, was turning bitterly critical.

W.S.C.: If you attack me I shall strike back and remember, while you have a 3.7 inch gun I have a 12 inch gun . . . [He] is so farseeing now that we have lost his services.

SPEECH
At St James's Place, London, on June 12, after a recital of Hitler's European atrocities.

W.S.C.: It is upon this foundation that Hitler, with his tailored lackey Mussolini at his tail and Admiral Darlan* frisking by his side, pretends to build out of hatred, appetite, and racial assertion a new order for Europe. Never did so mocking a fantasy obsess the mind of mortal man.

THE SECOND WORLD WAR, VOL. III

A Minute of June 14, to Minister of Agriculture.

W.S.C.: Have you done justice to rabbit production? Although rabbits are not by themselves nourishing, they are a pretty good mitigation of vegetarianism. They eat mainly grass and greenstuffs, so what is the harm in encouraging their multiplication in captivity?

BBC BROADCAST

On June 22, on Hitler's invasion of Russia.

W.S.C.: At four o'clock this morning Hitler attacked and invaded Russia. All his usual formalities of perfidy were observed with scrupulous technique . . .

I see advancing . . . in hideous onslaught the Nazi war machine, with its clanking, heel-clicking, dandified officers, its crafty expert agents fresh from the cowing and tying-down of a dozen countries. I see also the dull, drilled, docile, brutish masses of the Hun soldiery plodding on like a swarm of crawling locusts . . .

JOHN SPENCER

Just before leaving to deliver a broadcast, his official car broke down, so he ordered a cab to take him from 10 Downing Street to the BBC. On arriving he asked the cab driver to wait for him for 20 minutes while he gave the broadcast.

Cab Driver: Sorry, Guv'nor, but I must hurry home to the Missus, we want to hear the Prime Minister's broadcast.

The cab fare was three shillings. W.S.C. handed the cab driver fifteen shillings and told him to keep the change.

Cab Driver: To hell with the Prime Minister! I'll wait.

---

* Jean François Darlan, Admiral of the Fleet, and Vice Premier during Vichy regime.

HOUSE OF COMMONS

During a Secret Session on June 25, discussing the harsh language he used to subordinates.

W.S.C.: If we win, nobody will care. If we lose, there will be nobody to care.

HOUSE OF COMMONS

It was said that he never resented the resentment of those to whom he had been rude.

W.S.C.: I do not think . . . any expression of scorn or severity which I have heard used by our critics, has come anywhere near the language which I have been myself accustomed to use, not only orally, but in a continued stream of written minutes. In fact, I wonder that a great many of my colleagues are on speaking terms with me.

(A virtuoso of invective, his descriptions of other politicians, although sometimes unfair, were unforgettable. Stanley Baldwin was 'a countrified businessman who seemed to have reached the Cabinet by accident'; Clement Attlee, 'a modest man. He has every reason to be modest.' Of Selwyn Lloyd, when Conservative Secretary of State for Foreign Affairs [1955–1960], 'Mr Celluloid,' and seeing him with a colleague: 'Ah, the Minister Without Portfolio and the Portfolio Without a Minister.'

Though he and Aneurin Bevan greatly respected each other, for thirty years they delighted in exchanging insults. W.S.C. called Bevan 'a merchant of discourtesy,' 'a Minister of Disease in need of psychiatric treatment,' 'a squalid nuisance.' Bevan responded by tagging W.S.C. 'the entertainer of the House of Commons,' 'the bogeyman of the country,' 'a political chameleon,' 'a piece of political cheese.')

and

EAR-WITNESS

W.S.C.: (*of Hitler*): A victim carrying the traumas of juvenile frustration.

EAR-WITNESS

General Smuts (*to W.S.C.*): I wish you had more religion in you, Winston.

W.S.C.: What do you mean? I dare say I have appointed more bishops than any other Prime Minister in history.

EAR-WITNESS

It was told that when he offered R. A. Butler, a Munich man, and before that, an independence-for-India man, the Presidency of the Board of Education, Butler said there was no post he would rather have.*

W.S.C.: That confirmed my worst suspicions. [Butler ran the Ministry of Education, very ably, 1941–1945.]

EAR-WITNESS

His personal assistant, Commander C. R. Thompson, once asked him his secret in managing to give so many speeches a day with only subject headings as guides.

W.S.C.: It isn't nearly as difficult as you think. I just start my mouth off talking and leave it.

(His close friend Lord Birkenhead once said of him, 'Winston spent the best years of his life writing his impromptu speeches.')

HOUSE OF COMMONS

On July 29.

W.S.C.: Except for our Fighting Services, we have been driven back to a large extent from the carnivore to the herbivore. That may be quite satisfactory to the dietetic scientists who would like to make us all live on nuts, but undoubtedly it has produced, and is producing a very definite effect upon the energetic output of the heavy worker.

also

EAR-WITNESS

During the war, when one-course meals were the rule, he was boyishly

---

* Rt. Hon. Richard Austen Butler, British Conservative statesman, served in many Government posts, including those of Under Secretary for India, 1932–1937; Under Secretary of State for Foreign Affairs, 1938–1941; and ultimately as Foreign Secretary, 1963–1964. Twice disappointed of the Premiership.

TWO CELLARS. "I THOUGHT THAT WOULD WARM YOU, SIR: I AM SORRY NOT TO BE ABLE TO MANAGE A LITTLE MORE COAL AS WELL."

delighted by the sight of a noble salmon sent by a friend.
W.S.C.: That is indeed a magnificent fish; I must have some of him. No! No! I will have meat. Carnivores will win this war!

EAR-WITNESS

When Lord Woolton, Chairman of the Conservative Party, once stalked out of a Cabinet meeting.
W.S.C.: God save us from that ennobled haberdasher.*

EAR-WITNESS

In August, on the battleship 'Prince of Wales' on the way to Iceland, he was racked by a heavy cough. Sir Richard Pim, in charge of W.S.C.'s Map Room, came upon him smoking his cigar and looked surprised.
W.S.C.: Well, what the eye doesn't see the heart doesn't grieve over and the doctor is at the other end of the ship!

* Lord Woolton had run a huge chain of clothing stores.

ATLANTIC MEETING

At the Atlantic Meeting in Placentia Bay in August each British sailor on the 'Prince of Wales' received from the 'Augusta' a white carton containing an orange, two apples, two hundred cigarettes and half a pound of cheese, with the message 'The President of the United States sends his compliments and best wishes.' As the presents were being issued W.S.C. insisted on lining up American and British sailors together for a picture.

W.S.C.: (*waving his cigar at the group*): More tooth!

EAR-WITNESS

On August 12, to FDR.

W.S.C.: The wretched Hun has not only sunk our ships but put my initials [W.C.] on the debris.

ATLANTIC MEETING

On the 'Prince of Wales' steaming homeward from Placentia Bay he was the guest of a group of midshipmen in the gunroom.

A member of the crew: Tell us the true story of Hess,* Sir.

W.S.C.: The true story of Hess . . . is that a certain gentleman thought he had only to come over here and put a knot in the lion's tail and lead that noble creature back to Germany. He was er— mistaken.

THE SECOND WORLD WAR, VOL. III

On August 28, Prime Minister to Chancellor of the Exchequer.

W.S.C.: How much gold have we actually got left in this island or under our control in South Africa? Don't be alarmed: I am not going to ask you for anything.

HOUSE OF COMMONS

On September 30.

W.S.C.: Nothing is more dangerous in wartime than to live in the

---

* Rudolf Hess, Deputy Führer in Hitler's Cabinet Council; third in succession to Hitler; made solo flight to Scotland, 1941; life sentence as war criminal, 1945.

temperamental atmosphere of a Gallup Poll, always feeling one's pulse and taking one's temperature. I see that a speaker at the weekend said that this was a time when leaders should keep their ears to the ground. All I can say is that the British nation will find it very hard to look up to leaders who are detected in that somewhat ungainly posture.

EAR-WITNESS

During a showing of the film 'Oliver Twist' at Chequers his beloved and inseparable French poodle, Rufus, sat on his lap. At the very moment Bill Sikes was coaxing his dog to the edge of the water to drown it and put the police off his track, W.S.C. covered Rufus's eyes with his hand

W.S.C.: Don't look now, dear, I'll tell you all about it afterwards.

THE SECOND WORLD WAR, VOL. III

A Minute of October 3.

W.S.C.: . . . Neither is the expression 'Stay Put' really applicable to the districts where fighting is going on. First of all, it is American slang; secondly, it does not express the fact. The people have not been 'put' anywhere. What is the matter with 'Stand Fast' or 'Stand Firm'? Of the two I prefer the latter. This is an English expression and it says exactly what is meant . . .

HOUSE OF COMMONS

His November tribute to the Speaker of the House, Captain the Rt. Hon. Edward Fitzroy, on the occasion of his Golden Wedding.

W.S.C.: I arise to commit an irregularity. The intervention which I make is without precedent, and the reason for that intervention is also without precedent, and the fact that the reason for my intervention is without precedent is the reason why I must ask for a precedent for my intervention.

HOUSE OF COMMONS

Sir Percy Harris, Liberal Deputy Leader, had said that criticism of Government in wartime was necessary. It was the life-blood of democracy.

W.S.C.: There was a custom in ancient China that anyone who wished to criticize the Government had the right to memorialize the Emperor, and provided he followed that up by committing suicide, very great respect was paid to his words, and no ulterior motive was assigned. That seems to me to have been from many points of view a wise custom, but I certainly would be the last to suggest that it should be made retrospective.

INDEPENDENT MEMBER

A. P. Herbert, Independent Member of Parliament, wrote a poem for W.S.C.'s sixty-seventh birthday on November 30.

Many happy returns of the day
To the father of purpose and plan
To the one who was first in the fray
Never doubted, or rested, or ran,
To the Voice of Old Britain at bay,
To the Voice of young men in the van,
To the Voice of new worlds on the way—
To 'We must—and we will—and we can!'
May he live to hear History say,
'This was their finest man.'

and

Just returned from Washington and a conference with President Roosevelt, W.S.C. met A. P. Herbert in the Smoking Room of the House of Commons and thanked him for the poem, reciting it letter perfectly. As Members swarmed around him offering him a sherry, he declined it.

W.S.C.: No, I am going to lunch at Buckingham Palace and it would not look well if I were to slither under the Royal table!

EAR-WITNESS

The day after Pearl Harbor at a Chiefs of Staff meeting one of the chiefs still advocated a cautious approach to the United States.

W.S.C.: Oh! that is the way we talked to her [the US] while we were still wooing her; now that she is in the harem, we woo her quite differently.

also

After the United States joined Britain and her Allies against Germany in

World War I W.S.C. was asked what he thought of the splendid Americans.
W.S.C.: What do you expect me to do? Kiss them on all four cheeks?

HOUSE OF COMMONS
On December 11.
W.S.C.: Those who fight the Germans fight a stubborn and resourceful foe, a foe in every way worthy of the doom prepared for him.

EAR-WITNESS
Rapping a General for inadvertently releasing a censored item to the Press on the North African campaign.
W.S.C.: These gentlemen of the Press were listening carefully to every word you said—all eagerly anxious for a tiny morsel of cheese which they could publish. And you go and give them a whole ruddy Stilton.

THE LATE LORD MELCHETT
A transport expert, Mr Frank Pick, Chairman of the London buses, served as Director General of Information under the Minister of Information, Alfred Duff Cooper. At a meeting, the Director General informed W.S.C. that he had turned down a plan to publish a clandestine newspaper to subvert the enemy, on a point of ethics. Although conscious of many failings through life he did not think he had ever committed a mortal sin and was unwilling to be associated with one. Thus he had made it a rule of businessman's ethics—in contrast to a politician's—always to let his right hand know what the left hand was doing. W.S.C. grew angry and grasped the hand of Clement Attlee sitting next to him—pointing to the Director General.
W.S.C.: Shake him by the hand! Shake him by the hand! You can say to St Peter that you have met the perfect man.
(The next day W.S.C. went to inspect the defences at Dover.)
W.S.C.: If I am stricken down by enemy action, I hope that, when I appear before my Maker, it will serve me in good stead to have been so recently in the company of a man without sin.

(A short time afterward the same transport expert was quoted in a Cabinet paper.)

W.S.C.: *(writing on its margin)*: Must we hear more from this impeccable bus conductor?

(Later, Duff Cooper sent up a memorandum to W.S.C. announcing that the Director General had been relieved of his post. Dipping his pen in red ink reserved for such occasions, W.S.C. margined the memorandum.)

W.S.C.: The responsibility for the appointment of the Director General of Information belongs to the Minister of Information, but—as for me—never let that impeccable bus driver darken my door again.

EAR-WITNESS

During a wartime Cabinet meeting, as a free-trader he flared when restrictive agricultural proposals were under discussion.

W.S.C.: Thou shalt not grow thy daily bread! That is a terrible new commandment.

AMERICAN PRESS CONFERENCE

On his December arrival in the US the Press came aboard for interviews. The ship's officer was delegated to ask him if the photographers could 'shoot' him.

W.S.C.: Certainly. They can photograph me from the bottom up.

also

After he had expressed his relief that Russia was driving Hitler back in the East, Edward Folliard, a Southern-born reporter for the Washington Post *asked one of the first questions.*

Edward Folliard: Does the Prime Minister feel that America's entry into the war was another great climacteric?

W.S.C.: I sho' do.

EAR-WITNESS

The Free French seized the Vichy-controlled islands of St Pierre and Miquelon, off Newfoundland, on Christmas Eve, after having made an ambiguous statement under British and US pressure that had been taken to mean that the operation had been cancelled. There followed violent criticism of de Gaulle from the US State Department. W.S.C. was asked why Canada had not expelled the Vichy Minister there.

W.S.C.: A courtyard likes to have window.

and

Learning that the seizure of the islands had been ordered by General de Gaulle.

W.S.C.: (*to his aide Brendan Bracken*): What is the oppose of *Vive la France?*

THE SECOND WORLD WAR, VOL. III

On the Americans. After Pearl Harbor and US entry in World War II.

W.S.C.: Silly people and there were many   might discount the force of the United States. Some said they were soft, others that they would never be united. They would fool around at a distance. They would never come to grips. They would never stand blood letting. They would be just a vague blurr on the horizon to friend and foe. Now we should see the weakness of this numerous but remote, wealthy, and talkative people. But I had studied the American Civil War . . . American blood flowed in my veins.

also

W.S.C.: . . . unfathomable mixture of loquacity, affability, senti-mentality, rightfeeling, vigour and weakness, efficiency and muddle.

also

W.S.C.: The bigger the Idea the more wholehcartedly and obstinately do they throw themselves into making it a success. It is an admirable characteristic—provided the Idea is good.

also

SPEECH

On December 26, to a Joint Session of the US Congress with one thousand persons jammed into the Galleries, five thousand outside and cheers from both isolationist and internationalist members of Congress.

W.S.C.: I cannot help reflecting that if my father had been American and my mother British, instead of the other way around, I might have got here on my own . . . In that case this would not have been the first time you would have heard my voice . . . I should not have needed any invitation but if I had, it is hardly likely that

Herblock in The Washington Post

it would have been unanimous . . . I owe my advancement entirely to the House of Commons, whose servant I am. In my country, as in yours, public men are proud to be the servants of the State and would be ashamed to be its masters. On any day, if they thought the people wanted it, the House of Commons could by a simple vote remove me from my office. But I am not worrying about it at all.*

also

BBC BROADCAST

On receiving the Honorary Degree of Doctor of Law of the University of Rochester, New York, June 16, 1911.

W.S.C.: The great Burke[†] has truly said, 'People will not look forward to posterity who never look backward to their ancestors'; and I feel it most agreeable to recall to you that the Jeromes were rooted for many generations in American soil, and fought in [General George] Washington's armies for the independence of the American Colonies and the foundation of the United States. I expect I was on both sides then. And I must say I feel on both sides of the Atlantic Ocean.

also

EAR-WITNESS

As a guest of Mr John D. Rockefeller II on March 8, 1946, W.S.C. accompanied General Eisenhower[‡] to Williamsburg, Virginia, where he was to speak to the Virginia General Assembly. One of the General's historic-minded young aides asked if he might brief W.S.C. for the occasion with a two-page profile on Mr Rockefeller.

W.S.C.: (*after perusing it*): Hmmm! You number your Rockefellers. We number our Georges!

and

---

* After the speech, the wife of a Congressman described the scene: 'When Mr Churchill appeared before Congress it was as if the British Empire had walked into the room.'
† Edmund Burke, 1729–1797; British statesman and orator; advocated liberalism toward American Colonies.
‡ Gen. Dwight D. Eisenhower, Chief of War Plans Division, 1941; Commander in Chief, Allied Forces in Western Europe, December, 1943; 34th US President, 1953–1961.

In the same speech.

W.S.C.: I read the other day that an English nobleman, whose name is new to me, has stated that England would have to become the 49th state of the American Union. I read yesterday that an able American editor had written that the US ought not to be asked to re-enter the British Empire. It seems to me and I dare say it seems to you, that the path of wisdom lies somewhere between these scarecrow extremes.

and

W.S.C., 'half American and all British', an expert on the Revolution of 1776 and the Civil War, was once asked to address a patriotic gathering at Yorktown, Virginia, honouring the part that city played in the Revolution.

W.S.C.: I would be glad to oblige but not to celebrate!

SPEECH

On December 30, in Ottawa, speaking to the Canadian Parliament, he referred to the Fall of France and the words of defeatist Marshal Henri Pétain,* who told the French, 'in three weeks England will have her neck wrung like a chicken' by Hitler.

W.S.C.: But their Chief [General Weygand[†]] misled them. When I warned them that Britain would fight on alone, their Chief told their Prime Minister that in three weeks, England would have her neck wrung like a chicken—Some chicken! Some neck![‡]

and

W.S.C.: We have not journeyed across the centuries, across the oceans, across the mountains, across the prairies, because we are made of sugar candy.

---

* Henri Philippe Pétain, 1856–1951; French Commander-in-Chief, 1917–1918; Chief of French State, 1940–1944 (France in German hands); after Allied Liberation, sentenced to life imprisonment.
† Maxime Weygand, French General; commanded in France during retreat, 1940; military commander in North Africa, 1940–1941; Governor General of Algeria.
‡ Hans Engen, the Norwegian Ambassador to the US, wrote me in 1965, 'It was in a chicken-house somewhere in Norway that I listened by clandestine radio to Winston Churchill's speech before Parliament in Ottawa when he made his priceless remarks about the chicken and its neck. We were a group of underground fighters who used to meet there to listen to the news from London. The Churchillian phrases made no visible impression on the 'legal residents' of the chicken-house. The poor rooster did not even hear them, since he was soundly asleep on a crate. Every time we came to hear the news, he made such a terrible noise, that our only means of making him shut up was to put him to sleep by hypnosis. When the news was over, a couple of slaps over the neck would wake him up.'

1942

THE SECOND WORLD WAR, VOL. III

President Roosevelt persuaded Ambassador to the US Mr Litvinov to include a clause providing for religious freedom in the United Nations Pact.*

W.S.C.: Later on the President had a long talk with him alone about his soul and the dangers of hell fire. The accounts which Mr Roosevelt gave us on several occasions of what he said to the Russian were impressive. Indeed, on one occasion I promised Mr Roosevelt to recommend him for the position of Archbishop of Canterbury if he should lose the next Presidential election.

ROOSEVELT AND HOPKINS, AN INTIMATE DIARY

President Roosevelt, who was eager to continue discussions at the White House on the draft declaration of the United Nations Pact sealing the first Washington (Arcadia) Conference, wheeled himself into W.S.C.'s room. There he found his guest, in the words of Harry Hopkins,† 'stark naked and gleaming pink from his bath,' his valet waiting to wrap him in a towel. Faced with this vision President Roosevelt started to put his wheel chair in reverse.

W.S.C.: *(to F.D.R.)*: Pray enter—the Prime Minister of Great Britain has nothing to hide from the President of the United States.

also

THE SECOND WORLD WAR, VOL. III

W.S.C.: The President was wheeled in to me on the morning of January 1. I got out of my bath, and agreed to the draft [United Nations Pact].‡

EAR-WITNESS

During the same visit to Washington, W.S.C. was walking through the British Embassy corridors, and passed a Foreign Office official, Mr Evelyn

---

* Maxim Litvinov, 1876–1951; Russian Communist leader; Soviet ambassador to US, 1941–1943.
† Harry L. Hopkins, 1890–1946; American politician; President Roosevelt's personal envoy to Britain and Russia, 1941; his Special Assistant, 1942–1945.
‡ Later queried on the veracity of the story W.S.C. said that President Roosevelt knew as well as he that there were 'necessary concealments' between countries. William Jones, Brigadier Sir Leslie Hollis's secretary, delivering the documents to W.S.C., attested to the truth of the incident.

Shuckburgh, carrying a sheaf of cables.

W.S.C.: Young man, are there any of those papers you should show me?

Mr Shuckburgh: I think not, Sir.

W.S.C.: (*stomped down the hallway and suddenly stopped*): Then, young man, are there any of those papers you should not show me?

CHURCHILL BY HIS CONTEMPORARIES

Just as he was about to enter the ocean at Palm Beach, where he had gone for a few days' rest in January, a Security Officer shouted at him that a fifteen-foot shark had been sighted near the shore but that it was of a harmless sand variety.

W.S.C.: (*diving into the water*): I'm not so sure about that. I must see his identity card before I trust myself to him.

HOUSE OF COMMONS

On January 27.

W.S.C.: To hear some people talk . . . the way to win the war is to make sure that every power contributing armed forces and every branch of these armed forces is represented on all the councils and organizations . . . that everybody is fully consulted before anything is done. That is . . . the most sure way to lose a war. You have to be aware of the well-known danger of having 'more harness than horse . . .'

THE SECOND WORLD WAR, VOL. IV

A Minute of January 27, to First Lord.

W.S.C.: Is it really necessary to describe the *Tirpitz** as the *Admiral von Tirpitz* in every signal? This must cause a considerable waste of time for signalmen, cipher staff and typists. Surely *Tirpitz* is good enough for the beast.

---

* Ship named for Alfred von Tirpitz, 1849–1930; German naval commander, First World War; created modern German navy.

HOUSE OF COMMONS

On a January 27 Vote of Confidence, carried in his favour by 464 to 1.
W.S.C.: When I was called upon to be Prime Minister, now nearly two years ago, there were not many applications for the job. Since then perhaps the market has improved.

THE SECOND WORLD WAR, VOL. IV

A Minute of January 30, to the Secretary of State for War. Critical of giving full information about the siege of Singapore, he asked for a stricter censorship.
W.S.C.: I asked General Wavell* some time ago to have a stricter censorship on Singapore. After all they are defending a fortress and not conducting a Buchmanite† revival.

WINTERTON'S NIGHTMARE‡

* General Archibald Percival Wavell, first Earl, Supreme Commander Allied Forces, Far East (1942).
† Buchmanite, a follower of the Oxford Group Movement, a religious movement founded in Oxford, England, by Frank N. D. Buchman (1878–1961), American evangelist, which featured extensive public 'testifying'.
‡ Edward Turnour, 6th Earl Winterton, 1883–1962; Conservative Member of Parliament for forty-seven years, baby of the house when elected 1904; Father of House on retiring, 1951: Lord Winterton, an Irish peer and thus eligible to sit in the Commons, was the leading Conservative critic of the Government; he and his Labour opposite number Emanuel Shinwell, were known as 'Arsenic and Old Lace'.

THE OBSERVER ('THE MAN I KNEW,' BY LORD ATLEE)

After appointing William Temple Archbishop of Canterbury, W.S.C. was asked why he had chosen a Socialist.

W.S.C.: Because he was the only half-crown article in a six-penny-halfpenny bazaar.

HOUSE OF COMMONS

At a session in House of Commons there were suggestions from Labour members that high-level meetings with Marshal Stalin might win W.S.C. a kiss from the Soviet Leader. A Labour member, Hugh McGovern, reminded him that the Communist leader once met the Nazi Foreign Minister von Ribbentrop, Chiang Kai-shek and a Japanese ambassador whom he kissed on both cheeks.

W.S.C.: (*in the midst of a hilarious House*): Mr McGovern is as good a judge of such delights as I am.

HOUSE OF COMMONS

W.S.C.: Everybody has always underrated the Russians. They keep their own secrets alike from foe and friend.

THE WAR AND COLONEL WARDEN

On a wartime visit to London in May, Molotov and his Soviet colleagues were billeted at Chequers, the Prime Minister's country residence. At a ceremonial dinner, quail was served.

W.S.C.: (*to Commander C. R. Thompson*): Tell Crankshaw* that these miserable mice should never have been removed from Tutankhamen's tomb!

THE SECOND WORLD WAR, VOL. IV

The American aircraft carrier USS Wasp[†] *was made available at the request*

---

* Lt. Col. Sir Eric Crankshaw, Secretary of Government Hospitality Fund.
† She was sunk September 15, 1942, by Japanese torpedoes but all hands were saved.

of W.S.C. for a second trip with Spitfires for Malta's defence. On May 9,
1942, it delivered another crucial flight of these planes to Malta.
W.S.C.: *(in a message to the carrier)*: Who said a Wasp couldn't sting
twice?

BBC BROADCAST
On the German Army's trip to the outskirts of Moscow—and back.
W.S.C.: Then Hitler made his second grand blunder. He forgot
about the winter. There is a winter, you know, in Russia. For a good
many months the temperature is apt to fall very low. There is snow,
there is frost, and all that. Hitler forgot about this Russian winter.
He must have been very loosely educated. We all heard about it at
school, but he forgot it. I have never made such a bad mistake as
that.

THE SECOND WORLD WAR, VOL. IV
On May 22, just after the one thousandth day of the war.
W.S.C.: I have often tried to set down the strategic truths I have
comprehended in the form of simple anecdotes, and they rank this
way in my mind. One of them is the celebrated tale of the man
who gave the powder to the bear. He mixed the powder with the
greatest care, making sure that not only the ingredients but the
proportions were absolutely correct. He rolled it up in a large paper
spill, and was about to blow it down the bear's throat. *But the bear
blew first.*

THE SECOND WORLD WAR, VOL. IV
W.S.C.: In war it is not always possible to have everything go
exactly as one likes. In working with Allies it sometimes happens
that they develop opinions of their own.

THE SECOND WORLD WAR, VOL. V
*A Minute of May 30, Prime Minister to Chief of Combined Operations on
prefabricated ports to be ferried across the Channel for the invasion of
Europe. They became known later as 'Mulberries'—the synthetic floating*

harbours sunk as breakwaters that later figured at the Normandy beaches.[*]

W.S.C.: . . . they *must* float up and down with the tide. The anchor problem must be mastered. The ships must have a side-flat cut in them, and a drawbridge long enough to overreach the moorings of the piers. Let me have the best solution worked out. Don't argue the matter. The difficulties will argue for themselves.

EAR-WITNESS

In Washington in June, on his second visit to the White House, he was handed a telegram by President Roosevelt which bore the dire message that the Eighth Army was in retreat and Tobruk had fallen with 25,000 men taken prisoner.

W.S.C.: I am the most miserable Englishman in America—since Burgoyne.[†]

and

During a heated moment in Anglo-American discussions he remembered his Iroquois Indian ancestry.

W.S.C.: (*to an Aide*): Tell them I was here before they were!

EAR-WITNESS

Desmond Morton, his civilian aide, summoned to Chequers early one Sunday morning during the darkest days of the war, suspected a serious military crisis. Instead he found W.S.C. surrounded by glum-faced military and civilian advisers. Off in a corner, by himself, sat a prim little stranger with a briefcase across his knees.

W.S.C.: Come here, Desmond, drink this and tell me what you think of it.

(Mr Morton protested it was too early; that he did not like to drink before lunch.)

W.S.C.: Never mind, try this.

(After sipping the drink, Mr Morton admitted it was a drinkable but not a remarkable Scotch.)

W.S.C.: It was made from seaweed three weeks ago by the

---

[*] In 1917, in a note to David Lloyd George, W.S.C. described his idea for tanks to be carried by ship and landed on shore.

[*] General John Burgoyne, 1722–1792, British general who surrendered.

TRIAL GROUPING

remarkable little man in the corner. The question is what are we to do with this formula [holding it aloft]? Flood the market with cheap whisky and make a killing? But what then? Some wretch will discover the formula, and the Scotch whisky trade will be ruined forever.

(Much discussion and debate for and against followed. W.S.C. sat silent. All awaited his decision. Without a word he leaned toward the fireplace and dropped the formula on to the blazing logs. Mr Morton considered this one of the hardest decisions his chief had to make during the war.)

HOUSE OF COMMONS

In July, during a No Confidence motion with 475 votes to 25 in his favour.
W.S.C.: I have not made any arrogant, confident, boasting predictions at all. On the contrary, I have stuck hard to my 'blood, toil, tears and sweat', to which I have added muddle and mismanagement, and that, to some extent, I must admit is what you have got out of it.

MR CHURCHILL'S SECRETARY

After one of her typing errors which caused W.S.C. to explode and her tears to flow.

W.S.C.: Good Heavens, you mustn't mind me. We're all toads beneath the harrow, you know.*

HOUSE OF COMMONS

Mr Hore-Belisha:[†] What about the Churchill tank?

W.S.C.: This tank, the A.22, was ordered off the drawing-board, and large numbers went into production very quickly. As might be expected, it had many defects and teething troubles, and when these became apparent the tank was appropriately rechristened the 'Churchill'. These defects have now been largely overcome.

THE MEMOIRS OF ANTHONY EDEN

After W.S.C. initiated the idea that Anthony Eden[‡] should go to the Middle East, he reversed his decision on how Eden's position would appear:

W.S.C.: . . . like a great blue-bottle buzzing over a huge cowpat!

KING-HALL NEWS LETTER

To Sir Stephen King-Hall

W.S.C.: There is much gratitude towards us because we stood alone. It will not last. When we have beaten the 'Narzees' we shall have to take our coats off and work for our livings. Never forget, King-Hall! We have to import 50 per cent of what we eat! If the scrunch came, I very much doubt whether, notwithstanding our admirable constitutional arrangements, it would be easy to arrange in an amicable manner which half of the population should eat and which should starve.

---

* A reference to Kipling's lines:
'The toad beneath the harrow knows
Exactly where each tooth-point goes;
The butterfly upon the road
Preaches contentment to the toad.'

† Leslie Hore-Belisha, MP, Secretary for War, 1937–1940.

‡ Anthony Eden, Secretary of State for Foreign Affairs in Churchill's War Cabinet, 1940–1945.

EAR-WITNESS

As the war progressed he became tortured by requests from each of his war ministers for tanks, planes and supplies.

W.S.C.: (*to General Ismay, his Chief of Staff*): It's the same old story, Pug, too many piglets and not enough teats.

EAR-WITNESS

Friend [to W.S.C.]: Winston! how wonderfully your new grandson resembles you!

W.S.C.: All babies look like me. But then, I look like all babies!

THE WAR AND COLONEL WARDEN

Lunching on his favourite cold beef sandwiches while flying to Cairo in August.

W.S.C.: The bread must be wafer thin. It is nothing more than a vehicle to convey the filling to the stomach.

also

'NONSENSE, MADAM—ALL BABIES LOOK LIKE ME'

Herblock *in* The Washington Post

189

EAR-WITNESS

Three months earlier, on a Clipper flying to the US.

W.S.C.: (*to the Steward on the Clipper*): The clock is going to do some funny things while we are in the air; it is either going to go backwards or forwards, but that is of little consequence, my stomach is my clock and I eat every four hours!*

also

EAR-WITNESS

During a coffee-break at an Allied staff meeting in the Pentagon in Washington, he ordered tea which was brought to him in tea bags.

W.S.C.: (*in disgust, dropping the sopping bags into the hand of an astonished WAC*): War tea in bandages!

EAR-WITNESS

In Cairo. In August, before the Battle of El Alamein, he decided General Montgomery should take command of the Eighth Army in North Africa. Back in London he boiled with strategic plans on how the campaign should be fought and called General Montgomery to London for consultations.

W.S.C.: General, I think you would be well advised to study the science that Americans call logistics. That is to say, the correct disposition of your ships and lorry trains, so that your men in the front lines may get everything they need.

General Montgomery: Prime Minister, I am sure you are right, but I am wondering if I should become personally involved in such purely technical matters, because, after all you know they say that familiarity breeds contempt.

W.S.C.: I perceive your point, General, but I would like to remind you that without a degree of familiarity, we could not breed anything!

---

* Not unmindful that Napoleon had chicken served him every four hours, W.S.C. solved the problem of time lost or gained on transatlantic flights to his own satisfaction by being fed a steak every four hours.

THE SECOND WORLD WAR, VOL. IV

On Soviet banquets held in Moscow to honour the British and Americans.

W.S.C.: Silly tales have been told of how these Soviet dinners became drinking-bouts. There is no truth whatever in this. The Marshal and his colleagues invariably drank their toasts from tiny glasses, taking only a sip on each occasion. I had been well brought up.

and

On an August visit to Stalin.

W.S.C.: One hour's conversation drew to its close . . . Stalin said, 'You are leaving at daybreak. Why should we not go to my house and have some drinks?' I said that I was in principle always in favour of such a policy.

and

Before a talk with Stalin W.S.C. discussed his reasons for backing the White Russian Revolution of 1918 against the Soviets.

W.S.C.: Have you forgiven me?

Marshal Stalin: All that is in the past; and the past belongs to God.

THE MEMOIRS OF ANTHONY EDEN

(At the Cairo Conference in August, Foreign Secretary Anthony Eden impressed upon W.S.C. the importance of meeting the Minister of Defence M. Panayotis Kanellopoulos. Churchill was reminded of it by Sir Alexander Cadogan, permanent Under Secretary of State for Foreign Affairs. Later, summoned to W.S.C.'s bathroom, Cadogan heard strange words oozing between the splashings and soapings of his bathing.)

W.S.C.: Can-tellopoulos, Cant-tell-opoulos, Can-tellopoulos, all right, I'll see him!

THE SECOND WORLD WAR, VOL. IV

Complaining of the slowness of repairing British military equipment in the Tura Caves,* near Cairo.

W.S.C.: But I had my tables of facts and figures and remained dissatisfied. The scale was far too small. The original fault lay with the Pharaohs for not having built more and larger Pyramids. Other responsibilities were more difficult to assign.

SPEECH

In Edinburgh, October 12.

W.S.C.: I have myself some ties with Scotland which are to me of great significance—ties precious and lasting. First of all, I decided to be born on St Andrew's Day—and it was to Scotland I went to find my wife . . . I commanded a Scottish battalion of the famous 21st Regiment for five months in the line in France in the last war. I sat for fifteen years as the representative of 'Bonnie Dundee', and I might be sitting for it still if the matter had rested entirely with me.

SPEECH

At Westminster Central Hall, London on October 31 on Field Marshal Smuts; 'the greatest Prime Minister of South Africa.'

W.S.C.: He and I are old comrades. I cannot say there has never been a kick in our gallop. I was examined by him when I was a

---

* The Caves of Tura were created by the quarrying of the stones of the Pyramids and used during the war for British military repair shops.

prisoner-of-war, and I escaped; but we made an honourable and generous peace on both sides, and for the last forty years we have been comrades working together.

also

EAR-WITNESS

On a weekend at Chartwell, Field Marshal Smuts brought with him a gift of South African brandy which Lady Churchill asked the butler to serve.

W.S.C.: (*raising his glass to Field Marshal Smuts*): this is most excellent, my dear General, but it isn't brandy!*

SPEECH

At the Lord Mayor's Luncheon at the Mansion House.

W.S.C.: We mean to hold our own. I have not become the King's First Minister in order to preside over the liquidation of the British Empire.

and

W.S.C.: General Alexander, with his brilliant comrade and lieutenant, General Montgomery, has gained a glorious and decisive victory [at El Alamein] in what I think should be called the Battle of Egypt. [Field Marshal Erwin] Rommel's Army has been defeated. It has been routed. It has been very largely destroyed as a fighting force.

. . . Now this is not the end. It is not even the beginning of the end. But it is, perhaps, the end of the beginning.

also

THE SECOND WORLD WAR, VOL. IV

Earlier; W.S.C.'s August 10, 1942, Directive to Field Marshal Sir Harold Alexander, Commander in Chief, Middle East.

1) Your prime and main duty will be to take or destroy at the earliest opportunity the German-Italian Army commanded by Field Marshal Rommel, together with all its supplies and

---

* A reference to Marshal Canrobert's comments while watching the Charge of the Light Brigade, 'Magnificent, but not war.'

establishments in Egypt and Libya.

2) You will discharge or cause to be discharged such other duties as pertain to your Command without prejudice to the task described in paragraph 1, which must be considered paramount in His Majesty's interests.

Winston S. Churchill

(Six months later, February 1943, Field Marshal Sir Harold Alexander to Prime Minister.)

Sir: The Orders you gave me on August 10, 1942, have been fulfilled. His Majesty's enemies, together with their impedimenta, have been completely eliminated from Egypt, Cyrenaica, Libya, and Tripolitania. I now await your further instructions.

W.S.C.: Well, obviously we shall have to think of something else!

HOUSE OF COMMONS

On November 11.

W.S.C.: I am certainly not one of those who need to be prodded. In fact, if anything, I am a prod.

EAR-WITNESS

A story without words. On a Saturday afternoon, a time which W.S.C. usually spent at Chequers, Lord Mancroft, serving as a staff officer at the War Office, was lying on his stomach on the floor of the anteroom at 10 Downing Street, tunic unbuttoned, cap and Sam Browne belt beside him, busy working with coloured pencils like a pavement artist on W.S.C.'s situation maps. To his surprise he saw W.S.C. approaching with General William H. Simpson, Commander of the Ninth Army in Europe. As Lord Mancroft started to clamber to his feet W.S.C. waved him down and walked rapidly towards the War Room—paused at the threshold—turned around, put his hand in his pocket, took out a penny and threw it into the Staff Officer's cap! Lord Mancroft still treasures that penny.

HOUSE OF COMMONS

Admiral Darlan, the Vichy second-in-command, who was on a visit to Algiers, threw in his lot with the Allies and was accepted by General Eisenhower. His former co-operation with the enemy had been hotly criticized. *As part of the invasion of North Africa, General Henri Giraud had been helped by submarine to escape from France. He had fought bravely in 1940, escaped from the Germans into unoccupied France early in 1942, and it was thought he would dissuade the French in Algeria from resisting the Allied landing.*

W.S.C.: We all thought General Giraud was the man for the job, and that his arrival would be electrical. In this opinion, General Giraud emphatically agreed.

also

HOUSE OF COMMONS

The British and American governments had made a tentative deal with French Admiral Darlan, Pétain's deputy, who, quite coincidentally, was in North Africa at this moment, to facilitate the invasion of North Africa. In December, a storm arose over it in the House of Commons. W.S.C. noted that the French attached great significance to the hierarchical order of command and that the understanding with Darlan was very useful from this point of view.

W.S.C.: I entreat the members of the House to remember that God in his infinite wisdom did not make Frenchmen in the image of Englishmen.

HOUSE OF COMMONS

Responding when asked to rename the Minister of Defence and the Secretary of State for War, on the ground that their titles were illogical.

W.S.C.: We must beware of needless innovation, especially when guided by logic.

1943

EAR-WITNESS

Discussing the appointment of a First Sea Lord (in particular, Admiral of the Fleet Sir Philip Vian, who was responsible for the attack on the 'Altmark' in a Norwegian fiord before Hitler invaded Norway).

W.S.C.: Would not Admiral Vian be a suitable person?

Civil Servant: The trouble is that he does not get on with foreigners.

W.S.C.: I think that he gets on very well with them. He kills them!

[But the Admiral was not appointed.]

EAR-WITNESS

During January meetings with the French at Casablanca, he was reluctant to talk to General Auguste Noguès, Resident-General of Morocco. He doubted his loyalties but was persuaded to ask the General to dine. It was a night with a full moon.

W.S.C.: (*to General Noguès, after breaking a painfully long silence*): *Avez-vous telephone Berlin?*

General Noguès: (*flustered*): Absolutely, no!

(more silence.)

W.S.C.: *Au clair de la lune! Si vous bombardez nous—nous bombardez vous!*[*]

ADVENTURE IN DIPLOMACY

During the Casablanca Conference President Roosevelt and W.S.C. lived in the Moses Taylor villa, 'la Saadia'. After viewing a glorious panorama of the Atlas Mountains from the villa's tower roof, W.S.C. insisted that President Roosevelt be carried up to enjoy the thrilling view. Later they lunched with American Vice-Consul Kenneth Pendar in the villa.

W.S.C.: (*to Mr Pendar*): What a wonderful country, this Morocco. This sunlight, this wonderful air, these flowers. We English have always needed a place like this to come to for sunshine. Now Pendar, why don't you give us Morocco, and we shall give you India. We shall even give you Gandhi, and he's awfully cheap to keep, now that he's on a hunger strike.[†]

EAR-WITNESS

During the Casablanca Conference US Security officers hoped to dissuade W.S.C. from visiting the Casbah, fearing he might contract a disease and pass it on to President Roosevelt. An American officer was chosen to transmit their concern to him.

W.S.C.: Young man, I have no intention of visiting the Casbah. But if I had, it would not be for the purpose you obviously have in mind. But were I to visit the Casbah for that purpose, my relations

---

[*] By the light of the moon! If you bomb us—we bomb you!
[†] Mahatma Gandhi was on a hunger strike from February 9 to March 2.

with the President of the United States are not such that any disgrace so contracted would be passed on to him.

THE SECOND WORLD WAR, VOL. IV
On General de Gaulle.

W.S.C.: I could not regard him as representing captive and prostrate France, nor indeed that France had a right to decide freely the future for herself. I knew he was no friend of England. But I always recognized in him the spirit and conception which, across the pages of history, the word 'France' would ever proclaim. I understood and admired, while I resented, his arrogant demeanour. Here he was—a refugee, an exile from his country under sentence of death, in a position entirely dependent upon the goodwill of the British Government, and also now of the United States. The Germans had conquered his country. He had no real foothold anywhere. Never mind; he defied all. Always, even when he was behaving worst, he seemed to express the personality of France— a great nation, with all its pride, authority and ambition. It was said in mockery that he thought himself the living representative of Joan of Arc, with whom one of his ancestors is supposed to have served as a faithful adherent. This did not seem to me as absurd as it looked.

also

THE WAR MEMOIRS OF CHARLES DE GAULLE
General de Gaulle, of W.S.C.

General de Gaulle: . . . Without him my efforts would have been futile from the start . . . by lending me a strong and willing hand when he did . . . [he] vitally aided the cause of France.

but

US FOREIGN RELATIONS DOCUMENT: PROBLEMS WITH DE GAULLE
At the Casablanca Conference.

F.D.R.: I do not know what to do with de Gaulle.

W.S.C.: I am no more enamoured with him than you are but I

would rather have him on the committee than strutting about as a combination of Joan of Arc and Clemenceau.

also

CHURCHILL: TAKEN FROM THE DIARIES OF LORD MORAN

Of General de Gaulle.

W.S.C.: Like a female llama who had been surprised in her bath.

also

EAR-WITNESS

At Casablanca.

W.S.C.: (*to General de Gaulle*): *Mon Général, il ne faut pas obstacler la guerre!*[*]

also

Writhing in impatience at General de Gaulle's stubbornness at the Casablanca Conference.

W.S.C.: (*to his aide, Brendan Bracken*): *You* may have your single cross to bear but *I*—I have the double cross of Lorraine.

Brendan bracken: But . . . remember, Winston . . . he thinks of himself as the reincarnation of St Joan.

W.S.C.: (*grinning*): Yes, but *my* Bishops won't burn him!

and

EAR-WITNESS

After a very stormy interview with General de Gaulle, W.S.C. made it clear that if the General continued to be an obstacle he would not hesitate to break with him finally.

W.S.C.: (*interrupting his interpreter and facing up to General de Gaulle*): *Si vous m'obstaclerez, je vous liquiderai.*[†]

and

General de Gaulle attempted to claim for the Free French blocked gold held on

---

[*] 'One must not put obstacles in the path of waging the war.'
[†] 'If you obstruct me, I will liquidate you.' This outburst is said to have occasioned the General's only smile during World War II.

the French account by the Bank of England. W.S.C. was advised not to discuss this with the General but leave it to the experts. Inevitably, General de Gaulle brought it up.

W.S.C.: *Mon cher Général, quand je me trouve en face de la vieille dame de Threadneedle Street, je me trouve toujours impotent.**

and

SPEECH

Fifteen years later on W.S.C.'s 84th birthday General de Gaulle honoured him with the Order of Liberation—a twin-barred Cross of Lorraine.

General de Gaulle: I want Sir Winston to know this—today's ceremony simply means that France knows what she owes him.

MEMOIRS OF LORD ISMAY

After the US agreed to the invasion of Sicily, as the first step in conquering Italy, the British planners pressed to take Sardinia first. The Chiefs of Staff and W.S.C. were against the plan, anxious that operations against Sicily go forward without delay.

W.S.C.: I absolutely refuse to be fobbed off with a sardine.

and

W.S.C.: North Africa is a springboard, not a sofa.†

EAR-WITNESS

Determined to avoid a disaster paralleling the Dardanelles, he established a Combined Operations involving commando units under Admiral Sir Roger Keyes. Before the assault on Italy, he recommended seaborne landings.

W.S.C.: Why crawl up the leg like a harvest bug from the ankle upwards? Let us strike rather at the knee.

---

* 'When I find myself with the Old Lady of Threadneedle Street, [the Bank of England] I am always impotent.' (He meant *impuissant*, ie, powerless.)

† Aneurin Bevan, bitter Opposition critic of the wartime Coalition Government, said that the Allied Command, in this approach to the conquest of Italy, was 'like an old man approaching a young bride—fascinated, sluggish and apprehensive.'

PRESS CONFERENCE
In Cairo, on February 1.

W.S.C.: I always avoid prophesying beforehand, because it is much better policy to prophesy after the event has already taken place.

THE SECOND WORLD WAR, VOL. IV
On his attack of pneumonia.

W.S.C.: . . . the doctors . . . said I had pneumonia, to which I replied, 'Well, surely you can deal with that. Don't you believe in your new drug?' Doctor [Guy] Marshall said he called pneumonia 'The old man's friend'. 'Why?' I asked. 'Because it takes them off so quietly.' I made a suitable reply.

IMITATION
THE
SINCEREST
FLATTERY

THE SECOND WORLD WAR, VOL. IV
While recuperating from pneumonia.

W.S.C.: A gentleman, Mr Thomson, kindly presented me with a lion . . . 'Rota' was the lion's name . . . He was a male lion of fine quality, and in eight years became the father of many children. The assistant secretary, who had been with me in the airplane, came with some papers. He was a charming man, highly competent, but physically on the small side. Indulging in chaff, I now showed him a magnificent photograph of 'Rota' with his mouth open, saying, 'If there are any shortcomings in your work I shall send you to him. Meat is very short now.' He took a serious view of this remark. He repeated to the office that I was in a delirium.

also

In a letter to the Duke of Devonshire, President of the London Zoo.

W.S.C.: You are quite right in your assumption that I do not want the lion at the moment either at Downing Street or at Chequers owing to the Ministerial calm which prevails there . . . I consider you personally bound to receive the lion at Chatsworth [the Duke's country house] should all else fail.

EAR-WITNESS

Love for his black swans, the carp he hand fed with maggots, his French poodles, parakeets and cats found its way into discussions on bringing Turkey into the war.

W.S.C.: We must start by treating them purry purry, puss puss, then later we shall harden.

EAR-WITNESS

A W.S.C. anecdote current on both sides of the Atlantic had it that W.S.C. sent Anthony Eden, later Lord Avon, on a mission to bring Turkey into the war.

Eden (in a cable to W.S.C.): Progress slow. What more can I tell Turkey?

W.S.C. (to Eden): Tell them Christmas is coming!*

also

---

* From Lord Avon's letter to me, January 19, 1966: 'I am sure that Sir Winston did not make the delightful Turkey comment when speaking to me. The only time when Turkey was a leading topic as I set out on one of my missions abroad was in the early months of 1941. At that period we did *not* want the Turks in the war on our side, because we had no help to give them. All we had we were giving to Greece, which was already threatened. There is however this possibility. It was agreed at the Foreign Secretary's Conference in Moscow in 1943 that I should try to get Turkey into the war in negotiation in Cairo on my way home. I failed, but Sir Winston may well have sent this message to cheer me in my effort.'

THE MEMOIRS OF ANTHONY EDEN

Bidding farewell to President Inönü of Turkey after the December Cairo Conference, W.S.C. received an embrace from the President. Drawing this to Eden's attention, he was told that this was little enough exchange for 15 hours' hard argument. However (no doubt recollecting Gallipoli), as he went to bed, W.S.C. said to daughter Sarah:

W.S.C.: Do you know what happened to me today, the Turkish President kissed me. The truth is I'm irresistible. But don't tell Anthony, he's jealous.

F.D.R.: HIS PERSONAL LETTERS

President Franklin Roosevelt and W.S.C. met in ten conferences during World War II and exchanged over one thousand communications, including many personal ones.

March 19.

Dear Winston:

I did not know you came to the United States when you were at the baby carriage age, nor did I know you had visited Amenia. It is in Duchess County about twenty miles back of Hyde Park.

My best to you.

(W.S.C. replied that his first visit to America had been in December 1895, when he was too big for any baby carriage.* Actually W.S.C.'s first visit to the American continent was in 1895 as a war correspondent when he touched New York on his way to Cuba during the Rebellion. His first actual visit to the United States was in December 1900.)

President Roosevelt [Replied]:

For former Naval Person;

Some Baby!

Roosevelt

BBC BROADCAST

On the Four-Year Plan.

W.S.C.: We cannot have a band of drones in our midst, whether they come from the ancient aristocracy, the modern plutocracy, or the ordinary type of pubcrawler.

---

* He was born in 1874.

HOUSE OF COMMONS

In reply to the suggestion that church bells be used to warn of an invasion.

W.S.C.: We have come to the conclusion that this particular method of warning was redundant and not well adapted to the present conditions of war. For myself, I cannot help feeling that anything like a serious invasion would be bound to leak out.

and

Mr. Austin Hopkinson, M.P.: How can the news possibly leak out when it is an offence to spread alarm and despondency?

W.S.C.: Factual statements of that kind, especially if well-intentioned, would not fall into that category.

THE SECOND WORLD WAR, VOL. IV

A Minute of April 23, to Sir Edward Bridges, Brigadier Ian Jacob for Defence Committee (Supply) and others.*

W.S.C.: The idea of having a spear-point or battering-ram of heavy armoured vehicles to break the enemy's front and make a hole through which the lighter vehicles can be pushed has a very high military significance. A certain number of such vehicles should be attached to armies, and possibly even to corps, in each theatre. The wart hog must play his part as well as the gazelle . . . What has happened to the amphibious tank? Surely a float or galosh can be made to take a tank of the larger size across the Channel under good conditions once a beach landing has been secured.

BROADCAST

On May 14 from the US on the third anniversary of Britain's Home Guard for a possible invasion.

W.S.C.: . . . when imagining the horrors of a Hun invasion, there rose that last consoling thought which rises naturally in unconquerable races and in unenslavable men resolved to go down fighting—you can always take one with you.'

*Secretary to the Cabinet, 1938–1946.

SPEECH

To the US Congress on May 19.

W.S.C.: The proud German Army has by its sudden collapse, sudden crumbling and breaking up, . . . once again proved the truth of the saying, 'The Hun is always either at your throat or your feet.'

and

W.S.C.: It may not have escaped your attention that I have brought with me to this country and to this conference Field Marshal Wavell* and the other two commanders-in-chief from India. Now . . . they have not travelled all this way simply to concern themselves about improving the health and happiness of the Mikado of Japan.

also

EAR-WITNESS

Dining at the British Embassy he referred to Field Marshal Wavell—also a guest.

W.S.C.: You don't think I brought Far Eastern Commanders to Washington for the sake of the Son of—er—Heaven, I mean the Mikado.

SPEECH

To the US Congress.

W.S.C.: . . . in North Africa, we builded better than we knew. The unexpected came to the aid of the design and multiplied the results. For this we have to thank the military intuition of Corporal Hitler.†
We may notice . . . the touch of the master hand.

EAR-WITNESS

Of Field Marshal Montgomery, the hero of the Desert War, he wrote: 'This vehement and formidable General—a Cromwellian figure—austere, severe, accomplished, tireless—his life given to the study of war, who has attracted to

---

* Archibald Percival Wavell, first Earl Wavell, 1883–1950; soldier, writer; Commander of British Forces in Middle East, 1939–1941; of British Forces in India, 1941, 1942–1943; Viceroy and Governor General of India, 1943–1947.
† W.S.C. often referred to Hitler as corporal Schicklgruber, the name of his paternal grandmother that was used for a time by his father.

himself in an extraordinary degree the confidence and devotion of the Army.'
But he sometimes differed with his teetotalling, deeply religious General, once
in a parody on his own words.

W.S.C.: In retreat indomitable; in advance invincible; in victory insufferable!

and

During the North African campaign, German General Wilhelm von Thoma[*]
was captured by the Eighth Army. His captor, General Montgomery, invited
him to dine in his GHQ trailer caravan, which caused a furore in Britain.

W.S.C.: I sympathize with General von Thoma. Defeated, humiliated, in captivity, and [a long pause for dramatic effect] dinner with General Montgomery.

EAR-WITNESS

On his leading wartime critics, Mr Aneurin Bevan and Mr Emanuel
Shinwell.[†]

W.S.C.: Bevan finds it hard to conceal his pleasures at our defeats. Shinwell, though he tries hard, finds it equally difficult to hide his pleasure at our victories.

and

During one debate on Allied command appointments he was interrupted by
Mr Shinwell.

Mr Shinwell: All I say to him now is that the discussions about the Mediterranean and the discussions about the whole command have been taking place simultaneously.

W.S.C.: They may have been taking place simultaneously but one ended before the other. That sometimes happens in horse racing.[‡]

PRESS CONFERENCE

On May 25, in Washington, DC. Discussing how a wobbling Italy would
be treated.

W.S.C.: All we can do is to apply the physical stimuli which we have

---

[*] Wilhelm von Thoma, German general; Field Commander of the Afrika Corps; captured by British, 1942, after battle of El Alamein.
[†] Emanuel Shinwell, MP; later, under Labour Government, Minister of Fuel and Power, 1945–1947; Secretary of War, 1947–1950; Minister of Defence, 1950–1951.
[‡] W.S.C. and Shinwell both loved horse racing and, when on speaking terms, gossiped about it.

at our disposal to bring about a change of mind in these recalcitrant persons. Of this you may be sure: we shall continue to operate on the Italian donkey at both ends, with a carrot and with a stick.

and

At another Washington, DC, Press Conference.

W.S.C.: Signor Mussolini's position is indeed unenviable. The organ-grinder has managed to get his head in the monkey's collar.[*]

COLLIER'S

W.S.C.: A popular vote in favour of intoxicants would not justify me, if I were an American citizen, in pouring whisky down the throats of the stalwarts of the Anti-Saloon League; neither does a vote in the other direction entitle them to make me drink lemonade.

CHURCHILL BY HIS CONTEMPORARIES

After lunching superbly, he congratulated his host.

W.S.C.: It is perhaps as well that I was not accompanied by my colleague, the Minister of Aircraft Production [Sir Stafford Cripps], for there is a man who habitually takes his meal off a handful of peas, and, when he gets a handful of beans, counts that his Christmas feast!

EAR-WITNESS

In June, dining in Carthage with General Eisenhower, W.S.C. referred to its acoustically perfect amphitheatre.

W.S.C.: Yes, I was speaking from where the cries of Christian virgins rent the air whilst roaring lions devoured them—and yet— I am no lion and certainly not a virgin!

---

[*] In a good example of 'the sincerest form of flattery', Aneurin Bevan in 1956 reworked W.S.C.'s comment. As he turned from baiting Selwyn Lloyd to assail Anthony Eden, who had just entered, he asked, 'Why are we throwing things at the monkey, now that the organ grinder's here?'

HOUSE OF COMMONS

June 8, returning from the US and North Africa.

W.S.C.: I must acknowledge with gratitude the extraordinary kindness with which I have been treated in the House and out-of-doors throughout the land. That is a very great help in these days of continued crisis and storm.

THE SECOND WORLD WAR, VOL. V

A Minute of July 11, to Foreign Secretary, on War Marriages.

W.S.C.: About King Peter's [of Yugoslavia] marriage, we should recur to first principles. The whole tradition of military Europe has been in favour of 'les noces de guerre' [war marriages], and nothing could be more natural and nothing could be more becoming than that a young king should marry a highly suitable princess on the eve of his departure for the war. Thus he has a chance of perpetuating his dynasty, and anyhow of giving effect to those primary instincts to which the humblest of human beings have a right.

Against this we have some tale, which I disbelieve of a martial race, that the Serb principle is that no one must get married in wartime. *Prima facie* this would seem to condone extra-marital relations. Then a bundle of Ministers that has been flung out of Yugoslavia are rolling over each other to obtain the shadow offices of an émigré Government. Some are in favour of the marriage, some are not. The King and the Princess are strongly in favour of it, and in my view in this tangle they are the only ones whose opinions should weigh with us.

The Foreign Office should discard eighteenth century politics and take a simple and straightforward view . . . We might be back in the refinements of Louis XIV instead of the lusty squalor of the twentieth century . . . My advice to the King . . . will be go to the nearest Registry Office and take a chance. So what?

EAR-WITNESS

During the War, security measures had to be taken because of W.S.C.'s presence at the White House. Before leaving for the Quebec Conference in August, he was cautioned not to disclose how he was going to get there from

Washington. He telephoned to the Canadian Prime Minister Mackenzie King from the White House.

W.S.C.: They won't let me tell you how I'm going to travel. You know security measures. So all I can tell you is that I'm coming by puff-puff, if you know what I mean.

THE SECOND WORLD WAR, VOL. V

A Minute of August 8, to General Ismay.

W.S.C.: Operations in which large numbers of men may lose their lives ought not to be described by code-words which imply a boastful and overconfident sentiment, such as 'Triumphant', or, conversely, which are calculated to invest the plan with an air of despondence, such as 'Woebetide', 'Massacre', 'Jumble', 'Trouble', 'Fidget', 'Flimsy', 'Pathetic', 'Jaundice'. They ought not to be names of a frivolous character, such as 'Bunnyhug', 'Billingsgate', 'Aperitif', and 'Ballyhoo'. They should not be ordinary words often used in other connections, such as 'Flood', 'Smooth', 'Sudden', 'Supreme', 'Fullforce', and 'Fullspeed'. Names of living people— Ministers or Commanders—should be avoided; eg 'Bracken'.

2. After all, the world is wide, and intelligent thought will readily supply an unlimited number of well-sounding names which do not suggest the character of the operation or disparage it in any way and do not enable some widow or mother to say that her son was killed in an operation called 'Bunnyhug' or 'Ballyhoo'.

3. Proper names are good in this field. The heroes of antiquity, figures from Greek and Roman mythology, the constellations and stars, famous racehorses, names of British and American war heroes, could be used, provided they fall within the rules above.

also

EAR-WITNESS

Learning that a quite minor operation named 'Pinprick' was being laid on in the China-India-Burma Theatre, under Colonel Dean Rusk, Chief of Plans and Operations under General Joseph Stilwell, Theatre Commander.

W.S.C.: Never 'Pinprick'! Rename it 'Grapple'.

EAR-WITNESS

Dining at the British Embassy in Washington in August of 1943, following the Quebec Conference, he responded to the complaints of an Army supply General on the lack of trucks.

W.S.C.: Why do you want lorries? In my day, soldiers used to walk to battle. Now they go in lorries. And the lorries are transported by tank transports. I suppose when they get to the battlefield, a butler gets out of the transport, bows to the tank and says, 'Here is the battlefield, your Lordship.'

also

MEMOIRS OF LORD ISMAY

Protesting at the amount of equipment that modern armies demand.

W.S.C.: When I was a soldier, infantry used to walk and cavalry used to ride. But now the infantry require motor-cars, and even the tanks have to have horse boxes to take them to battle.

SPEECH

He believed so firmly in continuity yoked to tradition that when the House of

Commons snuff box, in use ever since the eighteenth century, was destroyed in the May 10, 1941 Blitz, depriving members of their pinch of snuff, he replaced it with one from the Marlborough collection at Blenheim. Later on March 2, 1944, before the Royal College of Physicians:

W.S.C.: I confess myself to be a great admirer of tradition. The longer you can look back, the farther you can look forward. This is not a philosophical or political argument—any oculist will tell you this is true.

BROADCAST

From Quebec. To Canada and the Western Allies.

W.S.C.: A supreme commander of the South-East Asia front has been chosen . . . As Chief of Combined Operations Lord Louis [Mountbatten] has shown rare powers of organization and resourcefulness . . . I will venture to call him 'a complete triphibian' . . . equally at home in three elements—earth, air and water—and also well accustomed to fire.

THE WAR AND COLONEL WARDEN

At a September White House lunch party given by F.D.R. for W.S.C., a guest, Mrs Ogden Reid, Vice President of the New York Herald Tribune, *was known by W.S.C. to believe that the people of India had been badly oppressed under British rule.*

W.S.C.: (*to Mrs Reid*): Before we proceed further let us get one thing clear. Are we talking about the brown Indians in India, who have multiplied alarmingly under the benevolent British rule? Or are we speaking of the red Indians in America who, I understand, are almost extinct?

EAR-WITNESS

On September 2, as the honoured guest of the Overseas Press Club, he was discussing with the Chairman, Barnet Nover, the Spanish Civil War in which he first favoured the rebels but changed when the Germans and Italians intervened.

W.S.C.: I am a royalist, you know.

Mr Nover: Monarchy is all right if the Monarch doesn't overstep his limits. That doesn't happen in Britain.

W.S.C.: Yes! We know what to do with him if he does, and it can be unpleasant.

and

A reporter putting a question to him was asked by the Chairman to speak up louder so he could be heard.

W.S.C.: Loud, but not menacingly.

F.D.R.: HIS PERSONAL LETTERS

W.S.C. discussed the possibilities of Basic English with F.D.R. at the Quebec Conference. They agreed that 'it has tremendous merit in it.' President Roosevelt, on June 5, 1944, wrote Cordell Hull 'If Stalin, Chiang Kai-shek and I had had . . . Basic English our conferences would have been . . . easier . . . than having . . . interpreters and . . . would soon take the place of French as the 'so-called' language of diplomacy.' But in a letter to W.S.C. which he never sent he concluded: 'I wonder what the course of history would have been if, in May 1940, you had been able to offer the British people only blood, work, eye water and face water; which I understand is the best that Basic English can do with five famous words.'

also

HOUSE OF COMMONS

On November 4.

W.S.C.: Basic English is not intended for use among English-speaking people, but to enable a much larger body of people who do not have the good fortune to know the English language to participate more easily in our society.

SPEECH

At Harvard University on September 6.

W.S.C.: We have learned to fly. What prodigious changes are involved in that new accomplishment. Man has parted company with his trusty friend the horse and has sailed into the azure with the eagles, eagles being represented by the infernal—I mean internal—combustion engine. Where, then, are those broad oceans, those vast staring deserts? They are shrinking beneath our very eyes. Even elderly Parliamentarians like myself are forced to acquire a high degree of mobility.

and

On September 6.

W.S.C.: I like to think of British and Americans moving about freely over each other's wide estates with hardly a sense of being foreigners to one another . . . It would certainly be a grand convenience for us all . . . I say, let us go into this together. Let us have another Boston Tea Party about it!

THE SECOND WORLD WAR, VOL. V

General Sir Henry Maitland ('Jumbo') Wilson, Commander in Chief,
Middle East, was selected in September to hold the Greek island of Leros
with comparatively few troops.

W.S.C.: (*to General Wilson*): This is the time to play high. Improvise and dare.

later

He improvose and dore.

EAR-WITNESS

At the White House during the War, he danced a jig in his 'zoot suit' when
there was good news.

W.S.C.: I wore a suit like this to the Kremlin once. It didn't go well. They thought I was pushing democracy too far.

THE SECOND WORLD WAR, VOL. V

Adapting from a speech made by F.D.R. at the 1936 Democratic
Convention:

W.S.C.: When I hear people talking in an airy way . . . of throwing modern armies ashore here and there as if they were bales of goods . . . I marvel at the lack of knowledge . . . of conditions of modern war . . . This class of criticism which I read in the paper reminds me of . . . the sailor who jumped into a dock to rescue a small boy from drowning. About a week later this sailor was accosted by a woman who asked, 'Are you the man who picked my son out of the water the other night?' The sailor replied modestly, 'That is true, ma'am.' 'Ah,' said the woman, 'you are the man I am looking for. Where is his cap?'

EAR-WITNESS

British and Free French forces entered Syria and Lebanon on June 8, 1941.
General Georges Catroux, Free French High Commissioner in the Middle
East, declared both countries independent. After the 1943 election in
Lebanon, the Free French objected to changes in the Constitution. On
November 11, they suspended it, dismissed the Government, arrested the
President and dissolved the Chamber of Deputies. The British and the
Americans protested the coup; there was disorder. As the Free French were
responsible for law and order under the Lyttleton–de Gaulle Agreement, and
the British were fighting a war, the dilemma was acute. To avoid trouble with
General de Gaulle W.S.C. decided to send Desmond Morton to Beirut as his
Special Representative.
Desmond Morton: What shall I do, Prime Minister?
W.S.C.: Take my aircraft and a case of Scotch for 'Jumbo' [General
Sir Henry Maitland Wilson, British Commander in charge], a case
of arak for Riad el-Sohl [deposed Prime Minister] and six cases of
champagne for the Frenchman.
A reconciliation was effected promptly!

THE SECOND WORLD WAR, VOL. V

As 1943 drew to its close, W.S.C. and F.D.R. decided to meet in Cairo before
a conference with Stalin at Teheran. It was a journey that was to keep W.S.C.
from Britain for nearly three months because of illness. En route to the
rendezvous he received word from President Roosevelt that his security officers
had advised him that Cairo was too vulnerable to German air attack from Crete
and Rhodes. As W.S.C. had received assurances from the military that there
was adequate air protection in Cairo, he cabled F.D.R., aboard the 'Iowa.'
W.S.C.: See St John chapter XIV verses 1 to 4.*

---

* 'Let not your heart be troubled; ye believe in God, believe also in me.
In my Father's house are many mansions: if it were not so, I would have told you. I go to prepare a place for you.
And if I go and prepare a place for you, I will come again, and receive you unto myself; that where I am, there ye may be also.
And whither I go ye know, and the way ye know.'

and

W.S.C.: On reading this [the message] through more carefully after it had gone, I was a little concerned lest, apart from a shadow of unintended profanity, it should be thought I was taking too much upon myself and thus giving offence. However, the President brushed all objections aside and our plans were continued, unchanged.

THE SECOND WORLD WAR, VOL. V

*At the end of the November Teheran Conference, discussing 'Overlord.'**

W.S.C.: 'In wartime,' I said, 'truth is so precious that she should always be attended by a bodyguard of lies.' Stalin and his comrades greatly appreciated this remark when it was translated, and upon this note our formal conference ended gaily.

ROOSEVELT AND HOPKINS, AN INTIMATE HISTORY

On the eve of his sixty-ninth birthday, November 29.

W.S.C.: (*to Averell Harriman†*): I . . .insist . . . that I be host at dinner tomorrow evening. I think I have one or two claims to precedence. To begin with, I come first in seniority and alphabetically. In the second place, I represent the longest established of the three governments. And, in the third place, tomorrow happens to be my birthday.

THE SECOND WORLD WAR, VOL. V

During the December Cairo Conference with its crucial decisions to be taken, he visited the Sphinx with President Roosevelt.

W.S.C.: I could not bear his leaving without seeing the Sphinx . . . We motored there . . . and . . . Roosevelt and I gazed at her for some minutes in silence. She told us nothing and maintained her inscrutable smile. There was no use waiting longer.

---

* 'Overlord,' code name for planned cross-Channel invasion of France.
† W. Averell Harriman, US Ambassador to Russia, 1943–1946; US Ambassador to Great Britain, 1946; Governor of State of New York, 1955–1959; Ambassador-at-Large, 1965.

EAR-WITNESS

Dr Guy Pulvertaft attended him during his illness in North Africa in 1943. To take blood tests, his ears had been pricked so many times the doctors told him they were puzzled where to turn next for more blood samples.

W.S.C.: Never let it be said that I have a human vampire and refuse to feed him. It is true that I have two ears, but I also have ten fingers and ten toes—and—and an infinite expanse of bottom!

EAR-WITNESS

After several bouts with pneumonia he delighted in the sulfa drug, M and B, that knocked the virus from him. (He also delighted in referring to his doctors, Lord Moran and Dr Bedford, as M and B.) He discovered that the most agreeable way of taking these drugs was through whisky or brandy, which drew protests from his nurse.

W.S.C.: Dear Nurse, pray remember that man cannot live by M and B alone.

CHURCHILL: TAKEN FROM THE DIARIES OF LORD MORAN

Later, on June 27, 1946, after consulting Sir Alexander Fleming, discoverer of penicillin, on a staphylococcus infection which had resisted penicillin.

W.S.C.: The bug seems to have caught my truculence. This is its finest hour.

THE WAR AND COLONEL WARDEN

In Carthage, where he was recuperating, a Christmas service was conducted by a British Army chaplain. Mrs Churchill, who attended, later told of a white dove that flew into the tin hut where the service was held, and lighted on the altar just as the Blessing was being pronounced.

W.S.C.: An ecclesiastical hoax!

also

ASSIGNMENT: CHURCHILL

W.S.C.: The ruins of Carthage are close by. The sound of the Romans and Hasdrubal [Carthaginian General]. What better place could I die than here? Here in the ruins of Carthage?

THE SECOND WORLD WAR, VOL. V

W.S.C.: . . . I for one, being an optimist, do not think peace is going to be so bad as war, and I hope we shall not try to make it as bad. *and*
W.S.C.: How much easier it is to join bad companions than to shake them off.

1944

EAR-WITNESS

During a wartime session in the House of Commons, although W.S.C. was becoming a bit deaf, he was trying hard to follow the words of an expert who was speaking in a droning voice.
W.S.C.: (*to his neighbour*): What's he talking about?
Neighbour: Buffer stocks.
W.S.C.: Butterscotch! Let's wind this up and get back to the war.

HOUSE OF COMMONS

A member suggested that the House should toast, 'Death to all Dictators and Long Life to all Liberators among whom the Prime Minister is First.'

W.S.C.: It is very early in the morning.

THE SECOND WORLD WAR VOL. IV

After his pneumonia attack in Carthage during World War II, W.S.C. on Christmas Eve, December 24, 1943 summoned five Commanders-in-Chief to probe his strategic concept of a landing at Anzio, which, if successful, could have brought victory closer, but ended unsuccessfully because he was unable to procure enough landing craft from the United States.

W.S.C.. I intended to throw ashore a hell-cat and all I got was an old stranded whale.

EAR-WITNESS

While Mrs Churchill was heading various War Relief Committees, Irving Berlin, the American song writer, gave her such generous help that when he visited London with his musical 'This Is the Army,' she mentioned it to her husband. The name 'Berlin' rang a bell with W.S.C., recalling a member of the British Embassy staff in Washington whose contributions to official despatches from America he found exceptionally perceptive. So he asked his wife to invite Berlin to lunch. As Mrs Churchill had never heard of Isaiah Berlin,* she wondered why in his busy life her husband would want to meet the composer. But she invited him to lunch with only a few friends, among them author Harold Nicolson and the Duchess of Buccleuch. From the moment of his arrival composer Irving Berlin was subjected to a volley of searching questions on American politics to which he could give only the most amorphous answers.

W.S.C.: Do you think President Roosevelt will be re-elected this year?

Irving Berlin: Well, Sir, in previous years I voted for him myself but this year I'm not so sure.

(If W.S.C. was surprised by the American accent he did not show it, perhaps assuming American citizens were employed at the British Embassy.)

---

* Sir Isaiah Berlin, author and Professor of Social and Political Theory, Oxford University; Fellow of All Souls; First Secretary, British Embassy staff in Washington, 1942–1945; on British Staff at Embassy in Moscow, 1945–1946.

W.S.C.: What do you consider to be the most important piece of work that you have done for us lately?

Irving Berlin: 'I'm Dreaming of a White Christmas.'

(At this W.S.C. fell into a sullen and gloomy silence. Though an aide whispered to him, 'Wrong Man,' he would not give up.)

W.S.C.: Mr Berlin, when do you think the European war is going to end?

Irving Berlin: Sir, I shall never forget this deathless honour. When I go back to my own country I shall tell my children and my children's children that in the early spring of 1944, the Prime Minister of Great Britain asked me, a little song writer, when the European war would end.

(At last W.S.C. showed extreme irritation. The meal ended in confusion and cross purposes. Irving Berlin returned to the Savoy Hotel and an appointment with Sir Alexander Korda, the British film producer, and reported that he thought Winston Churchill the greatest man alive but somehow they had not clicked. Later the comedy of errors was revealed to W.S.C., to his enormous delight.)

W.S.C.: *(on finally meeting Sir Isaiah)*: I fear that you will have heard of the grave solecism I was so unfortunate as to have perpetrated!!*

SPEECH

At Royal College of Physicians on March 2.

W.S.C.: As you can see from the excellent speech [by his personal physician Lord Moran] . . . we divide our labours; he instructs me in the art of speaking, and I teach him how to cure pneumonia . . . I do not profess to be very deeply acquainted with the science of medicine. I am a surgeon myself; my experiences in medicine have been vivid and violent and completely absorbing while they were going on.

---

* Years earlier, W.S.C.'s son Randolph, learning that the *New York Times* Soviet expert, Walter Duranty, was at the Savoy Hotel in London, invited him to lunch. But it was comedian Jimmy ('Schnozzle') Durante who arrived, to Randolph's initial confusion and later delight. Randolph managed one-upmanship on his father by lunching the following day with Walter Duranty.

HOUSE OF COMMONS

Mr Richard Stokes, Labour MP for Ipswich constantly attacked W.S.C.'s wartime leadership and was particularly critical of the quality and performance of British tanks, suggesting that a German Mark VI Tiger and British A22 be brought into the House of Commons yard and tested there.

W.S.C.: I think the trouble and expense involved, though not very great, is still more than is justified to satisfy the spiteful curiosity of my Hon. Friend.

Another MP suggested W.S.C. should man the Churchill tank and Mr Stokes the German model.

W.S.C.: I think it might be one way of settling the difference.

and

Later on April 10, Mr Stokes suggested in the House of Commons that if the two tanks were paraded, the untruthfulness of their relative merits might be exposed.

W.S.C.: Since the word 'untruthfulness' has been used, no one has been a greater contributor than the Hon. Member.

MEMOIRS OF LORD ISMAY

A few weeks before D-Day he asked General 'Pug' Ismay, his Chief of Staff, to give him all the data on weather, time and conditions that prevailed when William the Conqueror landed on the shores of England. General Ismay, caught off-guard and quite unprepared for such a request, murmured lamely something about '1066.'

W.S.C.: (*patting General Ismay on the head*): Pug, you should have been in your basket ages ago!

also

EAR-WITNESS

During the most tense moments of decision before D-Day.

W.S.C.: (*to his assistant private secretary John Peck*): Get me the moon. I MUST have the moon.*

---

* It was some moments before Mr Peck could collect himself from the shock of wondering whether his Chief had cracked under the strain. It was the Nautical Almanac he sought for the phases of the moon, which had a strong bearing on the tides governing weather conditions—a determining factor in the date for the projected invasion of the French coast.

EAR-WITNESS
Vic Oliver, the late music-hall comedian, once the husband of W.S.C.'s daughter Sarah, asked him which three men he judged to be the world's greatest.

W.S.C.: President Roosevelt, Marshal Stalin, and Mussolini.

Vic Oliver: Why Mussolini?

W.S.C.: (*grinning*): Of them all, Mussolini is the greatest. He had the courage to have his son-in-law shot!

HOUSE OF COMMONS
Two hundred MPs desired a badge to be issued to honourably discharged servicemen.

W.S.C.: I was not aware of it. I have the greatest respect for the opinion of any Hon. Member of the House, and especially of two hundred.

EAR-WITNESS
Before France was liberated, there were discussions on whether China should be asked to join the three powers—the United States, Britain and Russia.

W.S.C.: To include China? That would be a tripod with a pigtail.

HOUSE OF COMMONS
August 2, in a situation report on the War.

W.S.C.: . . . it is vain and idle for any one country to try to lay down the law . . . or to trace frontiers or describe the delicate instruments by which these frontiers will be maintained without further bloodshed; . . . the man who sold the hyena's skin while the beast lived was killed in hunting it.

CHURCHILL: TAKEN FROM THE DIARIES OF LORD MORAN
Before W.S.C. departed for Italy, his personal physician, Lord Moran, advised him to take as an anti-malaria precaution a yellow pill called mepacrine. He refused, citing similar refusals by King George VI and Field

Marshal Alexander.* *Lord Moran counter-punched with figures citing the loss through malaria of the effective strength of two infantry divisions in the Sicilian campaign who had not taken mepacrine.*

Lord Moran: General Alexander suggests the doctors keep their pills. I venture to wonder if General Alexander's views on medical matters have the same value as mine on military affairs.

W.S.C.: Most Immediate. Secret.

Telephone Message 6th August 1944 from the Prime Minister to Lord Moran.

In view of your salvo, all surrender unconditionally and hoist the yellow flag.†

THE SECOND WORLD WAR, VOL. VI, ENGLISH EDITION

On August 12 W.S.C., entertaining Marshal Tito at dinner in Naples, noticed that the Marshal was accompanied by two 'ferocious-looking' bodyguards, who were excluded from all meetings that the Marshal attended.

W.S.C.: On the way out from the dining room I did a very foolish thing. I saw before me five yards away the two formidable guardians [of Marshal Tito] who had once again been excluded. I have a very large oblong gold cigar case which belonged to Lord Birkenhead and was given to me by his family after his death. This was in my right-hand pocket. I grasped it firmly and marched toward them. Arrived within two yards I drew it from my pocket as if it were a pistol. Luckily they grinned with delight and we made friends. But I do not recommend such procedure in similar cases.

THE MEMOIRS OF ANTHONY EDEN

While he was sharing rooms with Foreign Secretary Anthony Eden to attend the Paris anniversary celebration of the 1918 Armistice, a telegram arrived which Eden took to the door of his chief's bathroom.

---

* Sir Harold Alexander, later Earl Alexander of Tunis, Commander in Chief, Allied Armies in Italy, 1943–1944; Field Marshal, 1944; Supreme Allied Commander, Mediterranean Theatre, 1944–1945; Governor General of Canada, 1946–1952.

† A reference to the quarantine flag displayed by ships harbouring infectious disease.

W.S.C.: Come in, come in; that is, if you can bear to see me in a gold bath* when you only have a silver one.

THE SECOND WORLD WAR, VOL. VI

On an August visit to Rome, he met the leaders of war-torn Italy's many political parties.

W.S.C.: (*to one group*): What is your party?

Answer: We are the Christian Communists.

W.S.C.: [I replied] . . . 'It must be very inspiring to your party having the Catacombs so handy.'

They did not seem to see the point, and, looking back, I am afraid their minds must have turned to the cruel mass executions which the Germans had so recently perpetrated in these ancient sepulchres. One may however be pardoned for making historical references in Rome.

EAR-WITNESS

After watching the result of an artillery barrage at a forward observation post in the Thirteenth Corps area in Italy.

W.S.C.: This is rather like sending a rude letter and being there when it arrives.

THE SECOND WORLD WAR, VOL. VI

W.S.C.: The topic that bulked the largest at this audience [with Pope Pius XII], as it had done with his predecessor eighteen years before, was the danger of Communism. I have always had the greatest dislike of it; and should I ever have the honour of another audience with the Supreme Pontiff, I should not hesitate to recur [revert] to the subject.

SECOND QUEBEC CONFERENCE

It was agreed after conferences that Poland's eastern frontiers should be fixed along the Curzon Line with minor modifications. But how far west should

---

* The gold fixtures had been installed by Hermann Goering during the Nazi occupation of France.

they be extended to make up to Poland for the loss of her eastern territories? W.S.C. fought hard against giving Poland too much German territory, questioning whether what was left of Hitler's Reich was capable of absorbing and feeding the Germans who would be displaced.

W.S.C.: It would be a great pity to stuff the Polish goose so full of food that it died of indigestion.

HOUSE OF COMMONS

Later, after the Potsdam Conference, in a survey of the war involving the future settlement of former Polish territory, W.S.C. was torn between awareness of the bravery of the Poles and the stubbornness of some leading exile leaders.

W.S.C.: There are few virtues that the Poles do not possess—and there are few mistakes they have ever avoided.

PRESS CONFERENCE

At the Second Quebec Conference in September he was asked to comment on an announcement of Colonel Robert McCormick, anti-British owner of the Chicago Tribune, that if Britain behaved she might be eligible to become one of the United States.

W.S.C.: What do you mean? Great Britain and the United States all one? Yes, I'm all for that, and you mean me to run for President?

and

W.S.C.: I read some of the papers when I am over here, these great big papers about an inch thick—very different from the little sheets with which we get on in Great Britain.

EAR-WITNESS

On a visit to the White House following the Quebec Conference a young lady is said to have asked him what he thought of the United States.

W.S.C.: Toilet paper too thin, newspapers too fat!

THE WAR AND COLONEL WARDEN

After the Liberation and a visit to Italy he flew home to London, alarmed to learn that the population of Barbary apes that roamed the Upper Rock of

Gibraltar was dropping off in numbers. Legend has it that if the apes ever leave Gibraltar Britain's rule there will end. When they began to decrease during World War II the Governor of Gibraltar, Lt. General Sir Frank Mason-McFarlane, ignored the situation. Not W.S.C. He ordered the apes to be placed on the garrison ration strength and an NCO appointed to look after them.

W.S.C.: The establishment of the apes on Gibraltar should be 24 and every effort should be made to reach this number as soon as possible and maintain it thereafter.[*]

HOUSE OF COMMONS

On September 28.

W.S.C.: When Herr Hitler escaped his bomb on 20 July he described his survival as providential; I think that from a purely military point of view we can all agree with him, for certainly it would be most unfortunate if the Allies were to be deprived in the closing phases of the struggle, of that form of warlike genius by which Corporal Schicklgruber has so notably contributed to our victory.

and

W.S.C.: I always hate to compare Napoleon with Hitler, as it seems an insult to the great Emperor and warrior to connect him in any way with a squalid caucus boss and butcher.

and

W.S.C.: The United States is a land of free speech; nowhere is it freer, not even here where we sedulously cultivate it even in its most repulsive forms.

HOUSE OF COMMONS

After Herbert Morrison,[†] then Home Secretary, had submitted a well-reasoned memorandum on town and country planning.

W.S.C.: Ah! Yes! I know—town planning—densities, broad vistas, open spaces. Give to me the romance of the 18th-century alley, with its dark corners, where footpads lurk.

---

[*] After this was reported by the Governor of Gibraltar to the Consul General to Spanish Morocco, twenty seasick apes were sent to Algeciras bringing the number up to full strength.
[†] Herbert Morrison, Deputy Prime Minister, 1945–1951; Deputy Leader of the Opposition, 1951–1955.

HOUSE OF COMMONS

On October 31, on prolongation of Parliament.

W.S.C.: I thought it right to touch upon matters of . . . importance to our constitutional procedure . . . Mr Jorrocks[*] said of fox-hunting that it was the image of war without its guilt, and only five and twenty per cent of its danger. Something like this might be said of a General Election.

HOUSE OF COMMONS

On November 12.

W.S.C.: If I am accused of this mistake, I can only say with M Clemenceau on a celebrated occasion: 'Perhaps I have made a number of other mistakes of which you have not heard.'

HOUSE OF COMMONS

On December 5, when asked to explain the nature of British American Lend-Lease payments.

W.S.C.: I must thank the Hon. Gentleman [Emanuel Shinwell, Labour MP] for making me acquainted with the word 'outwith', . . . For the benefit of English Members I must say that it is translated, 'outside the scope of'. I thought it was a misprint at first.

(After Mr Shinwell asked for more elucidation.)

W.S.C.: I think my Hon. Friend is going a little outwith the question which he put.

HOUSE OF COMMONS

On December 8, after the ELAS (military wing of Greek Communist Party) uprising in Greece, which sparked a civil war and intervention of British forces under General Scobie,[†] W.S.C. was accused in the House of Commons of helping install Greek reactionaries and suppressing democratic forces. A Motion of Censure on his Premiership was introduced into the House of Commons.

W.S.C.: Democracy is not based on violence or terrorism, but on

---

[*] Jorrocks, a grocer-sportsman character in *Jorrocks' Jaunts and Jollities* by R. S. Surtees, published 1831–1834.
[†] Sir Ronald Scobie, General Officer commanding in Greece, 1944–1946.

reason, on fair play, on freedom, on respecting the rights of other people. Democracy is no harlot to be picked up in the street by a man with a tommy-gun. I trust the people, the mass of the people, in almost any country, but I like to make sure that it is the people and not a gang of bandits . . . who think that, by violence, they can overturn the constituted authority.

and

Pausing during his long speech on the crisis in Greece.

W.S.C.: At this point I will take a little lubrication, if it is permissible. I think it is always a great pleasure to the Noble Lady, the Member for the Sutton Division of Plymouth [American-born, teetotalling Nancy, Lady Astor] to see me drinking water.

and

Responding to Mr Aneurin Bevan's interruption on the question of the intervention of British troops in Belgium.

W.S.C.: I should think it was hardly possible to state the opposite of the truth with more precision . . . The Hon. Member must learn to take as well as to give. There is no one more free with interruptions, taunts, and jibes than he is. I saw him—I heard him, not saw him—almost assailing some of the venerable figures on the bench immediately below him. He need not get so angry because the House laughs at him: he ought to be pleased when they only laugh at him.

and

Responding to an interruption from Emanuel Shinwell, Labour MP.

W.S.C.: I do not challenge the Hon. Gentleman when the truth leaks out of him by accident from time to time.

and

Teasing Mr Willie Gallacher, the Communist MP, on his failure to gain support in the House.

W.S.C.: The Hon. Member should not get so excited . . . I was eleven years a fairly solitary figure in this House and pursued my way in patience and so there may be hope for the Hon. Member.

and

Responding to an interruption by Willie Gallacher.

W.S.C.: I will not be interrupted by a Member of this House who consents to be used as the pawn and utensil of a foreign power.

and

Later, in 1947.

W.S.C.: (*to Mr Gallacher*): Shut up, Moscow!

Mr Gallacher (*to W.S.C.*): Shut up, Voice of Wall Street!

EAR-WITNESS

In December, W.S.C. flew to Athens to help the Greeks, worn from Nazi occupation, to combat the communist-led Greek ELAS rebellion. Before he received the prospective Regent, Archbishop Damaskinos, on board the cruiser Ajax *lying off Phaleron, he met with advisers.*

W.S.C.: This Archbishop? I suppose he is an ambitious, scheming, political Mediterranean prelate?

Mr Harold Macmillan: I believe so!

W.S.C.: Good! We can use him!

and

Of General Plastiras.*

W.S.C.: Has he feet of clay?

also

THE WAR AND COLONEL WARDEN

After instructing British troops under General Scobie to intervene against the Greek ELAS rebels, he met Captain J. W. Cuthbert, the commanding officer of the Ajax, *then in the harbour of Piraeus to support the British action.*

Captain Cuthbert: I hope, Sir, that while you are with us we shan't have to open fire . . . if we are asked to give supporting fire I must do so.

W.S.C.: Pray remember, Captain, that I came here as a cooing dove of peace, bearing a sprig of mistletoe in my beak—but far be it from me to stand in the way of military necessity.

1945   THE SECOND WORLD WAR, VOL. VI

In January, preparing for a Big Three Conference at Yalta.

W.S.C.: (*to President Roosevelt*): We shall be delighted if you will come to Malta. I shall be waiting on the quay. You will also see the inscription of your noble message to Malta of a year ago.

---

* General Nicholas Plastiras was asked by the Regent Archbishop Damaskinos to form a Coalition Government and took oath of office January 5, 1945.

Everything can be arranged to your convenience. No more let us falter! From Malta to Yalta! Let nobody alter!
and
W.S.C.: I elaborated this for private use:
No more let us alter or falter or palter
From Malta to Yalta, and Yalta to Malta.
and

W.S.C. suggested that a Combined British-American Military Chiefs and US Secretary of State Edward Stettinius might meet for a few days in Malta preliminary to Yalta, but President Roosevelt, anxious not to worry Stalin by such a preconference plan, vetoed the proposal, stating that the Yalta Conference ought not to take more than five or six days.

W.S.C.: I do not see any other way of realizing our hopes about world organization in five or six days. Even the Almighty took seven.
and

On February 5, at Yalta.

W.S.C.: Trying to maintain good relations with a Communist is like wooing a crocodile. You do not know whether to tickle it under the chin or beat it over the head. When it opens its mouth, you cannot tell whether it is trying to smile or preparing to eat you up.
and

EAR-WITNESS

Charles E. Bohlen, then a State Department officer, later US Ambassador to France, relates that at an afternoon meeting of the Foreign Ministers, during a report on the results of the morning session, W.S.C. misunderstood US Secretary of State Edward Stettinius' proposal to put the Japanese-mandated islands of the Pacific under trusteeship (thinking he was referring to a part of the British Empire).

W.S.C.: We will never tolerate the fumbling fingers of fifty nations prying into our heritage.

EAR-WITNESS

Sawyers, W.S.C.'s valet: (to W.S.C., who was looking for his hot water bottle): You are sitting on your hot water bottle. That isn't at all a good idea.
W.S.C.: Idea, it isn't an idea, it's a coincidence!

THE SECOND WORLD WAR, VOL. VI

At a state dinner on February 17, for King ibn-Saud at Fayum Oasis after the Yalta Conference.

W.S.C.: I had been told that neither smoking nor alcoholic beverages were allowed in the Royal Presence. As I was host at luncheon I raised the matter at once, and said to the interpreter that if it was the religion of his Majesty to deprive himself of smoking and alcohol, I must point out that my rule of life prescribed as an absolutely sacred rite smoking cigars and also the drinking of alcohol before, after, and if need be during all meals and in the intervals between them.

and

AMID THESE STORMS

Reflecting on his father's plea that he should avoid smoking.

W.S.C.: But consider! How can I tell that my temper would have been as sweet or my companionship as agreeable if I had abjured from my youth the goddess Nicotine?

also

EAR-WITNESS

At the Potsdam Conference a story went the rounds on the joint appearance of President Truman, Prime Minister Churchill and Marshal Stalin at the pearly gates. After greeting the three leaders, St Peter asked each of them to state his heart's desire. Stalin asked that every atom bomb plant in America be blown from the map; Truman that the Red Army and the Kremlin clique be blown sky-high. W.S.C. remained silent until St Peter came to him.

W.S.C.: Mine is a very simple wish. When the other gentlemen have been served, I'll have a cigar.

Theme for Triumph and Tragedy, *the sixth and last volume of his World War II Memoirs.*

W.S.C.:   How the Great Democracies
            Triumphed,
            and so
            Were able to Resume
            the Follies
            Which Had so Nearly
            Cost Them Their
            Life

HOUSE OF COMMONS

On March 7, to Lord Winterton.

W.S.C.: The Right Honourable Gentleman is a comparatively young Father of the House; he has many years of life before him. We still hope they may be years of useful life in this House, but unless in the future his sagacity and knowledge of the House are found to be markedly more superior to what he has exhibited today, I must warn him that he will run a very grave risk of falling into senility before he is overtaken by old age.

THE SECOND WORLD WAR, VOL. VI

On March 19.

W.S.C.: (*to Mr Assheton**): I notice in the newspaper that the Central Office or Party Chiefs have issued instructions that no one over seventy should be tolerated as a candidate at the forthcoming election. I naturally wish to know at the earliest moment whether this ban applies to me.

ASSIGNMENT: CHURCHILL

On March 25. Impatient to walk on the soil of conquered Germany, he visited Generals Eisenhower and Montgomery and units of the American Ninth Army on the west bank of the Rhine.

W.S.C.: (*writing in chalk on a shell*):

FOR HITLER PERSONALLY![†]

THE SECOND WORLD WAR, VOL. VI

On April 2. Urging a strike for Berlin, Vienna and Prague, to hold as much territory as possible until the Allies were reassured that the Soviets would honour their agreements.

W.S.C.: (*to General Eisenhower*): I deem it highly important that we should shake hands with the Russians as far to the east as possible.

---

[*] Rt. Hon. Ralph Assheton, Chairman of the Conservative Party Organization, 1944–1946.
[†] He was cheered when a 240-mm. gun fired his shell in the direction of Berlin.

THE SECOND WORLD WAR, VOL. VI

Prime Minister Churchill's Minute to the Minister of Agriculture, Minister of Food, and Minister of War Transport, April 3, 1945.

W.S.C.: On no account reduce the barley for whisky. This takes years to mature and is an invaluable export and dollar producer . . . It would be improvident not to preserve this characteristic British element of ascendancy.

HOUSE OF COMMONS

Of Herbert Morrison.

W.S.C.: I hope he is not going to lecture us today on bringing party matters and party feelings into discussions of large public issues. There is no man I can think of from whom such rebukes and admonitions come less well. I would not go so far as to describe him in words used by the Minister of Health Mr Aneurin Bevan a year ago when he was in an independent position, as, 'a third class Tammany boss'—I thought it was very much to be deprecated using disparaging expressions about important institutions of friendly countries,

and

HOUSE OF COMMONS

On May 12.

W.S.C.: I can assure the Right Hon. Gentleman [Mr Herbert Morrison] that the spectacle of a number of middle-aged gentlemen who are my political opponents being in a state of uproar and fury is really quite exhilarating to me.

and

On May 21.

W.S.C.: The Right Hon. Member for Lewisham, South [Mr Herbert Morrison], is a curious mixture of geniality and venom. The geniality, I may say after a great many years' experience, is natural to himself. The venom has to be adopted in order to keep on sides with the forces below the gangway.

and

Earlier, on November 11, 1947.

W.S.C.: Mr Herbert Morrison is a 'master craftsman'.

Mr Morrison: The Right Hon. Gentleman has promoted me.
W.S.C.: Craft is common both to skill and deceit.

EAR-WITNESS

On May 7, after General Ismay had given him the news of V-E Day.
General Ismay: That's that, Prime Minister!
W.S.C.: The eagle has ceased to scream, but the parrots will now begin to chatter. The war of the giants is over and the pigmies will now start to squabble.

A ROVING COMMISSION

1900 parallels 1945.
W.S.C.: Hitherto I had been regarded as a Jingo bent upon the ruthless prosecution of the war, and was therefore vilified by the Pro-Boers. I was now to get into trouble with the Tories . . . I must confess that all through my life I have found myself in disagreement alternately with both the historic English parties. I have always urged fighting wars and other contentions with might and main till overwhelming victory, and then offering the hand of friendship to the vanquished. Thus I have always been against the Pacifists

A FINE
TEAM—BUT
COULD DO
WITH A DASH
OF UNITY

during the quarrel, and against the Jingoes* at the close . . . Wherever we departed from it, we suffered; wherever we followed it, we triumphed . . . I always get into trouble because so few people take this line . . . As it is, those who can win a war well can rarely make a good peace, and those who could make a good peace would never have won the war. It would perhaps be pressing the argument too far to suggest that I could do both.

EAR-WITNESS

To Clement Attlee, during the July General Election.
W.S.C.: Well, I've tried 'em with pep, and I've tried 'em with pap, but I don't know what it is they want.

EAR-WITNESS

On July 26, the Map Room at 10 Downing Street had been converted into a news centre for the election results. W.S.C. realized from the earliest returns that the outlook was very bleak.
W.S.C.: (*to his aide Richard Pim*): This may well be a landslide and they have a perfect right to kick us out. That is democracy. That is what we've been fighting for—hand me my towel.
and
After W.S.C. lost the General Election, a caller sympathized with him that, 'At least while you held the reins you managed to win the race.'
W.S.C.: Yes, I won the race but they have warned me off the turf.
and
After his defeat it was suggested that he tour English cities and resign the leadership of the Conservative Party. He turned down both suggestions.
W.S.C.: I refuse to be exhibited like a prize bull whose chief attraction is his last prowess.
On an earlier occasion.
W.S.C.: Although always prepared for martyrdom, I preferred that it should be postponed.
and
W.S.C.: Some people tell me it [his defeat] is a blessing in disguise—but I must say the blessing is well disguised.

---

* Those who boast of patriotism, favouring more aggressive foreign policies.

EAR-WITNESS

One of W.S.C.'s prides at Chartwell was his Carnotic carp weighing two pounds each which he liked to paint Monet-style. One canvas of them was shown in the Academy and attracted the attention of some cranks who managed to go out to his ponds, throw in a hand grenade and kill the lot. On a visit of Lord Cherwell, 'The Prof' got quite wrought up over the sabotage.

Brigadier Lindemann: Winston, I think it's the dirtiest, filthiest, most cowardly thing I ever heard—what happened to those fish.

W.S.C.: Oh! I thought you were going to allude to the elections.

EAR-WITNESS

In 1895, W.S.C.'s grandmother, the Dowager Duchess of Marlborough, counselled her American daughter-in-law, Consuela Vanderbilt, bride of the ninth Duke of Marlborough, that she must have a child and it should be a son, as it would be 'intolerable to have that little upstart Winston become Duke.' When 'the little upstart,' then second, i.e., next in line for the dukedom, became Prime Minister he teased his son Randolph after they had a slight altercation.

W.S.C.: Randolph! If you don't behave, I'll take a peerage!*

and

At one of the darkest periods of his life, following his defeat by the Labour Government, he was offered the Order of the Garter by George VI.

W.S.C.: I could not accept the Order of the Garter from my Sovereign when I had received the order of the boot from his people.†

HOUSE OF COMMONS

After his rejection at the election.

W.S.C.: A friend of mine, an officer, was in Zagreb when the results of the late general election came in. An old lady said to him, 'Poor Mr Churchill! I suppose now he will be shot.' My friend was able

---

* His son was then planning a career in the House, and the possibility of succeeding to the Lords might have hobbled his political future.
† In *My Twenty Years in Buckingham Palace*, F. J. Corbitt records that W.S.C. reversed his decision, remembering his promise to Princess Elizabeth. 'If you are Prime Minister when I become Queen I would like you to be my first Garter Knight.' As Queen Elizabeth II she made him a Knight, April 24, 1953, and installed him June 14, 1954.

to reassure her. He said the sentence might be mitigated to one of the various forms of hard labour which are always open to His Majesty's subjects.

HOUSE OF COMMONS

On October 22, as leader of the Conservative Opposition.
W.S.C.: The inherent vice of Capitalism is the unequal sharing of blessings. The inherent virtue of Socialism is the equal sharing of miseries.
also

EAR-WITNESS

On the Labour Government's foreign policy.
W.S.C.: Dreaming all night of giving away bits of the British Empire, and spending all day doing it!
also

HOUSE OF COMMONS

As leader of the Opposition the Labour benches heckled him to 'Speak up, don't be afraid!' He answered them in a low tone which every member heard distinctly.
W.S.C.: I find I speak quite loud enough to silence any of YOU when I like!

SPEECH

On November 28 at a Conservative Party Meeting, he termed Sir Stafford Cripps 'One of the best brains brooding over our affairs,' but . . .
W.S.C.: Sir Stafford Cripps is under the profound delusion that he can build up an immense, profitable export trade while keeping everything at the minimum here at home. Look what he is doing to the motor car industry. It is astonishing so clever a lawyer should not have got his case up better. He is a great advocate of 'Strength through Misery'. He tried this theme on the public when he entered the Government in February, 1942. I did not like it. I preferred 'Strength through Victory', and that is what we got. And that is what we have got to get now . . .'

EAR-WITNESS

When asked how he would face his Maker over the decision to drop the atom bomb.

W.S.C.: I shall defend myself with resolution and with vigour. I shall say to the Almighty, why when nations were warring in this way, did You release this dangerous knowledge to mankind? The fault is Yours—not mine!

EAR-WITNESS

After his installation Geoffrey Francis Fisher, Archbishop of Canterbury, complained of the difficulties of living in Lambeth Palace, with its forty rooms but no furniture.

W.S.C.: Thirty-nine articles* [another term for chamber pots] and not a single bed to put them under.

EAR-WITNESS

While listening to a boring speech in the House of Commons on statistics, he saw an old Member with an antique ear trumpet leaning forward to hear the speech.

W.S.C.: (*in an aside to a colleague*): Who is that idiot denying himself natural advantages?

HOUSE OF COMMONS

One of his Conservative colleagues suggested that he would do better to stand on his dignity and not answer an attack levelled at him from a bitter Labour member.

W.S.C.: (*growling*): I know of no case where a man added to his dignity by standing on it.

EAR-WITNESS

During World War II, 'short-snorter' was a name given a member of an informal club to which a pilot, crew member, or passenger who had made a

---

* Since the reign of Queen Elizabeth I, every beneficed Anglican clergyman must swear to the Thirty-nine Articles, the basic tenets of the Church of England.

trans-oceanic flight was eligible. Each member carried a dollar bill (or pound note), autographed by at least two members, which had to be presented on demand or the forfeit of a dollar bill (or a pound note) to each member present.

W.S.C.: (*of much-travelled Cardinal, His Eminence Francis J Spellman, Archbishop of New York*): A worthy short-snorter.

ENJOYING CHARTWELL
1946-1951

In 1946, W.S.C. reached another milestone in his many lives. Lord Attlee, his Deputy Prime Minister in the wartime Coalition Government, has compared him to a layer cake. 'One layer is certainly seventeenth century. The eighteenth in him is obvious! There was the nineteenth century and a large slice, of course, of the twentieth century; and another curious layer which may possibly have been the twenty-first.' Again as in the thirties, W.S.C., for whom pleasure was as seductive as work, found time to eat and drink well. He farmed under the management of his son-in-law, Christopher Soames,* and raised Belted Galloway cattle, raced horses, painted, wrote books and received world figures. As Leader of the Conservative Opposition he continued harrying the Labour Party and won the Premiership once again in 1951. Chartwell, with its some five hundred acres of farm land and eighty acres of gardens, was bought by a group of W.S.C.'s friends in 1946, so he might live there tax free for his lifetime. It was to become a National Trust monument at his death.

* Assistant Military Attaché, British Embassy, Paris, 1946–1947; Parliamentary Private Secretary to Prime Minister W.S.C., 1952–1955; Parliamentary Undersecretary of State, Air Ministry, 1955–1957; Parliamentary and Financial Secretary of the Admiralty, 1957–1958; Secretary of State for War; Ambassador to France 1968–1972; Vice-President Commission of the European Communities, 1973–1977.

8TH JANUARY 1946	Awarded Order of Merit.
10TH JANUARY 1946	First General Assembly of the United Nations representing fifty-one nations met in London.
5TH MARCH 1946	Delivered historic speech at Fulton, Missouri, in which he coined the term, 'Iron Curtain.'
8TH MAY 1946	Arrived in Amsterdam on a visit to Holland at the invitation of Queen Wilhelmina.
27TH JUNE 1946	Published *Victory*.
19TH SEPTEMBER 1946	Spoke at Zurich for United States of Europe.
26TH SEPTEMBER 1946	Published *Secret Session Speeches*.
3RD OCTOBER 1946	Conservative Party Conference opened at Blackpool
6TH OCTOBER 1946	Announced decision to remain Leader of Conservative Party.
16TH OCTOBER 1946	Nazi leaders condemned to death at Nuremberg executed. Goering committed suicide.
23RD OCTOBER 1946	The General Assembly of the United Nations opened at Flushing Meadows, New York.
11TH NOVEMBER 1946	General Elections in France resulted in the Communists winning as the largest single party, with 159 seats in the National Assembly.
14TH MAY 1947	Advocated European Movement in a speech at the Royal Albert Hall, London.
5TH JUNE 1947	Secretary of State George C. Marshall spoke at Harvard University, urging the countries of Europe to unite in a common effort towards economic recovery.
20TH NOVEMBER 1947	Marriage in Westminster Abbey of Princess Elizabeth and Lieutenant Philip Mountbatten. Exhibited two paintings at the Royal Academy.
13TH JANUARY 1948	Mohondas K. Gandhi began a fast, attempting to bring about Hindu-Moslem unity and harmony in both India and Pakistan.
30TH JANUARY 1948	Mohondas K. Gandhi assassinated in New Delhi on his way to an evening prayer meeting.
APRIL 1948	Elected first Honorary Royal Academician Extraordinary.
7TH MAY 1948	Opened Congress of Europe at The Hague.
21ST JUNE 1948	Published *The Gathering Storm, Volume I of The Second World War*.
22ND JUNE 1948	King George VI relinquished title of 'Emperor of India.'
2ND NOVEMBER 1948	President Harry S Truman elected to his own term as President of the United States.
2ND DECEMBER 1948	Republic of Ireland Bill passed by the Dáil.
DECEMBER 1948	Published *Painting as a Pastime*.
20TH JANUARY 1949	President Truman began second term as President of the United States.

22ᴺᴰ JANUARY 1949	Peking surrendered to the Communists.
28–29ᵀᴴ JANUARY 1949	*De Facto* recognition accorded Israel by United Kingdom, France, Belgium, Netherlands, Luxembourg, Australia and New Zealand.
3ᴿᴰ FEBRUARY 1949	Awarded the Grotius Medal.
31ˢᵀ MARCH 1949	Addressed Massachusetts Institute of Technology.
4ᵀᴴ APRIL 1949	North Atlantic Treaty signed at State Department in Washington by Belgium, Canada, Denmark, France, Iceland, Italy, Luxembourg, Netherlands, Norway, Portugal, United Kingdom and United States.
18ᵀᴴ APRIL 1949	Republic of Ireland Act came into force, severing the remaining link with the United Kingdom, the British Commonwealth and Empire.
7ᵀᴴ JUNE 1949	United Kingdom ratified the North Atlantic Treaty.
27ᵀᴴ JUNE 1949	Published *Their Finest Hour, Volume II of The Second World War*.
10ᵀᴴ AUGUST 1949	Addressed first meeting of Council of Europe at Strasbourg.
25ᵀᴴ AUGUST 1949	Won first race with Colonist II.
1ˢᵀ OCTOBER 1949	Mao Tse-tung* announced the Nationalist Government of China overthrown and proclaimed the People's Republic as the sole Government of China.
26ᵀᴴ JANUARY 1950	Formal proclamation of the Republic of India within the Commonwealth of Nations.
27ᵀᴴ JANUARY 1950	Anglo-American Mutual Defence Assistance Agreement under the North Atlantic Treaty signed in Washington.
14ᵀᴴ FEBRUARY 1950	Thirty-year Treaty of Friendship, Alliance and Mutual Assistance between Russia and China signed by Marshal Stalin and Mao Tse-tung in the Kremlin.
19ᵀᴴ FEBRUARY 1950	Spoke at Edinburgh, suggested Summit meeting with Soviets.
23ᴿᴰ FEBRUARY 1950	Re-elected Conservative member for Woodford.
20ᵀᴴ JULY 1950	Published *The Grand Alliance, Volume III of The Second World War*.
11ᵀᴴ AUGUST 1950	At Council of Europe, Strasbourg, advocated a European Army.
9ᵀᴴ OCTOBER 1950	Visited Denmark and received prize from Sonning Foundation.
26ᵀᴴ OCTOBER 1950	French National Assembly approved its Government's proposals for the creation of a European army, but expressed its intention not to permit the re-creation of a German army or General Staff.

---

* Chinese Communist leader; Chairman, Chinese People's Republic, 1949–1959.

MY DEAR MR CHURCHILL

W.S.C.: The world would be better off it were inhabited only by animals.

and

After placing an unsigned advertisement in an English paper announcing one of his bulls for sale, he drew an inquiry from the Russians.

W.S.C.: (*to Christopher Soames*): Very difficult. Do you think the Russians know the bull belongs to me?

Christopher Soames: Probably not. Their intelligence can't be that good. After all—the advertisement only gave a box number.

W.S.C.: We cannot discriminate against the Russians over a bull. But they'll have to pay a good price to get it. I'm not going to have that poor fellow sent to Russia for nothing*

also

EAR-WITNESS

A visitor interested in animal husbandry who was taken about Chartwell asked if artificial insemination was being used on his herd.

W.S.C.: The beasts will not be deprived — not while I'm alive!

SPEECH

On February 26. At University of Miami, Florida.

W.S.C.: I am surprised that in my later life I should have become so experienced in taking degrees when as a schoolboy I was so bad at passing examinations. In fact, one might almost say that no one ever passed so few examinations and received so many degrees.[†]

and

Later, to the Massachusetts Institute of Technology on March 31, 1949.

W.S.C.: I have no technical and no university education, and have just had to pick up a few things as I went along.

---

* The price tag did indeed force the Russians out of the bidding.
† Honorary degrees from the colleges and universities of Oxford, Rochester (US). Queen's (Belfast), Bristol, Harvard, McGill, Brussels, Louvain, Miami, Westminster (Fulton, Missouri), Columbia, Aberdeen, Leyden, New York, Oslo, London, St Andrew's, Liverpool, Cambridge and Copenhagen.

EAR-WITNESS

On March 4, travelling by train with President Truman to the Fulton, Missouri speech, he noted the Presidential seal on the wall of the Presidential Club Car. Mr Truman explained that, before he took office, the eagle on the seal carried a quiver of warlike arrows in one talon and the ivy or olive branch of peace in the other, with its head turned toward the warlike quiver of arrows. As President he had requested that the Seal be changed so the eagle faced the olive branch of peace. Mr Clark Clifford had been charged with carrying it out, which meant changing all the existing seals of the office of President.

W.S.C.: (*To President Truman*): Why not put the eagle's neck on a swivel so that it could turn to the right or left as the occasion presented itself?

EAR-WITNESS

On March 6 just after the Fulton speech Henry R. Luce, President of Tim *Inc., gave a dinner at the Union Club in New York City honouring W.S.C. A senior editor of* Time *inquired of the honoured guest why at Yalta (February 4–11, 1945) he had supported bringing Russia into the war with Japan so late, with American sea and land power so ascendant in the Pacific. W.S.C. answered that he and President Roosevelt wished to end the war with a minimum of losses, citing the heavy casualties at Iwo Jima (February 19 to March 16, 1945) and Okinawa (April 1 to June 22, 1945).*

Senior Editor: (*to W.S.C.*): But sir, the Yalta meetings preceded both those battles.

W.S.C.: You are quite right. I'm glad I didn't make that mistake on the floor of the House of Commons!

EAR-WITNESS

His good friend, Lord Birkenhead, once said of him, 'Winston is a man of simple tastes, he is always prepared to put up with the best of everything.' And Mrs Churchill knew, 'if you want to keep Winston happy the first thing is to feed him well. He must have good dinner. It is essential to his happiness.' This embraced everything from his breakfast of eggs and bacon, cold cuts or fresh salmon followed by toast and black cherry jam, coffee or a glass of white wine, ending with a cup of cold consommé before retiring. To the last he loved his roast beef and Yorkshire pudding. On a certain occasion one of his clubs served his favourite meal beginning with petite marmite soup followed by filet of sole wrapped in smoked Scotch salmon smothered in tiny shrimp. Next a roast deer stuffed with pâté and truffles. The dessert was a pudding.

W.S.C.: My idea of a good dinner is, first to have good food, then discuss good food, and after this good food has been elaborately discussed, to discuss a good topic—with myself as chief conversationalist.

also

MY DEAR MR CHURCHILL

W.S.C.: My wife and I tried two or three times in the last forty years to have breakfast together, but it didn't work. Breakfast should be had in bed, alone.

and

W.S.C.: Stilton and port are like man and wife. They should never be separated. Whom God has joined together, let no man put asunder. No—nor woman either.

also

EAR-WITNESS

W.S.C.: Whatever the good earth has to offer, I am willing to take.

and

It is said that an elderly member of a club to which he belonged was judged too senile, as he continually dropped food over his tie, vest and jacket. W.S.C. was asked to join in voting him out of the club.

W.S.C.: Certainly not! His food looks so well on him.

EAR-WITNESS

*Much has been made of his zest for drink. He disliked cocktails ('I liked wine, both red and white, and especially champagne,' he wrote in one of his early works, and 'a small glass of brandy' and 'whisky in a diluted form'), but he liked to be thought a two-bottle man in the tradition of Pitt.**

---

* William Pitt, 1759–1806, 'the Younger Pitt'; Prime Minister at twenty-four; known as one of England's greatest Prime Ministers—and as a 'two-bottle man' for the quantities of port he consumed, and which killed him.

W.S.C.: (*travelling by train with 'the Prof.' [Lord Cherwell], his 'human slide rule'*): Prof! How many pints of champagne in cubic feet have I consumed in 24 years at the rate of a pint a day and how many railway carriages would it fill?

The 'Prof.' (*after rapid calculation*): Only a part of one.

W.S.C.: So little time and so much to achieve.

also

A ROVING COMMISSION

W.S.C.: I had been brought up and trained to have the utmost contempt for people who get drunk—except on very exceptional occasions and a few anniversaries.

also

THE STORY OF THE MALAKAND FIELD FORCE

On champagne.

W.S.C.: A single glass of champagne imparts a feeling of exhilaration. The nerves are braced; the imagination is agreeably stirred; the wits become more nimble. A bottle produces a contrary effect. Excess causes a comatose insensibility. So it is with war; and the quality of both is best discovered by sipping.

also

EAR-WITNESS

W.S.C.: I've often been the better for it—seldom the worse.

MY 21 YEARS IN THE WHITE HOUSE

At the White House during an Anglo-American meeting, W.S.C. summoned a butler, Alonzo Fields, to the library.

W.S.C.: I need a little more to drink. You see I have a war to fight and I need fortitude for the battle. And there is one favour I hope you will do for me.

A. Fields: Yes, Sir?

W.S.C.: I hope you will come to my defence if someday, someone should claim that I am a teetotaller.

also

THE WAR AND COLONEL WARDEN

On a trip to America, his valet, Sawyers, rushed to the bridge of the HMS Duke of York *exhorting Captain Cecil Harcourt, 'The Prime Minister doesn't like the ship's water and I've run out of white wine!'*

W.S.C.: You can't make a good speech on iced water.

also

EAR-WITNESS

W.S.C.: I have a profound distaste for skim milk and no deep rooted prejudice about wine. So I have resolved the conflict in favour of the latter.

also

MY YESTERDAY, YOUR TOMORROW

W.S.C.: (*to Scotsman, Lord Boothby*): I find alcohol a great support in life. Sir Alexander Walker, who keeps me supplied with your national brew, told me that a friend of his, who died the other day, drank a bottle of whisky a day for the last 10 years of his life. He was 85!

also

I WAS WINSTON CHURCHILL'S PRIVATE SECRETARY

On a wartime visit to Washington, DC, though he hated dial telephones, he lifted a receiver and gave his order, thinking he was talking on the British Embassy house phone.

W.S.C.: (*to his secretary Miss Moir*): I've just asked the Washington operator for a glass of sherry . . . I'm afraid I gave her rather a shock.

also

CLARK CLIFFORD

On the train to Fulton, Missouri, on March 4, President Truman, Press Secretary Charlie Ross, Clark Clifford and W.S.C. were playing poker at 2.30 a.m.

W.S.C.: If I were to be born again, there is one country of which I would want to be a citizen. There is one country where a man knows he has an unbounded future.

Q.: Which?

W.S.C.: The USA, even though I deplore some of your customs.

Q.: Which, for instance?

W.S.C.: You stop drinking with your meals.

also

THE LIFE OF F. E. SMITH

Earl Haig's diaries reveal that he and his wife counted the number of glasses of brandy their guests drank. The present Lord Birkenhead, lunching with W.S.C., was pressed by his host to take a second brandy.

W.S.C.: Have another glass, my dear boy. I shan't write it down in my diary.

also

EAR-WITNESS

After a public banquet towards the end of his term as wartime Premier, he found himself seated next to the Iraqi Ambassador, Daud Pasha al-Haidari. Calling for a whisky and soda he suggested the Ambassador might join him in a nightcap but was turned down by the non-drinking Moslem envoy whose religion prohibits drinking alcohol.

W.S.C.: What? You don't drink? Good God . . . I mean Jesus Christ . . . I mean Allah!

and

Six years later, dining on the presidential yacht 'Williamsburg' with President Truman during the 1952 Potomac Conference in Washington, DC, he sat between Secretary Dean Acheson and Mutual Security Administrator W. Averell Harriman. All through the meal iced water was drunk, and the wine glasses remained empty. Not until the end of the meal were the goblets filled for toasts to King George VI.

W.S.C.: (*to his Ambassador, Sir Oliver Franks*): I could have respected the ancient tradition of a dry Navy, but this tantalizing business of the empty wine glass—and then this matter of too little and too late—I hope you don't follow such barbarous practices in *your* house [the British Embassy], Franks!

and

On his trip to Washington, DC, January 1952, he was offered a second drink at a dinner at the British Embassy.

W.S.C.: I accept it for many reasons. One, because I am thirsty, and another, because I have gotten more out of alcohol in the course of my life—than alcohol has gotten out of me!

and

Later in January 1952, after seeing Princess Elizabeth and the Duke of Edinburgh off to East Africa, King George VI suggested to W.S.C. that, as it was chilly, a little whisky might be permissible.

W.S.C.: When I was younger I made it a rule never to take strong drink before lunch. It is now my rule never to do so before breakfast.

and

After asking his personal physician, Lord Moran, whether a liqueur was permitted him after lunch.

Lord Moran: Do you want it or need it?

W.S.C.: I neither want it nor need it but I should think it pretty hazardous to interfere with the ineradicable habit of a lifetime.

SPEECH

On May 7, receiving the Freedom of Westminster.

W.S.C.: The human story does not always unfold like an arithmetical calculation on the principle that two and two make four. Sometimes in life they make five or minus three; and sometimes the blackboard topples down in the middle of the sum and leaves the class in disorder and the pedagogue with a black eye. The element of the unexpected and the unforeseeable is what gives some of its relish to life and saves us from falling into the mechanical thraldom of the logicians.

SIR JOHN FOSTER, MP

Bored during a long speech in the House, he dropped his head on his chest and closed his eyes. The Labour MP who was speaking protested that his Right Honourable Opponent was asleep.

W.S.C.: I wish to God I were!

also

EAR-WITNESS
A Labour MP: Must you fall asleep when I am speaking?
W.S.C.: No, it is purely voluntary.

EAR-WITNESS
Of the Labour Government.
W.S.C.: What is the use of being a famous race and nation if at the end of the week you cannot pay your housekeeping bills?

EAR-WITNESS
W.S.C.'s room in the House of Commons was near a Member whose loud shouting so disturbed him he sent a secretary to discover the source.
Secretary (*to W.S.C.*): It's Mr Ernest Brown [Member for Leith], sir, speaking to his constituency.
W.S.C.: Go and ask him why he doesn't use the telephone.

HOUSE OF COMMONS
On June 5. Debate on Foreign Affairs under the Labour administration.
W.S.C.: None of us likes the Franco regime, and, personally, I like it as little as I like the present British administration, but between not liking a government and trying to stir up a civil war in a country, there is a very wide interval. It is said that every nation gets the government it deserves. Obviously, this does not apply in the case of Britain.
and
W.S.C.: There are no people in the world who are so slow to develop hostile feelings against a foreign country as the Americans and there are no people who, once estranged, are more difficult to win back. The American eagle sits on his perch, a large strong bird with formidable beak and claws. There he sits motionless and Mr Gromyko[*] [Soviet delegate to the United Nations] is sent day after day to prod him with a sharp-pointed stick—now his neck, now under his wings, now his tail feathers. All the time the eagle keeps

[*] Andrei A. Gromyko, Minister of Foreign Affairs in USSR since 1957.

quite still. But it would be a great mistake to suppose that nothing is going on inside the breast of that eagle.

HOUSE OF COMMONS
On August 1.
W.S.C.: The Right Hon. and Learned Gentleman, the President of the Board of Trade [Sir Stafford Cripps] spoke of the past twenty-five years as being the most unkind or unhappy Palestine has known. I imagine that it would hardly be possible to state the opposite of the truth more compendiously.

SPEECH
Though W.S.C. was made Lord Warden of the Cinque Ports by George VI on December 30, 1941, he was not officially installed until August 1946. In his acceptance speech he referred to his war years when he held office as Prime Minister, Minister of Defence and Lord Warden.
W.S.C.: No dispute ever arose between the Lord Warden and the Minister of Defence . . . if any unfortunate division had occurred we should have both gone to the Prime Minister who, I may tell you in confidence, was very much on our side.

SPEECH
At Blackpool on October 5.
W.S.C.: The amount of needless suffering, vexation and frustration his [Aneurin Bevan's] prejudices have caused cannot be measured. There is, however, a poetic justice in the fact that the most mischievous month in wartime has also become in peace the most remarkable administrative failure.
and
W.S.C.: And now the British housewife, as she stands in the queues to buy her bread ration, will fumble in her pocket in vain for a silver sixpence. Under the Socialist Government nickel will have to be good enough for her. In future we shall still be able to say: 'Every cloud has a nickel lining.'

HOUSE OF COMMONS

On October 23, discussing foreign affairs.

W.S.C.: It is very easy for foreign observers in a position of perfect detachment to abuse a Government which is struggling against a Communist conspiracy, fomented and supported by outside intrigues. An armed Communist advances upon you, you react against him; therefore you are a reactionary.

Of the Socialists—'I have always though they had got hold of an error—a fallacy—that the State could produce better than the individual—but I say during the War when we worked together—they did not flinch—they did not whimper—they did not retreat.' W.S.C. once referred to Mr Attlee's 'concise, massive statesmanlike contribution to world affairs.'

but

HOUSE OF COMMONS

As it was hard for him to realize he was no longer Prime Minister, a Labour Member was quick to remind him that he must face the fact that his place had been taken by Clement Attlee.

W.S.C.: (*in an aside and glaring at Prime Minister Attlee*): Indeed, I am facing the fact—such as it is!

also

SIR JOHN FOSTER, MP

Some time after his defeat by Labour, he was reminded that Prime Minister Attlee was doing rather well in high office.

W.S.C.: Yes! Like the grub that feeds on the Royal Jelly and thinks it's a Queen Bee!

also

EAR-WITNESS

When it was announced that Mr Attlee had cancelled a projected trip to Australia.

W.S.C.: He is afraid that when the mouse is away, the cats will play.

HOUSE OF COMMONS

On December 6, on Government Policy—a Motion of Censure.

W.S.C.: The course of my remarks now reaches the President of the Board of Trade [Sir Stafford Cripps].Everyone knows the distinguished talents which the Right Hon. Gentleman brings unstintedly to the services of his fellow countrymen. No one has made more sustained exertions to contribute to the common pot and few take less out of it than he does. I have got my vegetarian too, my honoured friend Lord Cherwell. These ethereal beings certainly do produce a very high level and a very great volume of intellectual output, with the minimum of working costs in fuel . . . Human beings, happily for them, do not have to direct all their bodily functions themselves. They do not have to plan in advance how many heartbeats they are to have in the next 24 hours or what relation their temperature or blood pressure should bear to those heartbeats. They do not have to decide, as a part of the daily routine, what secretions are to be made by the liver or kidneys. No official quota is set for lymph or bile. Otherwise I fear the President of the Board of Trade would find he had overdrawn his account very much. Providence has relegated these problems to the subconscious mind and left the commanding sphere to human reason

also

EAR-WITNESS

W.S.C.: Ah, Stafford—his career takes him to the left and his conscience to the right and they are like two squirrels chasing each other's tails in a cage.

and

An earlier dig at vegetarian Sir Stafford while addressing the troops in the desert during the war.

W.S.C.: Here we are marooned in all these miles of sand—not a blade of grass or a drop of water or a flower—how Cripps would have loved it.

also

After Sir Stafford gave up smoking cigars an editor ran a picture of him smoking one.

W.S.C.: (*to the Editor*): Cripps no longer smokes a cigar.

Editor: Is that so important?

W.S.C.: Very important, that cigar was his last contact with humanity.

and

W.S.C.: (*of Sir Stafford Cripps*): Wearing his look of injured guilt.

HOUSE OF COMMONS

On December 6, on Government Policy.

W.S.C.: The Right Hon. Gentleman [Aneurin Bevan] threatened us the other night with the disclosure of certain scandals if we asked questions about figures—'putrefying corpses,' he called them for which his predecessors . . . were responsible . . . We cannot have a Minister of Health living among a lot of putrefying corpses.

and

W.S.C.: Last night the Hon. Member for Bilston [Mr Will Nally] drew an affecting picture of my personal position; the noble stag was dying, the curs were at his throat; his own friends behind him were hogs . . . Let me reassure him . . . I only remain in politics because I think it is my duty to try to prevent the great position we won in the war being cast away by folly . . . The hoots and howls of the curs—the hounds as the Hon. Member for Bilston put it— do not worry me . . . I must say that the maiden glance of the Hon. Member for Bilston at the House of Commons should impress us somewhat with the unfavourable impression we produce upon him. Here are hogs, there are hounds. I trust that a longer experience of this Chamber will make him realize that both these branches of the animal kingdom have their virtues.

HOUSE OF COMMONS

During a debate on December 13.

W.S.C.: . . . We recognize that it is the duty of the Government to decide. In international matters it is always our desire to associate ourselves, so far as possible, with them. I very much regret that we cannot do so on this occasion. The task falls to me, as Leader of the Conservative Party, to give advice to my Hon. Friends as to what our conduct should be in this present bleak and difficult situation. It would be a great pity and would weaken us for our future tasks, which are heavy, if we all voted in different Lobbies on a question of this kind.

Sir Waldron Smithers: Why?

W.S.C.: My Hon. Friend asks why. I would have thought that even the simplest process of ratiocination would enable him to supply the answer to that. We therefore thought it better and wiser to abstain as a body.

Hon. Members: Why?

W.S.C.: For this reason. We thought it better and wiser to abstain as a body, and that is the course we intend to pursue.

Mr Bevin:* How can you pursue it when you are sitting still?

W.S.C.: We are discussing the movements of the mind, and not the much more bulky shiftings of the human body (Laughter).

HOUSE OF COMMONS

On December 12, referring to Sir Stafford Cripps in a debate on India.

W.S.C.: At any rate, the Right Hon. and Learned Gentleman can defend himself. No one more than he has taken responsibility in this matter, because neither of his colleagues could compare with him in that acuteness and energy of mind with which he devotes himself to so many topics injurious to the strength and welfare of the State.

and

On the problems of Hindu-Moslem co-operation in India.

W.S.C.: If the bride or bridegroom fails to turn up at church, the result is not what, to use an overworked word, is called a 'unilateral' wedding. The absolute essence of the matter is that both parties should be there.

EAR-WITNESS

When his opinion was sought after the publication of Elliott Roosevelt's book, As He Saw It.

W.S.C.: A butler's eye view.

---

* Then Secretary of State for Foreign Affairs.

EAR-WITNESS

During one of his illnesses, as his trained nurse left his room bearing the bed pan she heard him chuckling.

Nurse: I don't see anything funny about taking out a bed pan.

W.S.C.: It's the first time that a motion [movement] of mine has been carried out since the Labour Government came in.

1947   EAR-WITNESS

In an interview with Dorothy Thompson.

Dorothy Thompson: History will place you among the world's great men.

W.S.C.: That depends on who writes the history.

A ROVING COMMISSION

Musing as an author.

W.S.C.: It was great fun writing a book. It built an impalpable crystal sphere around one of interests and ideas. In a sense one felt like a goldfish in a bowl; but in this case the goldfish made his own bowl . . .

and

On his two-volume masterpiece, The River War, *on the loss and reconquest of the Sudan.*

W.S.C.: I affected a combination of the style of [Thomas] Macaulay and [Edward] Gibbon, the staccato antitheses of the former and the rolling sentences and genitival endings of the latter; and I stuck in a bit of my own from time to time.

also

HOUSE OF COMMONS

During a debate in the House, issues involving mistakes made at Yalta and Potsdam were revived.

W.S.C.: Let us stop our melancholy recriminations and apply ourselves to the business at hand. Let us leave hindsight to history—that history which I am now, myself, in the process of writing!

also

EAR-WITNESS

He worked with a team of researchers, historians and secretaries on his six-volume World War II memoirs, which later won him a Nobel Prize for Literature and were translated into eighteen languages.

W.S.C.: (*to Lord Beaverbrook**): What are you doing?

Lord Beaverbrook: Writing.

W.S.C.: What are you writing about?

Lord Beaverbrook: Me.

W.S.C.: A good subject. I've been writing about me for fifty years and with excellent results.

and

EAR-WITNESS

Earlier, during an Anglo-American wartime meeting in Washington, John McCrae, of the American publishing house of E. P. Dutton & Co, Inc, made an appointment with W.S.C. at the White House to negotiate a possible contract for his World War II memoirs. Ushered into the bedroom he found him sitting in bed clad in a nightshirt. After stating the amount of advance Dutton's was prepared to make, Mr McCrae was staggered to hear W.S.C. ask for ten times the amount, then dive under the bedclothes to recover some lost object, with only a large, pink expanse of bottom showing.

John McCrae: Well, Mr Churchill, I thought I had lost you for a moment!

W.S.C.: You haven't lost *me*, you've lost the book!

and

On November 2, 1949.

W.S.C.: Writing a book was an adventure. To begin with, it was a toy, an amusement; then it became a mistress, and then a master, and then a tyrant. The last phase is that just as you are about to be reconciled to your servitude, you kill the monster, and fling him to the public.

---

* William Maxwell Aitken, First Baron Beaverbrook, Baronet, PC, 1879–1964; Canadian–British business tycoon, politician and writer, Churchill's Minister for Aircraft Production (1940-41), Minister of Supply (1941-42), Minister of War Production (1942) and Lord Privy Seal (1943-45).

MR. CHURCHILL AND FRIEND.

WINSTON. "WE HAVE BOTH MADE HISTORY AND WE HAVE BOTH WRITTEN IT. LET US EXCHANGE HEADGEAR."

MY DEAR MR CHURCHILL

W.S.C.: I write a book the way they built the Canadian Pacific Railway. First I lay the track from coast to coast, and after that I put in all the stations.

SPEECH

His response on receiving the Chesney Gold Medal at the Royal Service Institute.

W.S.C.: Certainly I have been fully qualified as far as writing of books about wars is concerned; in fact already in 1900 I could boast to have written as many books as Moses, and I have not stopped writing them since, except when momentarily interrupted by war, in all intervening periods.

also

EAR-WITNESS

The magazine Life *paid him $2 million for the serial rights for his memoirs of World War II.*

W.S.C.: I feel that I am not writing a book but developing a property

HOUSE OF COMMONS

On March 12, on the alleged determination of the Labour Government to control people's lives through bureaucrats, just as the prison authorities control the inmates of Wormwood Scrubs through jailers.

W.S.C.: The Socialist ideal is to reduce us to one vast Wormwood Scrubbery.

SPEECH

At the Albert Hall on April 18.

W.S.C.: Now I travel about a certain amount myself, and I am received with much kindness by all classes, both in Europe and America. But when I am abroad I always make it a rule never to criticize or attack the Government of my own country. I make up for lost time when I come home.

HOUSE OF COMMONS

May 7, on the screening of Armed Forces report by the Chiefs of Staff to the Government.

W.S.C.: That is a curious phrase [screened] which has crept in. 'Sifted' would have been a more natural word, and would avoid any ambiguity with the word 'concealed'. 'Screened' is a modern vulgarism.

and

W.S.C.: I am glad that the Right Hon. Gentleman [Mr A. V. Alexander, Minister of Defence] did not pretend that the Chief of Staff were in agreement with what had been done. He used the word 'consulted'. Well, one can always consult a man and ask him 'Would you like your head cut off tomorrow?' and after he has said, 'I would rather not', cut it off. Consultation is a vague and elastic term.

EAR-WITNESS

On August 9, on the Labour Government.

W.S.C.: The Island is beset by a tribe of neurotic philosophers who, on awakening, begin each day by thinking what there is of Britain that they can give away, and end each day by regretting what they have done.

SPEECH

On September 10, to the International Congress of Physicians at the Guildhall.

W.S.C.: Fanned by the fierce winds of war, medical science and surgical art have advanced unceasingly, hand in hand. There has certainly been no lack of subjects for treatment. The medical profession at least cannot complain of unemployment through lack of raw material.

and

W.S.C.: I have been inclined to feel from time to time that there ought to be a hagiology of medical science and that we ought to have saints' days to commemorate the great discoveries which have been made for all mankind, and perhaps for all time—or for whatever time may be left to us. Nature, like many of our modern statesmen, is prodigal of pain. I should like to find a day when we can take a holiday, a day of jubilation when we can fête good Saint Anaesthesia and chaste and pure Saint Antiseptic. I would not venture in a company so distinguished as this to pretend to any qualifications to judge who should figure in this list, but if I had a vote I should be bound to celebrate, among others, Saint Penicillin, whom I see represented here, and Saints M & B, both invaluable figures, to whom I was introduced during the war in good time by Lord Moran, and but for whose benediction I might be regarding your present troubles, if not otherwise preoccupied, from a more serene sphere.

BROADCAST

The Al Smith* Memorial in a broadcast to New York, October 14.

W.S.C.: I had followed Al Smith's contest for the Presidency with keen interest and sympathy. I was in the fullest agreement with his attitude on prohibition. I even suggested to him a slogan—'All for Al and Al for All.'

HOUSE OF COMMONS

On October 28.

W.S.C.: I repeat . . . that our policy is an adequate basic standard—within just laws, let the best man win. [Laughter] The crackling of thorns under a pot does not deter me.[†]

and

An exchange with Hugh Gaitskell over the policy of fewer baths to conserve fuel which particularly annoyed W.S.C., who revelled in two hot baths daily.

W.S.C.: I will conclude my strictures in the social and domestic field . . . by reading the latest economies proposed by the Minister of Fuel and Power, who represents, I believe, Socialist intellectualism and the old school tie.[‡] He advocated a policy of fewer baths. I

---

[*] Alfred E. Smith, 1873–1944; American political leader; Governor of the State of New York, four terms; Democratic presidential candidate, 1928.

[†] Ecclesiastes VII:6. 'For as the crackling of thorns under a pot, so is the laughter of a fool.'

[‡] Mr Hugh Gaitskell, an 'old school tie' from Winchester, famous for its distinguished scholarship. Entered Parliament, 1945; Chancellor of Exchequer, 1950–1951; Leader of Labour Opposition, 1955–1963.

really must read the words which he is reported to have used, as I think they constitute almost a record. 'Personally, I have never had a great many baths myself, and I can assure those who are in the habit of having a great many, that it does not make a great difference to their health if they have less. As to their appearance, most of that is underneath, and nobody sees it.' When Ministers of the Crown speak like this on behalf of His Majesty's Government, the Prime Minister and his friends have no need to wonder why they are getting increasingly into bad odour. I had even asked myself, when meditating upon these points, whether you, Mr Speaker, would admit the word 'lousy' as a Parliamentary expression in referring to the Administration, provided, of course, it was not intended in a contemptuous sense, but purely as one of actual narration!

Sitting opposite Sir Stafford Cripps, a strict vegetarian and teetotaller, at a dinner on November 13, 1947, to his hostess:

W.S.C.: I am glad I am not a herbivore. I eat what I like, I drink what I like, I do what I like . . . and *he's* the one to have a red nose.

HOUSE OF COMMONS

Speech on November 11, on Parliament Bill defining the true purposes of democracy.

W.S.C.: The Right Hon. Gentleman [Mr Herbert Morrison] has an obvious unconcealable, well known relish for petty dictatorship. He has many good qualities, but he should always be on guard against his propensity and love to cat-and-mouse the people from morning until night.

and

W.S.C.: Many forms of Government have been tried, and will be tried in this world of sin and woe . . . No one pretends that democracy is perfect or all-wise. Indeed, it has been said that democracy is the worst form of Government except all those other forms that have been tried from time to time.

and

W.S.C.: There are, I must admit, moments when I am sorry for the Lord President of the Council [Mr Herbert Morrison] a man outpassed at the moment by his competitors, outdated even by his prejudices, scrambling along trying to regain popularity on an obsolete issue and on an ever-ebbing tide. I hope he will not mind my quoting or adapting some lines, although they are of a martial character, about his position:

'Crippses to right of him. Daltons* to the left of him,
Bevans behind him, volleyed and thundered! . . .
What tho' the soldiers knew
Some one had blunder'd . . .
Then, they came back, but not the four hundred.'[†]

and

W.S.C.: If there was a General Election tomorrow the Socialist majority would vanish. If they wait another year, they themselves will vanish for a considerable period, 'unwept, unhonoured and unsung—and unhung.'[‡]

and

W.S.C.: No government has ever combined so passionate a lust for power with such incurable impotence in its exercise.

and

An early stricture on Socialists, at the start of his career:
W.S.C.: They are not fit to manage a whelk stall.

and later, of Socialism:
W.S.C.: A Government of the duds, by the dud, and for the duds.

1948   BBC BROADCAST
On Politics, February 14.
W.S.C.: Dr Dalton, the practitioner who never cured anyone, in his 'rake's progress' at the Exchequer.

and

Attacking Socialist mismanagement.
W.S.C.: They keep the British bulldog running round after his own tail till he is dizzy and then wonder that he cannot keep the wolf from the door.

---

* Hugh Dalton, Chancellor of the Exchequer, 1945–1947; Chancellor of the Duchy of Lancaster, 1948–1950.
† Parodying Alfred, Lord Tennyson's 'Charge of the Light Brigade'. Almost 400 Labour MPs had been elected in the 1945 landslide.
‡ Based on lines from Sir Walter Scott's 'Lay of the Last Minstrel'.

HOUSE OF COMMONS

On February 16.

W.S.C.: In regard to the representation of the House of Commons there are two principles which have come into general acceptance. The first is: 'One man, one vote'—there was an old joke about 'man embracing woman except where the contrary appears in the text' . . . and the second is 'one vote, one value.' The first has been almost entirely achieved . . . with regard to 'one vote, one value,' nothing like so much progress has been made.

SPEECH

On April 21, on the American loan, at the Royal Albert Hall.

W.S.C.: Nor should it be supposed as you would imagine, to read some of the left wing newspapers, that all Americans are multi-millionaires of Wall Street. If they were all multimillionaires that would be no reason for condemning a system which has produced such material results.

and

W.S.C.: However we may regard Sir Stafford Cripps's record there is no doubt he has shouldered the main weight of the Government's task. He has a brain which, at any rate, is something to begin with. He has also a conscience which, like the curate's egg,* is good in parts.

EAR-WITNESS

On May 1, at a Prime Minister's Commonwealth Conference, W.S.C. spotted Mr Havenga,† Finance Minister of the Union of South Africa, who had fought and been wounded many times in the Boer War.

W.S.C.: There he is—there he is, you see, full of British bullets and no animosity.

---

* Curate's egg: derived from a celebrated 1895 *Punch* cartoon of the new curate's first visit to the Bishop's Palace when he was served a bad egg. In response to his Right Reverend host's concern, the young curate replied, 'Oh no, my Lord, I assure you! Parts of it are excellent.'
† Nicolaas Christiaan Havenga, 1882–1957; at age 17 fought in Boer War against the British; later MP, Union of South Africa; then its Minister of Finance, 1924–1929, 1948–1953.

EAR-WITNESS

In the Smoking Room of the House of Commons, Wilfred Paling,
Postmaster General (1947–1950) in the Labour Government, was said to
have accused W.S.C. of being an arrogant, dirty dog.

W.S.C.: Well, look at what dirty dogs do to palings [fences].

SPEECH

At a Conservative Fête on June 26.

W.S.C.: Mr Herbert Morrison, in a momentary lapse into candour, and also, I may say, into accuracy, told us at Liverpool . . . that without American aid we should be facing one or two million unemployed . . . We may indeed ask ourselves how it is that capitalism and free enterprise if . . . out of date, enable the United States not only to support its vast and varied life and needs, but also to supply enormous sums to . . . other countries in distress.

SPEECH

Attack on Aneurin Bevan, Minister of Health, at Woodford Green, July 10,

W.S.C.: Here in inaugurating a National Health Service was a task which to most natures would have brought the balm of healing to the human heart. Instead he has chosen . . . to speak of at least half of his fellow countrymen as, 'lower than vermin', . . . We speak of the Minister of Health, but ought we not rather say Minister of Disease, for is not morbid hatred a form of mental disease, moral disease, and indeed a highly infectious form? Indeed, I can think of no better step to signalize the inauguration of the National Health Service than that a person who so obviously needs psychiatrical attention should be among the first of its patients . . . The odium of the words used by Mr Bevan will lie upon the Socialist Government as a whole. We . . . will not easily forget that we have been described as 'lower than vermin' and in common with the 10 million who voted Tory at the last election, we will take whatever lawful and constitutional steps are possible to free ourselves from further ill-usage by highly-paid Ministers of the Crown.

and

W.S.C.: I have no doubt that the highest exponents in the medical profession would concur that a period of prolonged seclusion and relief from any responsible duties would be an equal benefit to Mr Bevan and to the National Health Service.

HOUSE OF COMMONS
On the Criminal Justice Bill, comparing the horrors of life imprisonment with the equal horror of the death sentence.
W.S.C.: Hanging under English law, if properly conducted, is, I believe, an absolutely painless death.
Mr A. E. Stubbs: Try it.
W.S.C.: Well, it may come to that.

RANDOLPH S. CHURCHILL
In the still austere and food-rationed British winter of 1948, his son Randolph had been on a long lecture tour in America.
W.S.C.: (*in a cable to Randolph*): Come home, dear Randolph. We all await you—all except the fatted calf.

CHURCHILL BY HIS CONTEMPORARIES
Labour's Mr Richard Stokes kept up a running attack on W.S.C.'s strategy in World War II, especially concerning tanks. Late one evening as he left the Smoking Room of the House he bade goodnight to a group of Members, among them Stokes.
W.S.C.: (*to Richard Stokes*): Of course I've forgiven you. Indeed I agree with you very much that you are saying about the Germans. Very good. Such hatred as I have left in me—and it isn't much—I would rather reserve for the future than the past. H'mm—a judicious and thrifty disposal of bile.

HOUSE OF COMMONS
On October 28.
W.S.C.: I am sorry if personal jealousies, or other motives below the level of events, have led the Socialist Party at first to embark upon the unnatural plan of narrowing United Europe down to United Socialist Europe. I warned them at the very beginning that that was not the hopeful line of advance. I hope that their recent

publication, entitled, I think, 'Facing the Fact', or 'Face the Facts'.
[Honourable Members, interrupting: 'Feet on the Ground'—]
W.S.C.: 'Feet on the Ground'. If Honourable Gentlemen opposite were to persist very long in facing the facts they would find their feet on the ground. And they might very soon find the rest of their bodies [there] as well.

and

On November 16.

W.S.C.: Of the difference between Socialism and Communism if I may make another quotation from the past, I said a good many years ago: 'A strong dose either of Socialism or Communism will kill Britannia stone dead, and at the inquest the only question for the jury will be: Did she fall or was she pushed?'

and

On the Socialist Government's Bill to nationalize steel.

W.S.C.: . . . this is not a Bill, it is a plot; not a plan to increase production, but rather, in effect, at any rate, an operation in restraint of trade. It is not a plan to help our patient struggling people, but a burglar's jemmy to crack the capitalist crib.

SPEECH

At the University of London on November 18.

W.S.C.: We want some scientists, but we must keep them in their proper place. Our generation has seen great changes. We have parted company with the horse; we have an internal combustion engine instead and I wonder whether we have gained by the change.

HOUSE OF COMMONS

On December 1, on National Service Bill.

W.S.C.: I believe that the army would be better entrusted to men who are not engaged in the bitter strife of politics, nor should the War Office be regarded as a receptacle for ministerial failures.

EAR-WITNESS

The sensational Lynskey Tribunal in Britain involving a Junior Minister, John W. Belcher, Parliamentary Secretary to the Board of Trade in Prime

*Minister Attlee's Labour Government, involved $40,000 in bribes. Belcher
was later cleared, but was ruined.*
W.S.C.: (*paraphrasing*): It would not have happened had Mr Attlee
been alive.

1949   EAR-WITNESS

*A grey three-year-old French-bred horse, Colonist II, which W.S.C. bought
for £1,000 carried the chocolate and pink racing colours of his father, Lord
Randolph Churchill. It won at Ascot and took thirteen out of the twenty-four
races it entered, earning more than £13,000. In 1951, his trainer, Walter
Nightingall, suggested he put Colonist II to stud to make more money.*
W.S.C.: To stud? And have it said that the Prime Minister of Great
Britain is living on the immoral earnings of a horse?
and
*W.S.C. used to have serious talks with Colonist II before each race. Once it
came in fourth.*
W.S.C.: I told him this is a very big race and if he won it he would
never have to run again but spend the rest of his life in agreeable
female company. Colonist II did not keep his mind on the race!*
and
In the Smoking Room in the House of Commons.
A Labour MP: Why don't you sell your horse?
W.S.C.: Well, that is at least a piece of property which has increased
its value since it came under my control [laughter], a happy
contrast to the 'resources' frittered away by His Majesty's Ministers.
As a matter of fact, I was strongly tempted to sell the horse; but I
am doing my best to fight against the profit motive.

EAR-WITNESS

W.S.C.: Recovery in the former occupied countries of Belgium,
Holland, Denmark and Norway, has outstripped never occupied
Britain.

---

* One of W.S.C.'s racing friends described these pre-race sessions: 'It might be an exaggeration to describe the horse's face as apprehensive, but I noticed the same look from sluggish ministers after a
wartime Cabinet meeting. In any case, the horse gets into motion pretty fast and keeps glancing back
over his shoulder. Winston's oratory has been producing that same effect throughout the animal kingdom
for more than fifty years.'

SPEECH

At Massachusetts Institute of Technology, Boston, on March 31.

W.S.C.: In the nineteenth century Jules Verne wrote *Round the World in Eighty Days*. It seemed a prodigy. Now you can get around it in four; but you do not see much of it on the way. The whole prospect and outlook of mankind grew immeasurably larger, and the multiplication of ideas also proceeded at an incredible rate. This vast expansion was unhappily not accompanied by any noticeable advance in the stature of man, either in his mental faculties, or his moral character. His brain got no better, but it buzzed the more.

EAR-WITNESS

When the Republic of Ireland as an independent state divorced from the British Crown left the Commonwealth, under the Republic of Ireland Act of April 18, 1949, as a traditionalist but nonconformist he had his tease.

W.S.C.: As far as I can follow the matter . . . because it requires an effort of mental gymnastics—that the policy of the Dublin Government is that Ireland must be partitioned together and thus excluded into the British Commonwealth

SPEECH

Later, in a speech at the Mansion House, December 16, 1955, on becoming a Freeman of Belfast and Londonderry, he referred to a speech he made thirty years before.*

W.S.C.: I have a very strong feeling that the worst of Ulster's trials and anxieties are over. I may cherish the hope that some day all Ireland will be loyal because it is free, will be united because it is loyal, and will be united within itself and united with the British Empire.

EAR-WITNESS

In June, soon after US ambassador to London Lewis Douglas suffered the loss of an eye after a salmon fishing accident near Southampton, W.S.C. visited him at the American Embassy.

* Residence of the Lord Mayor of London.

FIRST LORD OF THE ADMIRALTY

W.S.C.: My dear Lew, you must not let this bother you, you must remember, Nelson had only one eye.

HOUSE OF COMMONS

On July 32, discussing the dismantling of Germany and bringing German generals to trial.

Mr Sidney Silverman:[*] I wonder what the Right Hon. Gentleman would say if he abandoned restraint.

W.S.C.: The Hon. Gentleman is always intervening. On this occasion he did not even hop off his perch.[†]

---

[*] Tiny, short-legged Labour Member of Parliament, crusader against capital punishment.

[†] It is the custom of the House of Commons for a Member to rise on asking a question.

HOUSE OF COMMONS

On August 17, on a Constitution in preparation for the Council of Europe.

W.S.C.: I will not prejudge the word of the committee, but I hope they will remember Napoleon's saying: 'A constitution must be short and obscure.' Until that committee reports, I think we should be well advised to reserve our judgment . . . To take a homely and familiar test, we may just as well see what the girl looks like before we marry her . . .

Ten ancient capitals of Europe are behind the Iron Curtain. A large part of this continent is held in bondage. They have escaped from Nazism only to fall into the other extreme of Communism. It is like making a long and agonizing journey to leave the North Pole only to find out that, as a result, you have woken up in the South Pole.

HOUSE OF COMMONS

On September 28.

W.S.C.: Again and again the Chancellor [Sir Stafford Cripps] was warned from this side of the House and by financial authorities outside that he was living in a fool's paradise. But all these warnings were in vain. I think he made some remark about 'Dismal Desmonds'.* Was that his phrase or did one of his colleagues achieve this alliterative gem?

SPEECH

At a Conservative Annual Conference at Empress Hall, Earl's Court, October 14.

W.S.C.: We are now threatened, besides the nationalization of steel, with that of insurance, sugar and cement. All of these thriving industries are to be disturbed, mauled and finally chilled and largely paralysed by the clumsy and costly grip of State bureaucracy . . .

But in all matters of good housekeeping the Socialists have proved themselves an effective substitute for some of the evils we overcame in the war. I expect there is many a housewife who looks back to those hard days with reflection, as she only wishes old

---

* Pink, plush, droopy-eared toy dog popular with British children before World War II.

269

Woolton* had it in his hands again. I was, of course, only quoting the housewife, because as a matter of fact he is quite a young fellow compared to me.

DAILY EXPRESS (AN INTERVIEW)

'When Churchill's in his seat, the Opposition breathes fire. When he is not, the Tory front bench has the venom of a bunch of daffodils,' wrote the Daily Express. Asked why he had not retired earlier . . .

W.S.C.: If you wish to play dog in the manger, you cannot leave your manger.

also

Before retiring as Prime Minister to be succeeded by Anthony Eden.

W.S.C.: I must retire soon. Anthony won't live forever.

HOUSE OF COMMONS

Speech on Economic Situation, October 27.

W.S.C.: The Socialist Party are very mealy-mouthed today, and the Chancellor of the Exchequer [Sir Stafford Cripps] is very delicate in his language. One must not say 'deflation', but only 'disinflation'. In a similar manner, one must not say 'devaluation', but only 'revaluation', and, finally, there is the farce of saying that there must be no increase in personal incomes when what is meant is no increase in wages. However, the Chancellor felt that a certain broad prejudice attaches to the word 'income' and that consequently no one would mind saying that incomes shall not increase—but wages, no. However, it is wages that he means. I am sure that the British electors will not be taken in by such humbug. I suppose that presently when 'disinflation' also wins its bad name, the Chancellor will call it 'non-disinflation' and will start again . . .

HOUSE OF COMMONS

On November 17, on recognizing Communist China.

W.S.C.: Ought we to recognize them or not? Recognizing a person

---

* Frederick James Marquis, first Earl of Woolton, first Baron Woolton; Minister of Food 1940–1943, when food rationing was introduced.

is not necessarily an act of approval. I will not be personal, or give instances. One has to recognize lots of things and people in this world of sin and woe that one does not like. The reason for having diplomatic relations is not to confer a compliment, but to secure a convenience.

also

EAR-WITNESS

W.S.C.: British policy has always been that you recognize when you are satisfied that the Government truly has control. It's not a question of whether you like them or not.

and

A year later, on a visit in the US, discussing the possibility of Britain's recognition of Red China.

W.S.C.: If you recognize the sow, why worry about the piglets?

also

HOUSE OF COMMONS

After the Korean War.

W.S.C.: I was, I think, the first in this House to suggest, in November 1949, recognition of the Chinese Communists . . . I thought it would be a good thing to have diplomatic representation. But if you recognize anyone it does not necessarily mean that you like him. We all, for instance, recognize the Right Hon. Gentleman, the Member for Ebbw Vale [Mr Bevan].

(In an aside)

W.S.C.: I recognize him as a fact!

PRESS INTERVIEW

On his seventy-fifth birthday, November 30.

W.S.C.: I am ready to meet my Maker. Whether my Maker is prepared for the great ordeal of meeting me is another matter.

also

MY YEARS WITH CHURCHILL

Meeting the Press at the door of his 28 Hyde Park Gate house.

Photographer: I hope, sir, that I will shoot your picture on your hundredth birthday.

W.S.C.: I don't see why not, young man. You look reasonably fit and healthy.

1950

SPEECH

In his Constituency at Woodford.

W.S.C.: Why should queues become a permanent, continuous feature of our life? Here you see clearly what is in their minds. The Socialist dream is no longer Utopia but Queuetopia. And if they have the power this part of their dream will certainly come true.

SPEECH

Election speech at the Town Hall in Leeds, February 4.

W.S.C.: I rejoice in the undoubted growing recovery of France, but I want to warn you that the kind of political whirligig under which France lives, which is such great fun for the politicians and for all the ardent parties into which they are divided, would be fatal to Britain. We cannot afford to have a period of French politics in Westminster.

SPEECH

Election speech at Cardiff, February 8.

W.S.C.: I hope you have all mastered the official Socialist jargon which our masters,* as they call themselves, wish us to learn. You must not use the word 'poor'; they are described as the 'lower income group'. When it comes to a question of freezing a workman's wages the Chancellor of the Exchequer speaks of 'arresting increases in personal income'. The idea is that formerly income tax payers used to be the well-to-do, and that therefore it will be popular and safe to hit at them. Sir Stafford Cripps does

---

* Sir Hartley, now Lord Shawcross, Attorney General, 1945–1951, who later became much more conservative, had been so injudicious as to say, 'We are the masters now.'

not like to mention the word 'wages', but that is what he means. There is a lovely one about houses and homes. They are in future to be called 'accommodation units'. I don't know how we are to sing our old song 'Home Sweet Home'. 'Accommodation Unit, Sweet Accommodation Unit, there's no place like our Accommodation Unit.' I hope to live to see the British democracy spit all this rubbish from their lips.

and

W.S.C.: In this period of 'hell for all except the profiteers' the expectation of life for all babies who had the courage to be born rose by nine years. That was an important fact to be borne in mind not only by the parents but by the baby. When the survivors of five years of hell went to the elementary schools in London it was found that they had gained an average of two inches in height and four pounds in weight compared with the standards before the First World War. How very surprising! The warm climate must have suited them. There was also a steady improvement in the food of the people, and a marked increase in the consumption of milk, cheese, butter, and eggs, and of fruit and vegetables. But I do not wish to make your mouths water.

SPEECH

Election speech at Usher Hall, Edinburgh, February 14.

W.S.C.: I doubt if it gives very much pleasure to the average Socialist when he wakes up in the morning to say to himself, 'Oho, I own the Bank of England, I own the railways, I own the coal mines.' But if it does give him any actual pleasure, he is certainly paying dearly for it. It may gratify his pride, but it makes a nasty hole in his pocket. In order that these Socialist enthusiasts may enjoy this little thrill in the morning, very large sums are being taken from them and their wives and families in taxes, or in prices, or in both.

HOUSE OF COMMONS

April 20. Reviewing the eighth meeting of the Consultative Council of the Brussels Treaty on Western Union and the installation of signal communications and division of the airfields collectively known as the infrastructure.

W.S.C.: As to this new word [infrastructure] with which he [Mr Shinwell, then Minister of Defence] has dignified our language, but which perhaps was imposed upon him internationally, I can only say that we must have full opportunity to consider it and to consult the dictionary.

HOUSE OF COMMONS

Attack on Socialist doctrines of the Labour Party, April 24.

W.S.C.: I always find these financial matters better explained by simple illustrations. I will take that which occurred to me the other day when I was looking at a cow, and I find that quite a different principle prevails in dealing with cows from that which is so applauded below the gangway opposite in dealing with rich men. It is a great advantage in a dairy to have cows with large udders because one gets more milk out of them than from the others. These exceptionally fertile milch cows are greatly valued in any well-conducted dairy and anyone would be thought very foolish who boasted he had got rid of all the best milkers, just as he would be thought very foolish if he did not milk them to the utmost limit of capacity, compatible with the maintenance of their numbers. I am quite sure that the Minister of Agriculture would look in a very different way upon the reduction of all these thousands of his best milkers from that in which the Chancellor of the Exchequer looks upon the destruction of the most fertile and most profitable resources of taxation. I must say the cows do not feel the same way about it as do the Socialists. The cows have not got the same equalitarian notions and dairy farmers are so unimaginative that they think mainly of getting as much milk as possible; they want a lot of political education.

HOUSE OF COMMONS

While speaking on the Schuman Plan for pooling European coal and steel, he took a dig at Hugh Gaitskell, Labour Leader and old boy of Winchester.

W.S.C.: In this Debate we have had the usual jargon about 'the infrastructure of a supra-national authority'. The original authorship is obscure; but it may well be that these words 'infra' and 'supra' have been introduced into our current political parlance by the band of intellectual highbrows who are naturally anxious to impress British labour with the fact that they learned Latin at Winchester. Although we may not relish the words, no one will wish to deny the old school tie contingent their modest indulgence in class self-consciousness.

EAR-WITNESS

After Labour's Mr John Strachey was transferred from Minister of Food to Minister of War.

W.S.C.: As Minister of Food he couldn't produce food—now as Minister of War, surely he won't be able to produce any war.

EAR-WITNESS

At a Council of Europe meeting at Strasbourg in August, Dr Hugh Dalton, formerly Labour's Chancellor of the Exchequer, was overheard whispering to W.S.C.

Dr Dalton: I see we're divided only by one Italian.

W.S.C.: That's not all that divides us!

HOUSE OF COMMONS

On September 19.

W.S.C.: After all there are millions of Conservative and Liberal trade unionists throughout the land, and I say to them from here— and my voice carries some distance—that they must not let themselves be discouraged in their national efforts by the political and party manoeuvres of a fanatical intelligentsia. The Home Secretary [Mr James Ede] is laughing; I did not mean to include him in the intelligentsia.

Mr Ede: I was quite sure the Right Hon. Gentleman did not. That was why I laughed.

W.S.C.: The Right Hon. Gentleman could surely find other things in life to laugh at besides those which do not include himself. Otherwise life might be rather gloomy for him.

SPEECH

At Copenhagen University, October 10.

W.S.C.: The first duty of a university is to teach wisdom, not a trade; character, not technicalities. We want a lot of engineers in the modern world, but we do not want a world of engineers.

HOUSE OF COMMONS

December 14, on the International situation.

W.S.C.: The argument is now put forward that we must never use the atomic bomb until, or unless, it has been used against us first. In other words, you must never fire until you have been shot dead. That seems to me a silly thing to say and a still more imprudent position to adopt.

EAR-WITNESS

There is the story of the little boy who lived near Chartwell and was taken there by his nanny to see 'the greatest man in the whole wide world.' W.S.C. had retired for his afternoon nap. While the little boy's nanny had her tea, the child sneaked off to look for his hero and found him reading in bed.

Little boy: Are you the greatest man in the whole wide world?

W.S.C.: Of course I'm the greatest man in the whole wide world. Now buzz off.

PRIME MINISTER AGAIN |
1951-1955

JANUARY 1951	Mr Aneurin Bevan, previously Minister of Health, appointed Minister of Labour. Resigned with other Ministers three months later over the issue of increased military spending.
9TH MARCH 1951	Mr Herbert Morrison appointed Foreign Secretary in place of Mr Ernest Bevin; Mr Bevin appointed Lord Privy Seal.
18TH MARCH 1951	Treaty setting up 'European Coal and Steel Community' (Schuman Plan) signed in Paris.
26TH MARCH 1951	Conference of American Foreign Ministers opened in Washington.
2ND APRIL 1951	General Eisenhower assumed effective command of Allied Treaty forces in Europe.
26TH APRIL 1951	The oil commission in Persia resolved to effect nationalization of Persian oil immediately.
2ND MAY 1951	Germany admitted to the Council of Europe.
25TH MAY 1951	United Nations forces in Korea advanced on all fronts; Thirty-eighth Parallel crossed on May 26.
3RD AUGUST 1951	Published *The Hinge of Fate*, Vol. IV of *The Second World War*.
19TH SEPTEMBER 1951	The Prime Minister announced in a broadcast speech that Parliament would be dissolved on October 5, and a General Election held on October 25; the new Parliament would meet on October 31.
20TH SEPTEMBER 1951	The North Atlantic Council meeting in Ottawa agreed to admission of Greece and Turkey to NATO.
27TH SEPTEMBER 1951	The refinery at Abadan came completely under Persian control; most of the staff of the Anglo-Iranian Oil Company left Abadan for Britain on October 3.
6TH OCTOBER 1951	Published *In the Balance*.
17TH OCTOBER 1951	The sixteenth British Parachute Brigade began arriving by air in the Suez Canal Zone from Cyprus.
26TH OCTOBER 1951	*New Government, Winston Churchill, Conservative Prime Minister*; also Minister of Defence.
31ST DECEMBER 1951	Sailed for Washington for talks with President Truman.
11TH JANUARY 1952	Visited Ottawa.

6TH FEBRUARY 1952	Death at Sandringham of HM King George VI.
8TH FEBRUARY 1952	HM Queen Elizabeth returned from Kenya and held her first Privy Council.
1ST MARCH 1952	W.S.C. handed Ministry of Defence to Field Marshal Alexander.
26TH JULY 1952	Abdication of King Farouk of Egypt.
3RD SEPTEMBER 1952	Published *The Second World War*, Vol. V, *Closing the Ring*.
3RD OCTOBER 1952	First British atomic bomb detonated in Monte Bello Islands.
4TH NOVEMBER 1952	General Eisenhower elected President of the United States.
5TH JANUARY 1953	Arrived in the US for discussions with President-elect Eisenhower.
20TH JANUARY 1953	Dwight D. Eisenhower sworn in as President of the United States.
24TH APRIL 1953	Made a Knight of the Garter.
24TH JUNE 1953	Suffered a slight stroke.
15TH OCTOBER 1953	Awarded the Nobel Prize for Literature 'for his mastery of historical and biographical description as well as for brilliant oratory in defending exalted human values.'
5–12TH DECEMBER 1953	Attended Bermuda Conference with President Eisenhower and French Premier Joseph Laniel.
26TH APRIL 1954	Published Vol. VI of *The Second World War, Triumph and Tragedy*.
14TH JUNE 1954	Installed as Knight of the Garter.
25TH JUNE 1954	Published *Stemming the Tide*. Began a visit to the US and Canada.
27TH JUNE 1954	Russia claimed construction of the first atomic power station.
29TH JUNE 1954	The Potomac Charter, a declaration on foreign policy, issued by W.S.C. and President Eisenhower.
30TH NOVEMBER 1954	Recovered from severe stroke to celebrate eightieth birthday in Westminster Hall and was presented with his portrait painted by Graham Sutherland.
28TH MARCH 1955	Made last speech as Prime Minister in House of Commons.
5TH APRIL 1955	Resigned as Prime Minister.
6TH APRIL 1955	*New Government, Anthony Eden, Conservative Prime Minister.*
7TH APRIL 1955	Mr Harold Macmillan became Foreign Secretary.
15TH APRIL 1955	Sir Anthony Eden announced a General Election to be held on May 26, which increased Conservative majority.
9TH OCTOBER 1955	Accepted the Freedom Award.
16TH OCTOBER 1955	Accepted the Williamsburg Award.
14TH DECEMBER 1955	Mr Hugh Gaitskell elected Leader of the Parliamentary Labour Party. Mr Herbert Morrison resigned as Deputy Leader.

1951

EAR-WITNESS

Food Minister, Gwilym Lloyd George (son of David Lloyd George), finding the British larder extremely low, decided the British could have no extra Christmas food rations and sent an explanatory memorandum to W.S.C. detailing the reasons.

W.S.C.: (*initialled the memorandum*): Scrooge!

MY YEARS WITH CHURCHILL

In February 1951, so many calls come in to Government offices (including Scotland Yard) asking if W.S.C. was dead, he gleefully issued a formal statement.

W.S.C.: I am informed from many quarters that a rumour has been put about that I died this morning. This is quite untrue.

HOUSE OF COMMONS

From a Conservative Party Political Broadcast.

W.S.C.: I resented Mr Stalin calling him [Mr Attlee] a warmonger. I thought this was quite untrue. It was also unfair, because the word 'warmonger' was, as you have no doubt heard, the one that many of Mr Attlee's friends and followers were hoping to fasten on me whenever the election comes . . . they were keeping that for my special benefit. Stalin has therefore been guilty, not only of an untruth, but of infringement of copyright. I think Mr Stalin had better be careful or else Mr [Sidney] Silverman will have him up for breach of privilege . . .

HOUSE OF COMMONS

On March 21.

W.S.C.: I remember well that my father . . . called Mr Gladstone 'An old man in a hurry'. That was in the year 1885, and sixteen years later Mr Gladstone was engaged in forming another Administration. I do not want to suggest that such a precedent will be repeated, for that would dishearten Hon. Members opposite.*

---

* Seven months later W.S.C., at seventy-seven, became Prime Minister for the second time.

HOUSE OF COMMONS
April 19, on North Atlantic Supreme Commander.

W.S.C.: Going back a long time to 27 March 1936 . . .the Prime Minister [Stanley Baldwin] said, according to the *Daily Herald*— 'We shall have to give up certain of our toys—one is "Britannia rules the Waves."' . . . As has been often pointed out, it is 'Britannia rule the Waves'—an invocation, not a declaration of fact. But if the idea 'Rule Britannia' was a toy, it is certainly one for which many good men from time to time have been ready to die.

HOUSE OF COMMONS
During a heated debate, April 19.

Emanuel Shinwell (*Labour*): . . . I am not prepared to rely exclusively on the views expressed by him [W.S.C.]. There are other Members of the House who are subordinate to him, but who, nevertheless, are entitled to express an opinion.

W.S.C.: Or insubordinate.

HOUSE OF COMMONS
Commenting on Prime Minister Attlee's return from the hospital to the leadership of the Labour Government, which the Conservatives hoped to overthrow.

W.S.C.: It is hard on any country when no one is looking after it. The Right Honourable Gentleman combines a limited outlook with strong qualities of resistance. He now resumes the direction and leadership of that cluster of lion-hearted limpets—a new phenomenon in our natural history, also a subject I could offer Mr Herbert Morrison for his fun fair—who are united by their desire to hold on to office at all costs to their own reputations and their country's fortunes, and to put off by every means in their power to the last possible moment any contact with our democratic electorate.

HOUSE OF COMMONS
On June 6.

W.S.C.: The object of Parliament is to substitute argument for fisticuffs.

SPEECH

To the Royal College of Physicians on July 10.

W.S.C.: . . . I must thank you for according me an Honorary Fellowship of the Royal College of Physicians. I also had the honour to be made a surgeon eight years ago, and now I can practise, in an honorary fashion, the arts of surgery and medicine. Unless there is a very marked shortage of capable men in both these professions, I shall not press myself upon you. No doubt in these difficult times it will be a comfort not only to the profession but to the nation at large that you have me in reserve. I have not yet taken any final decision as to which of these beneficent branches I should give priority to (in case an emergency arises). Being temperamentally inclined to precision and a sharp edge, it might be thought that I should choose the surgeon's role.

and

W.S.C.: It is arguable whether the human race have been gainers by the march of science beyond the steam engine. Electricity opens a field of infinite conveniences to ever greater numbers, but they may well have to pay dearly for them. But anyhow in my thought I stop short of the internal combustion engine which has made the world so much smaller. Still more must we fear the consequences of entrusting to a human race so little different from their predecessors of the so-called barbarous ages such awful agencies of the atomic bomb. Give me the horse!

EAR-WITNESS

A Senate Subcommittee, studying the needs of recipient NATO-Marshall Plan countries, visited W.S.C. at his 28 Hyde Park Gate London House. Its Chairman, Senator Theodore Green of Rhode Island, remarked on how much he liked a portrait of George III by Allan Ramsay* they had seen in the Foreign Minister's office.

W.S.C.: A remarkable man, Senator. We owe him a great debt of gratitude. If it weren't for his stubbornness we would not now be eligible for Foreign Aid!

---

* Allan Ramsay, 1713–1784; Scottish court painter to George III, 1767.

SPEECH
On July 21, at Woodford, referring to high taxes demanded for Britain's Welfare State.

W.S.C.: All the boastings of the Welfare State have to be set against the fact that more than what they have given with one hand has been filched back by the other.

MY YEARS WITH CHURCHILL
On a September holiday in Venice as the train approached the city he leaned from the window for a fuller view. A detective pulled him back in time to prevent his decapitation by a concrete post.

W.S.C.: Anthony Eden nearly got a new job then, didn't he?

SPEECH
During October Election at Liverpool.

W.S.C.: No doubt it takes two parties to make a quarrel and we certainly have done our duty in the Opposition.

SPEECH
During October Election.

W.S.C.: . . . the *Daily Mirror*, coined a phrase . . . which is being used by the Socialist Party . . . 'Whose finger,' they asked, 'do you want on the trigger, Attlee's or Churchill's?' I am sure we do not want any fingers upon any trigger. Least of all do we want a fumbling finger . . . I must now tell you that in any case it will not be a British finger that will pull the trigger of a Third World War. It may be a Russian finger, or an American finger, or a United Nations Organization finger, but it cannot be a British finger. Although we should certainly be involved in a struggle between the Soviet Empire and the free world, the control and decision and the timing of that horrible event would not rest with us.

BBC BROADCAST
On October 8.

W.S.C.: The difference between our outlook and the Socialist outlook on life is the difference between the ladder and queue. We are for the ladder. Let all try their best to climb. They are for the queue. Let each wait in his place in the queue?' 'Ah,' says the Socialists, 'our officials—and we have plenty of them—come and put him back in it, or perhaps put him lower down to teach the others.' And when they come back to us and say: 'We have told you what happens if anyone slips out of the queue, but what is your answer to what happens if anyone slips off the ladder?' Our reply is: 'We shall have a good net and the finest social ambulance service in the world.'

and

W.S.C.: I do not hold that we should rearm in order to fight. I hold that we should rearm in order to parley

EAR-WITNESS

During the General Election of 1951, he called his Party Leaders together to plot strategy.

W.S.C.: The road will be hard and uphill after a rake's progress, the resulting evils cannot be cured by a Parliamentary vote or a stroke of the Administrative pen.

and

During the Election campaign he was said to have silenced a pimply-faced young heckler by re-using Lord Rosebery's * *blast to his own son.*

W.S.C.: I have always admired a manly man and I rejoice in a womanly woman but I cannot abide a boily boy.

SPEECH

During the October Election. On the effect of the Bevanite split in the Labour Party and its effect on British world-wide influence.

W.S.C.: A Bevan-coloured Government or even a Bevan-tinted Government or tainted (to change the metaphor excusably) might well lead to our being left in the front line of danger without our fair share of influence upon the course of events.

also

* Archibald Philip Primrose, Lord Rosebery, 1847–1929; author-statesman who expressed three wishes: to be Prime Minister, to marry a Rothschild and to win the Derby. He realized all three, but remained a very glum man.

SPEECH

On October 12, at Woodford.

W.S.C.: Mr Attlee, speaking of the achievements of his Government, said he was not satisfied with what had been done. Here are his words: 'How can we clear up in six years the mess of centuries?' The mess of centuries! This is what the Prime Minister considers Britain and her Empire represented when in 1945 she emerged honoured and respected from one end of the world to the other by friend and foe alike after her most glorious victory for freedom. The mess of centuries—that is all we were. The remark is instructive because it reveals with painful clarity the Socialist point of view and sense of proportion. Nothing happened that was any good until they came into office. We may leave out the great struggles and achievements of the past—Magna Carta, the Bill of Rights, Parliamentary institutions, Constitutional Monarchy, the building of our Empire—all these were part of the mess of centuries. Coming to more modern times, Gladstone and Disraeli must have been pygmies. Adam Smith, John Stuart Mill, [John] Bright and [the Earl of] Shaftesbury, and in our lifetime, Balfour, Asquith and [John] Morley, all of these no doubt were 'small fry'. But at last a giant and a titan* appeared to clear up the mess of centuries. Alas, he cries, he has had only six years to do it in . . . Now the Titan wants another term of office.

also

SPEECH

Election address at Town Hall, Huddersfield, October 15.

W.S.C.: 'All men are created equal', says the American Declaration of Independence. 'All men shall be kept equal', says the British Socialist Party.

also

THE TIMES

During the October Election he spoke at St Andrew's Hall in Glasgow

---

* Attlee was very small, and although quite able, was extraordinarily dry and not usually given to over-statement.

belabouring the Labourites for—in his view, weakly—allowing the Persians
to nationalize their oil especially at Abadan, and arrangements also for
yielding to nationalist agitation in the Sudan.
W.S.C.: (*in an aside*): The record of the Labour Government is—
Abadan, Sudan, Bevan.
also

HOUSE OF COMMONS

On November 6, responding to Mr Attlee's attack on him which had brought
Labour members to their feet cheering.
W.S.C.: A great deal of his speech was made up of very effective
points and quips which gave a great deal of satisfaction to those
behind him. We all understand his position. 'I am their leader, I
must follow them.'
and
Opposing the abolition of University seats in the House of Commons in
which Mr Herbert Morrison indicated dissent.
W.S.C.: The Right Hon. Gentleman is shaking his head, but he
will have to shake it a great deal to shake off his personal
responsibility in this matter.

HOUSE OF COMMONS

On November 19, on importing cigars from hard currency areas.
W.S.C.: I have not for quite a time imported any cigars from hard
currency areas—I have nevertheless received some from time to
time!
also

A MINUTE

Earlier, in 1944.
W.S.C.: (*to Foreign Secretary Eden*): In regard to your minute about
raising certain legations to the status of embassies. I must say Cuba
has as good a claim as some of the other places—'la perla de las
Antillas'. Great offence will be given if all the others have it and this
large, rich beautiful Island, *the home of the cigar*, is denied.
also

MY DEAR MR CHURCHILL

W.S.C.: Tobacco is bad for love; but old age is worse.

He memorialized forever not only the 'V' sign but the cigar and smoked about nine cigars a day, none to the end, gluing a bit of paper around the tip of each which he called a 'belly bando.' His favourite was said to have been half-Havana, half-Virginia tobacco imported from John Rushmore in New York.

HOUSE OF COMMONS

As Prime Minister, and Minister of Defence, during a November 28 discussion on the recruitment of the Home Guard, W.S.C. was heckled by one of his Welsh antagonists, Labour Member Emryhs Hughes, son-in-law of Keir Hardie. *

Mr Hughes: Is the Right Hon. Gentleman aware that the Minister of Defence was absent from the first Home Guard Parade last night? Is he now on open arrest waiting court martial?

W.S.C.: I was pursuing my studies into the Welsh language.[†]

DANIEL SCHORR, CBS CORRESPONDENT

On December 3, at a dinner in London. Konrad Adenauer, Chancellor of the Federal Republic of Germany, was speculating with W.S.C., over coffee and cognac, about whether, if God were to create the world a second time, He would make any changes.

W.S.C.: He might put each nation on an island surrounded by a channel.

Chancellor Adenauer: That is an extremely British point of view!

W.S.C.: What would you do?

Chancellor Adenauer: If I were re-creating the world, I would suggest that this time we not put a limit on man's intelligence without putting a limit on man's stupidity.

W.S.C.: That would not do at all, because it would deprive me of many of my Cabinet members.

---

[*] Keir Hardie, 1856–1915, British Socialist and labour leader; organized miners into unions.
[†] He had just appointed a Minister for Welsh affairs—Sir David Maxwell-Fyfe, a Scot.

EAR-WITNESS

Referring to his old Liberal Party in the House of Commons.

W.S.C.: So few and so futile.

HOUSE OF COMMONS

During a December speech on defence estimates for the protection of Britain.

W.S.C.: Our country should suggest to the mind of a potential paratrooper the back of a hedgehog rather than the paunch of a rabbit.

THE SUNDAY TIMES (CHURCHILL'S ART OF GOVERNMENT BY VISCOUNT ECCLES)

As Minister of Works, Mr David Eccles discovered a proposal left by the Labour Government, to excavate emergency headquarters in case of World War III.

W.S.C.: Is this hole to accommodate key members of the Government in some future war? How many would it hold?

Mr Eccles: Seventeen thousand.

W.S.C.: And who pray will get them breakfast?

BBC BROADCAST

On the eve of his December trip to Washington, DC, as Prime Minister for the second time, to effect an American loan.

W.S.C.: We are resolved to make this Island solvent, able to earn its living and pay its way. We have no assurance that anyone else is going to keep the lion as a pet.*

1952   PRESS INTERVIEW

On the Verandah Grill of the Queen Mary *in New York Harbour.*

W.S.C.: The television has come to take its place in the world; as a rather old-fashioned person I have not been one of its principal champions, but I don't think it needs any champion. I think it can

---

* On January 6, 1959, he used this same sentence in a speech to the Woodford Conservative Association.

make its own way and I think it's a wonderful thing indeed to think that every expression on my face at this moment may be viewed by millions of people throughout the United States. I hope that the raw material is as good as the methods of distribution.

PRESS INTERVIEW

At a Washington, DC, press conference, he was asked what he thought about the role of women in the twentieth century.

W.S.C.: The position of women today it seems to me hasn't altered —except perhaps technically—since the days of Adam and Eve.

and

W.S.C.: What is the good of speaking one language if you can't put your differences to each other plainly? That is the great advantage of one language. One language is the biggest thing, as Bismarck said. The greatest development of the nineteenth century was that the United States was found definitely to speak only the— may I say it—the English language.

and

Asked how Britain was going to solve her dire economic distress.

W.S.C.: For 900 years minus 14, we have staved off, indeed, warded off invasions. During that time we had some difficulties. Sometimes during those times we couldn't pay our bills. But at least we kept them from being collected!

EAR-WITNESS

In January, on this first visit to Washington after becoming Prime Minister a second time, the European Defence Force was under discussion and exploration by all sides, especially the proposal that national uniforms should be scrapped in favour of a new European one.

W.S.C.: (*to Secretary of Defence Robert Lovett*): Oh, no! That would be a sludgy amalgam.

and

At another of these Potomac conferences, arguments arose over failure to agree about a standard rifle for the NATO forces. One meeting took place at the British Embassy.

Field Marshal Sir William Slim:* Well, I suppose we could experiment with a bastard rifle—partly American—partly British.
W.S.C.: Kindly moderate your language, Field Marshal, it may be recalled that I am myself partly British, partly American.
and

During the same talks on various NATO Army and Navy Commands, W.S.C. noticed Secretary of Defence Robert Lovett fixing him with his banker's eye.

Mr Lovett: Mr Churchill, who is going to command in the English Channel? I am told it was determined in Rome.
W.S.C.: Thank you for that crumb, Mr Lovett. I suppose the President and I should issue a joint communiqué that naval traffic in the Potomac will be under the supervision of the US Navy?

EAR-WITNESS

W.S.C.: A fanatic is one who can't change his mind and won't change the subject.

SPEECH

In Ottawa on January 14, at a State dinner to which all members of the Canadian Parliament were invited, the public address system went off. W.S.C. could not be heard and was told so by many voices in the audience shouting, 'Can't hear,' 'Speak up!' Thereupon he tore off the button microphone from his lapel and threw it on the floor.

W.S.C.: Since the resources of science have failed us, we shall now fall back on Mother Nature . . . I have been a leader of an Opposition. In a free country one is always allowed to have an Opposition . . . In England we even pay the Leader of the Opposition a salary of £2,000 a year to make sure that the Government is kept up to the mark.[†] I have no doubt that Mr Attlee . . . will devote himself to his constitutional task with the zeal which, under totalitarian systems, might well lead him to Siberia or worse.

---

* Chief of Imperial General Staff, 1948–1952; Governor General and Commander in Chief, Australia, 1953–1960.
† Oddly enough, Attlee had been the first Leader so paid, under the Ministers of the Crown Act, 1937.

MY YEARS WITH CHURCHILL

An over-enthusiastic lady asked if it didn't thrill him to realize that his speeches always brought overflow audiences.

W.S.C.: It is quite flattering . . . but whenever I feel this way I always remember that if instead of making a political speech I was being hanged, the crowd would be twice as big.

SPEECH

To a Joint Session of the United States Congress, Washington, January 17.

W.S.C.: But I am by no means sure that China will remain for generations in the Communist grip. The Chinese said of themselves several thousand years ago: 'China is a sea that salts all the waters that flow into it.' There is another Chinese saying about their country which is much more modern, it dates only from the fourth century . . . 'The tail of China is large and will not be wagged.' I like that one. The British democracy approves the principle of movable heads and unwaggable national tails.

HOUSE OF COMMONS

On March 5, on Defence.

W.S.C.: My first impression on looking round the scene at home in November as Minister of Defence [in addition to being Prime Minister] was a sense of extreme nakedness such as I have never felt before in peace or war—almost as though I was living in a nudist colony.

HOUSE OF COMMONS

When it was decided to return the Coronation Stone to Westminster Abbey, W.S.C., responding to an attack by Emrys Hughes, a Labour Member who had been travelling in Russia, teased him about the 'Red' Dean of Canterbury, who was said to be soft to Communists.*

Mr Hughes: Is the Prime Minister aware . . . that the Dean of Westminster is now wondering whether, on the Day of Judgement,

---

* The Very Reverend Hewlett Johnson, Dean of Canterbury, 1931–1963.

he will appear with the Prime Minister on a charge of accepting stolen property?

W.S.C.: I should have thought that the Hon. Member would be more concerned with the future of the Dean of Canterbury.

BBC BROADCAST

A political broadcast of May 3, on the weakening pound and resulting loss of buying power.

W.S.C.: Up to this moment I have been talking only about our buying power abroad. If we lose that we should be like a swimmer who cannot keep his head above water long enough to get a new breath. (No fun at all!)

THE TIMES OF LONDON

When he was shown about the French Parliament in the Palais Bourbon in 1952, he examined the MS. of Joan of Arc's trial, in the strongroom.

W.S.C.: You know, it wasn't our fault. The English were just working for the Burgundians [tapping the MS.] Probably you will find in there that the French called us 'Goddams'. It is still a term we use a good deal. It is a fine thing to keep these old conservative practices.

HOUSE OF COMMONS

Mr James Callaghan* pressed him upon the subject of the Allied Naval Commander in the Mediterranean. Under the Labour Government, as Leader of the Opposition, he appeared to have inclined slightly in one direction and, as Prime Minister once again, in another direction.

W.S.C.: My views are a harmonious process which keeps them in relation to the current movement of events.

HOUSE OF COMMONS

On May 6, on transferring the administration of foot-and-mouth disease in Scotland from the Ministry of Agriculture in London to Edinburgh.

---

* James Callaghan, Labour Member of Parliament; Chancellor of the Exchequer, 1964–1967; Home Secretary, 1967–1970 and 1974–1976; Prime Minister, 1976–1979.

Mr Robert Boothby: (*Member for Aberdeen, later Lord Boothby*): Is my Right Hon. Friend aware that there is a torrent of complaints from Scotland at the present time?

W.S.C.: I am sure my Hon. Friend would be fully capable of giving full vent to any such torrent, but the difficulty is that we are not sure that foot-and-mouth disease is as well educated on the subject of borders and questions arising out of them as he is.

Mr Boothby: I beg to give notice that I shall raise this matter at Adjournment.

W.S.C.: I am afraid I cannot undertake to be present when this new red herring is drawn across the border.

HOUSE OF COMMONS
On May 21.
W.S.C.: It is no part of my case that I am always right.

HOUSE OF COMMONS
Emrys Hughes MP, querying him on the effect on wild life of the atom tests on Monte Bello Islands near Australia.

W.S.C.: The report of a recent special survey showing that there is very little animal or bird life on Monte Bello Islands was one of the factors in the choice of the site for the test of the United Kingdom atomic weapon.

I should add, however, that an expedition which went to the islands 50 years ago reported that giant rats, wild cats and wallabies were seen, and these may have caused the honourable Member some anxiety. However the officer who explored the islands recently says that he found only some lizards, two sea eagles and what looked like a canary sitting on a perch.

Mr Hughes (*Labour Member*): Will the Prime Minister tell us whether any competent officer will go on this expedition. Is he aware that there are still civilized people in this country who are interested in bird and animal life? Will he get some report which will satisfy civilized human beings that no unnecessary destruction of wild life will take place.

W.S.C.: Certainly. I think everything should be done to avoid the destruction of bird life and animal life and also of human life.

HOUSE OF COMMONS
On June 24.

W.S.C.: I have always considered that the substitution of the internal combustion machine for the horse marked a very gloomy milestone in the progress of mankind.

MY YEARS WITH CHURCHILL
While he was wearing the uniform of Lord Warden of the Cinque Ports during a tour of duty, one of his epaulettes fell off. Unselfconsciously he continued minus one.

W.S.C.: (*later, to his valet Norman McGowan*): It's a good job I personally fasten my braces.
and
Bathing in his tub one morning, his mutterings and splashings were so thunderous they brought his alarmed valet to his side.

W.S.C.: I wasn't talking to you, Norman, I was addressing the House of Commons.
also

WAR AT THE TOP
While Brigadier Sir Leslie Hollis* was reading him some secret reports as he lay in his bath, he suddenly pinched his nose with his forefinger and thumb and disappeared under the water line, causing the Brigadier to stop reading.

W.S.C.: (*surfacing*): Why do you stop reading? Don't you know that water is a conductor of sound?

HOUSE OF COMMONS
On July 1, on being questioned as to why the British Government was not informed of a certain bombing in the Korean War.

W.S.C.: Yes, it should have been; indeed it was our intention to do it. It is only as the result of what in the United States is known as a Snafu†—which word I have added to my vocabulary—that you were not consulted about it.

---

* Assistant to General Ismay.
† Situation *Normal: All F***ed Up.*

HOUSE OF COMMONS
When the 'Red' Dean of Canterbury returned from Red China and Russia in July, claiming germ warfare had been used in Korea by the Americans, W.S.C. vetoed trying him for treason.

W.S.C.: Free speech carries with it the evils of all the foolish, unpleasant, venomous things that are said. But on the whole we would rather lump them than do away with it.

HOUSE OF COMMONS
On July 23.

W.S.C.: It is always wise to look ahead, but difficult to look farther than you can see.

HOUSE OF COMMONS
On November 4, on a Bill furthering the production of the iron and steel industry.

W.S.C.: Personally, Mr Speaker, I am always ready to learn, although I do not always like being taught.

HOUSE OF COMMONS
On November 18, on the Korean War.

Mr Lewis (*Labour Member*): Is the Prime Minister aware of the deep concern felt by the people of this country at the whole question of the Korean conflict? . . .

W.S.C.: I am fully aware of the deep concern felt by the Hon. Member in many matters above his comprehension.

HOUSE OF COMMONS
On December 4, on Motion of Censure.

W.S.C.: I have today to deal with a Motion of Censure and therefore I hope I shall be pardoned if I do not confine myself entirely to the uncontroversial methods which I usually practise.

HOUSE OF COMMONS

Responding to an attack, during the holiday season.

Mr William Ross* (*to W.S.C.*): What else can you say to a goose.

W.S.C.: I do not in the least mind being called a goose [in an aside] even at Christmas time. I've been called many worse things than that.

1953

PRESS CONFERENCE

On the RMS Queen Mary.

W.S.C.: You remember Fulton. I got into great trouble being a bit in front of the weather that time. But it's all come out since—I won't say right, but it's all come out.

Q: Do you have any thoughts of retiring?

W.S.C.: (*then seventy-eight*): Not until I'm a great deal worse and the Empire a great deal better.

SKETCHES FROM LIFE

In January, on his way to a vacation in Jamaica, he stopped off in
Washington, DC and was host at the British Embassy to President Truman,
British Ambassador Sir Roger Makins, Robert Lovett, W. Averell Harriman,
General Omar Bradley[†] *and Dean Acheson.*

W.S.C.: (*to President Truman*): Mr President, I hope you have your answer ready for that hour when you and I stand before St Peter and he says, 'I understand you two are responsible for putting off those atomic bombs.'

Robert Lovett: Are you sure, Prime Minister, that you are going to be in the same place as the President for that intertion?

W.S.C.: Lovett, my vast respect for the Creator of this universe and countless others gives me assurance that He would not condemn a man without a hearing.

Robert Lovett: True, but your hearing would not be likely to start in the Supreme Court, or, necessarily, in the same court as the President's. It could be in another court far away.

---

* Labour Member of Parliament; Secretary of State for Scotland, 1964–1970.
† Omar Bradley, Commander of US troops in invasion of France, June 1944; Chief of Staff, US Army, 1948–1949; Chairman, Joint Chiefs of Staff, 1949–1953.

W.S.C.: I don't know about that, but, wherever it is, it will be in accordance with the principles of the English common law.

Dean Acheson: Is it altogether consistent with your respect for the Creator of this and other universes to limit His imagination in judicial procedure to the accomplishment of a minute island, in a tiny world, in one of the smaller of the universes?

W.S.C.: Can you think of a better?

Dean Acheson: No, but I don't put myself in the position of the Creator of these universes.

W.S.C.: Well, there will be a trial by a jury of my peers. That's certain.

Dean Acheson: Oyez! Oyez! In the Matter of the Immigration of Winston Spencer Churchill, Mr Bailiff, will you empanel a jury?

Robert Lovett (*to General Bradley*): Are you Alexander the Great? *(Then followed the naming of a jury, among them Julius Caesar; Socrates; Aristotle; Voltaire, who was challenged as an atheist; and Oliver Cromwell, as not believing in the fundamental law. Then General George Washington was called.)*

W.S.C.: I waive a jury, but not *habeas corpus*. You'll not put me in any black hole.

EAR-WITNESS

Before flying off to Jamaica on the 'Sacred Cow,' lent him by President Truman, he conversed in the plane at the Washington, DC airport with one of his French-speaking aides about their mutual love and disappointment in some of the French.

W.S.C.: The French—the French—for 14 long years they have been living in ignominy—and—and—enjoying every moment of it.

CHURCHILL: TAKEN FROM THE DIARIES OF LORD MORAN

On February 24, three months before the Coronation of Queen Elizabeth II, began concerning himself with details of the Coronation.

W.S.C.: (*to Lord Moran, his physician*): The people in the stands at Hyde Park corner, by Byron's statue, will be there from seven in the morning till five in the evening. They [Coronation officials] were

seeing to their sanitary needs, but doing nothing for them in food and drink . . . Looking after their exports while neglecting their imports . . . and why? . . . Because alcohol had not been drunk in the royal parks for a hundred years, they were to have nothing to drink. I altered all that.

HOUSE OF COMMONS

On February 9, Stalin had accused a number of doctors, most of whom were Jewish, of seeking to poison leading members of the Soviet Government.

Mr Emrys Hughes (*Labour MP*): Has the Prime Minister forgotten that in at least half a dozen important speeches on the eve of the last Election he pressed for a meeting with Mr Stalin? Is he aware that earlier in this year Mr Stalin declared himself favourably towards a meeting? Why does he not unite with Mr Stalin, and invite President Eisenhower?

W.S.C.: I think we must try to understand the general position as it moves. We in this country would feel very severe domestic pre-occupations, making it difficult to have conversations with heads of Government, if for instance so many of our best doctors were being charged with poisoning so many of our best politicians . . . If all the other difficulties were swept away I could easily take my own medical adviser with me.

HOUSE OF COMMONS
On February 24. Questioned concerning a Member's Statement that economic planning was baloney.
W.S.C.: I should prefer to have an agreed definition of the meaning of 'baloney' before I attempted to deal with such a topic.

A LETTER
To the TUC (Trades Union Congress) on Adult Education, March 2.
W.S.C.: A man or woman earnestly seeking a grown-up life . . . will make the best of all pupils in this age of clatter and buzz, of gape and gloat.

HOUSE OF COMMONS
March 3, on the Cold War.
W.S.C.: What is called the Cold War—which is not a legal term—continues. What we are faced with is not a violent jerk but a prolonged pull.

HOUSE OF COMMONS
On March 5.
W.S.C.: I must now warn the House that I am going to make an unusual departure. I am going to make a Latin quotation. It is one which I hope will not offend the detachment of the old school tie and will not baffle or be taken as a slight upon the new spelling brigade. Perhaps I ought to say the 'new spelling squad' because it is an easier word. The quotation is, '*Arma virumque cano*,'* which, for

* *Aeneid*

the benefit of our Winchester friends, I may translate as 'Arms and the men I sing.' That generally describes my theme.

Mr Hugh Gaitskell (*Leeds, South*), *who had attended Winchester College*: Should it not be 'man', the singular instead of the plural?

W.S.C.: Little did I expect that I should receive assistance on a classical matter from such a quarter. I am using the word 'man' in a collective form which, I think, puts me right in grammar. Let me now come to arms, about which I believe there is no classical dispute.

SPEECH

Coronation Luncheon, Westminster Hall, London, March 27.

W.S.C.: We must be very careful nowadays—I perhaps all the more because of my American forebears—in what we say about the American Constitution. I will therefore content myself with the observations that no Constitution was ever written in better English.

also

ROOSEVELT AND HOPKINS, AN INTIMATE HISTORY

Earlier in July 1942, after arriving in London from the United States, Harry Hopkins reported to President Roosevelt, 'The Prime Minister threw the British Constitution at me with some vehemence. As you know, it is an unwritten document so no serious damage was done. Winston is his old self and full of battle.'

SPEECH

On April 23, to Honourable Artillery Company, at St George's Day Dinner.

W.S.C.: Now I must say something about the artillery. I've had very little help from our Chairman because he was mostly on the bow and arrow; after that we got to the musketoon and the tripod, and then there was the period when our artillery really came boldly out on the battlefield.

HOUSE OF COMMONS

On April 30, responding to critics of the United Nations offer of rewards for surrender of MIG fighters in Korea.

W.S.C.: It does seem to me very much better to bribe a person than to kill a person, and very much better to be bribed than to be killed.

HOUSE OF COMMONS

On May 1. Knighted by Queen Elizabeth II on April 24, 1953, he entered the House of Commons the following Friday and was given a rousing welcome, the traditional waving of papers and a rising of chorus of 'Hear! Hear!' from the Members. Emrys Hughes (Labour) caused laughter when he asked the Prime Minister whether he was not on the slippery slope to 'another place' (the only permissible term in the Commons for the House of Lords).

W.S.C.: Provided the term, 'another place' is used in its strictly Parliamentary sense, I am glad to give the assurance required!

HOUSE OF COMMONS

On May 11, after Colonel Nasser* ousted King Farouk in July 1952, and made himself dictator of Egypt.

W.S.C.: One of the disadvantages of dictatorships is that the dictator is often dictated to by others, and what he did to others may often be done back again to him.

HOUSE OF COMMONS

During a debate on Queen Elizabeth's title, an MP aware of Ireland's having left the British Commonwealth, asked W.S.C. if he realized that the Irish government objected to her title.

W.S.C.: Which Irish government?

MP: Is the Prime Minister aware that there is a strong feeling in Scotland about the Oath being taken to a Queen Elizabeth II on the ground of historical inaccuracy? In view of his great claim to historical accuracy himself, will he not do something to meet this very strong resentment in Scotland?

---

* Gamal Abdel Nasser, Prime Minister, later President of Egypt.

W.S.C.: I shall be very glad to hear from the Honourable Member if he will put his question in the pillar box.[*]

and

Mrs Jean Mann (*Labour MP*): Is the Prime Minister aware that . . . the Mint has decided to issue coins with 'Elizabeth II', and Scots who object to this title are placed in an awful dilemma?

W.S.C.: I hope that theoretical refinements will not stop the normal conduct of business.

EAR-WITNESS

In July, after the fall of the Italian Premier Alcide de Gaspari's Government, a friend told W.S.C., then growing deaf, that the Italian leader was planning to retire and read the works of Anthony Trollope.

W.S.C.: (*after a twenty-minute silence*): Tell me more about that trollop.

SPEECH

On October 10, at the Conservative Party Conference at Margate. On some figures produced by Food Minister, Mr Gwilym Lloyd George.[†]

W.S.C.: But he found time to work out this fact which I asked for because I knew it would be plain and simple and could be well understood even by collective ideologists (those professional intellectuals who revel in demand and polysyllables). Personally I like short words and vulgar fractions. Here is the plain vulgar fact.

and

W.S.C.: We have a deep respect for public opinion but we do not let our course be influenced from day to day by Gallup Polls, favourable though they may be. It is not a good thing always to be feeling your pulse and taking your temperature; although one has to do it sometimes, you do not want to make a habit of it. I have heard it said that a Government should keep its ear to the ground but they should also remember that this is not a very dignified attitude.

---

[*] Indignant Scotsmen had been blowing up post boxes carrying the royal designation because Elizabeth I, who had, after all, beheaded Mary Queen of Scots, had never ruled Scotland. 'Pillar Box' in W.S.C.'s usage means 'Post Box'.

[†] Later Viscount Tenby; son of David Lloyd George.

STATEMENT FROM 10 DOWNING STREET

On October 15, receiving notification that he was the first statesman and seventh Briton to be awarded the Nobel Prize for Literature.

W.S.C.: I notice that the first Englishman to receive the Nobel Prize was Rudyard Kipling and that another equally rewarded was Mr Bernard Shaw. I certainly cannot attempt to compete with either of those. I knew them both quite well and my thought was much more in accord with Mr Rudyard Kipling than with Mr Bernard Shaw. On the other hand, Mr Rudyard Kipling never thought much of me, whereas Mr Bernard Shaw often expressed himself in most flattering terms.

also

SPEECH

His December 10 speech of acceptance for the award was read in Stockholm by Lady Churchill.

W.S.C.: The roll on which my name has been inscribed represents much that is outstanding in the world's literature of the twentieth century. I am proud, but also I must admit, awestruck at your decision to include me. I do hope you are right. I feel we are both running a considerable risk and that I do not deserve it. But I shall have no misgivings if you have none.

HOUSE OF COMMONS

Explaining that even a Parliament with a small majority should run its course; that annual elections might turn the House into a 'vote-catching machine looking for a springboard'; and that he thought of the House as a wide-angle lens with a wide embrace of many fields.

W.S.C.: There is no doubt . . . that elections exist for the sake of the House of Commons and not the House of Commons for the sake of elections.

HOUSE OF COMMONS

On November 3.

W.S.C.: When I was a schoolboy, I was not good at arithmetic, but I have since heard it said that certain mathematical quantities when

they pass through infinity, change their signs from plus to minus—
or the other way round . . . This rule [the asymptotes of
hyperbolae] may have a novel application, and that when the
advance of destructive weapons enables everyone to kill everybody
else, nobody will want to kill anyone at all.

SPEECH

On November 9, at the Lord Mayor's Guildhall Banquet.
W.S.C.: I remember a saying I heard in my youth: 'Every word of
Daniel Webster* weighs a pound.' But that was before the days of
television.
and
W.S.C.: Where there is a great deal of free speech there is always
a certain amount of foolish speech.

EAR-WITNESS

*At a Cabinet meeting before the Bermuda Conference, colleagues tried to
persuade him to travel by sea to provide him with more rest and safety*
W.S.C.: I shall go to the airport. I shall board my plane. I shall go
to bed and take my pill. In the morning I shall wake up either in
Bermuda—or in Heaven [dramatic pause]—unless you gentlemen
have some other destination in mind for me.

1954   HOUSE OF COMMONS

*February 1 debate on whether to adopt the Belgian rifle as the standard army
rifle.*
Mr R. Paget, MP: If the Prime Minister will not tell us whether
the Americans have accepted the Belgian rifle, will he tell us
whether anybody has accepted it? Have the French? Have even the
Belgians? Are we not alone?
W.S.C.: I am not in the least alarmed by being shouted at. In fact,
I rather like it. The descendant of Paget's 'Examen'† will, I hope,

---

* Daniel Webster, 1782–1852; American lawyer and statesman; celebrated Congressional orator.
† A book first published in 1861, attacking the historian Macaulay and, by implication, defending the
first Duke of Marlborough. W.S.C. wrote an introduction to the 1934 edition, in which he managed the
essays so that the piece defending Marlborough appeared first.

be very careful and precise in his facts, and be careful in not misrepresenting and misquoting and otherwise defaming other people. He was a great defender of my ancestor.

SPEECH
On April 7, accepting in absentia an honorary Doctor of Laws degree from New York University.
W.S.C.: I am not a lawyer, but I have obeyed a lot of laws, and helped to make a few. Going back to 1776 you may have heard that as a lineal descendant on my Mother's side from a Captain in [General George] Washington's armies, I am a member of the Cincinnati. As I told them when admitted to the Society I must have been on both sides then. Certainly in judging that historic quarrel I am on both sides now. Sex was not born till protoplasm—or protozoa if you prefer—divided itself. But for this split the sexes would not have had all the fun of coming together again.

SPEECH
Before the English-Speaking Union, June 8.
W.S.C.: We have history, law, philosophy and literature; we have sentiments and common interest; we have a language which even the Scottish nationalists will not mind me referring to as English.

HOUSE OF COMMONS
On June 17, responding to Mr Norman Dodds, a Labour Member who suggested calling a summit meeting of US, USSR and Britain to improve international relations.
W.S.C.: Perhaps on this somewhat delicate topic I may be permitted by the House to take refuge in metaphor. Many anxieties have been expressed recently at the severe character of the course of the Grand National Steeplechase, but I am sure that it could not be improved by asking the horses to try to jump two fences at the same time.

HOUSE OF COMMONS

On June 17, responding to Labour Member Hector Hughes' suggestion to reconsider separating the Ministry of Agriculture from the Ministry of Fisheries to help solve problems.

W.S.C.: It would not, I feel, be a good arrangement to have a separate Department for every industry of national importance. These two industries have been long associated departmentally and, after all, there are many ancient links between fish and chips.

EAR-WITNESS

At a June 24 Press Conference in Washington, DC, he referred to Secretaries of State Dean Acheson and John Foster Dulles, saying 'I always had very pleasant relations with Mr Acheson although I did not always agree with him nor he with me. But so do I have with my friend, Mr Foster Dulles . . . and I have kept in close touch with him at all times.' But . . .

W.S.C.: (*during a difference with Mr Dulles*): He is the only case of a bull I know who carries his china closet with him.

PRESS CONFERENCE

At the Statler Hotel in Washington, DC, June 28.

Reporter: Sir Winston, do you think larger Conservative and Republican majorities in Congress—in Parliament and Congress— would improve US–British relations?

W.S.C.: I am all for a Conservative majority . . . I am not going to choose between Republicans and Democrats; I want the lot. Any British Government, Conservative or Socialist—I disagree with the Socialists—but Conservative or Socialist, will try hard to work with the United States. When they are in opposition they can't control their tail. It is hard enough to control your tail when you are in office!

and

Responding to a written question from Edward Folliard of the Washington Post at a Press Conference.

Q.: Sir Winston, in your communiqué at Quebec [September 1944] with Mr Roosevelt you spoke of 'blazing friendship' between our two countries. What is the temperature of that friendship now? [Laughter].

W.S.C.: What is the temperature of that friendship now? *Normal!* [Laughter and applause.]

HOUSE OF COMMONS

On July 14, during a review of foreign affairs.
Mr George Craddock (*Labour MP, calling out to W.S.C.*): Scandalous!
W.S.C.: We are still allowed to debate and not merely to yelp from below the Gangway.

HOUSE OF COMMONS

On July 14.
W.S.C.: The Hon. Member [Mr R. H. S Crossman, Labour MP] is never lucky in the coincidence of his facts with the truth.*

SPEECH

At Blackpool Conservative Party Conference October 9.
W.S.C.: I am sorry that Mr Attlee did not have more success in his trip abroad, but even our football team came a cropper in Moscow and they never meant to go to China. They did not, of course, represent the full strength of Britain and that may apply to Mr Attlee's team also.

SPEECH

At Lord Mayor's Banquet at the Guildhall, November 9.
W.S.C.: Personally I must confess that there was one quite old ruin which seemed to me to deserve at least as much attention as those which owed their destruction to Hitler. I am very glad . . . that we rescued the Temple of Mithras† from the progress of modern civilization, whether in its destructive or reconstructive form. I must congratulate you on having got a magnificent new roof over your

---

* Crossman later so misrepresented Churchill in another matter that he had to pay a large sum to a charity of Churchill's choice in lieu of paying libel damages.
† A Mithras temple dating from Roman times had just been discovered in the course of a nearby excavation and preserved only through private generosity.

heads and amid all the problems of housing for the people not to have left Gog and Magog* out in the cold.

and

W.S.C.: . . . we have found a strong measure of responsibility among many of the Leaders of the Opposition and among the strongest—I did not say the loudest—elements in their rank and file.

HOUSE OF COMMONS

On his eightieth birthday, November 30. After recovering from a severe stroke he spoke to both Houses of Parliament in Westminster Hall, where they had assembled to greet him. Clement Attlee, leader of the Opposition, keynoted the occasion with 'we have come here not to bury Caesar but to praise him.'

W.S.C.: I am very glad that Mr Attlee described my speeches in the war as expressing the will not only of Parliament but of the whole nation. It fell to me to express it, and if I found the right words you must remember that I have always earned my living by my pen and by my tongue. It was a nation and race dwelling all around the globe that had the lion's heart. I had the luck to be called upon to give the roar. I also hope that I sometimes suggested to the lion the right place to use his claws.

and

At the same ceremony he was presented with a startling portrait of himself by Graham Sutherland.

W.S.C.: The portrait is a remarkable example of modern art. It certainly combines force and candour.[†]

A CHURCHILL CANVAS

During lunch at 10 Downing Street, the subject of Spain entered the conversation. Lady Churchill told of a request she had from the Spanish Foreign Minister, Señor Ramon Suñer (pronounced 'Soonyaire'), who was thought to have been pro-Nazi and had asked her to help place his niece in a certain English convent.

---

* In Rev.XX: 7–9, Gog and Magog represent nations of the Earth deceived by Satan. They had been interpreted as giants, and their names given to huge gilt figures in the Guildhall.

† Lady Churchill, horrified, later destroyed it.

Lady Churchill: I hope this was not wrong diplomatically.

W.S.C.: (*who had seemed far away in his thoughts*): Well, we will know Suñer or later!

PROCONSUL

Earlier, when he was at Port Said he watched some high-level Arabs boarding a ship seeking an official they were there to greet.

One of the Arabs: Have you seen the Wazir?

W.S.C.: Yes, he was 'ere a minute ago but I can't see him now.

and

In January 1932, recuperating in Nassau from an injury he incurred when knocked down by a cab in New York, he was floating face down in the ocean near the beach where his daughter Diana was sunning.

Diana: There's a dead fish lying at the bottom of the sea.

W.S.C.: What kind of a fish?

Diana: I don't know; I think it's a turbot.

W.S.C.: Well, don't disturb it.

HOUSE OF COMMONS

In a December 1 debate on German Rearmament.

Mr Emanuel Shinwell, Labour MP: . . . In this field of foreign relations the Right Hon. Gentleman, like Caesar's wife, must be above suspicion. [Interruption.] I assure Hon. Members that any reference that I am suspecting the Right Hon. Gentleman of feminine qualities is quite wrong.

W.S.C.: It was Caesar's wife, not Caesar.

1955

EAR-WITNESS

Informed of the increase of vice in London, and the number of women loitering in doorways in Piccadilly.

W.S.C.: I wouldn't worry—when business is better they'll all be upstairs.

EAR-WITNESS

During the British Elections of May 1955, a debate was conducted over the

BBC on Christianity versus Atheism. W.S.C. reproved the BBC for allowing the new devices to spread such doubts. The BBC responded that their duty in the support of truth was to allow both sides to debate over their facilities.

W.S.C.: If then, there had been the same devices at the time of Christ, would the BBC give equal time on the air to Judas and Jesus?

SPEECH

On May 16, at Woodford. On Clement Attlee, leader of the Labour Opposition.

W.S.C.: His real struggle is less with the Tories than with his own Left Wing followers. His choice is therefore a hard one. The best he can do is to be a piebald . . . we should all rejoice that the Conservative Government took over in time to rescue it from the half-witted treatment which the Socialists had in store for . . . [the British steel industry].

SPEECH

Election address at Bedford on May 17.

W.S.C.: Some of the Socialists say that it [H bomb] should be made and tested, but not used until we have first been attacked by this kind of weapon. That would be like a man saying: 'I carry a pistol in self defence but you can trust me not to use it until I am shot dead.'

SIR JOHN FOSTER, MP

When votes are taken in the Division Lobbies of the House of Commons, Members pile into a narrow corridor, pushing and shoving their way past the clerk who takes the count. But when there was a very pronounced and steady pressure, not a shove, from the rear of the line, MPs knew that it was coming from W.S.C., forging his way forward, gaining three or four yards on the other Members. After one such effort, and judging him out of earshot, an MP remarked, 'It's wonderful to see Winston bulldozing his way through, in spite of his growing deafness and the din of the noisy lobby.'

W.S.C.: Partly by force, partly by favour!

EAR-WITNESS
To Canadian Prime Minister Lester Pearson.
W.S.C.: Never stand down when you can sit and never sit if you can lie down.

SIR JOHN ROTHENSTEIN
On a February visit to Chartwell Sir John Rothenstein, art historian and former Director of the Tate Gallery, declined the cigar offered him by his host, saying every man should have one virtue and his was not smoking.
W.S.C.: There is no such thing as a negative virtue. If I have been of any service to my fellow men, it has never been by self-repression, but always by self-expression.

EAR-WITNESS
Anthony Eden was rumoured to replace W.S.C. as Leader of the Conservative Party.
W.S.C.: When I want to tease Anthony, I remind him that Mr Gladstone formed his last administration at the age of 83.[*]
and

SKETCHES
Earlier, on February 18, 1952, he was looking out from the top floor of 10 Downing Street on to the small garden and beyond to the Horse Guards Parade with his guests, the Dean Achesons and Anthony Eden.
W.S.C.: (*Prodding Acheson in the ribs to indicate that mischief was afoot*): Give me your advice. You see how those plane trees . . . interfere with the view from here of the parade ground. They spoil an otherwise perfect spot to see the Trooping of the Colour. I'm thinking of having them taken away. What do you say?
Anthony Eden: My God, Winston. You can't do that. You don't own the place.
W.S.C.: (*with another delighted poke at Acheson*): Who's to stop me? What are you so excited about? I live here, don't I?

---

[*] Actually Gladstone was 82 when he formed his last administration.

Anthony Eden: That's just it. You only live here. You don't own it. It's just plain vandalism to cut down those trees.

W.S.C.: Ah! I see. I only live here, the life tenant, so to speak, and you inherit the place. What do they call you?—The remainderman, that's it.

Anthony Eden: (*to Dean Acheson*): The old boy got me that time!

BERNARD HAILSTONE

Over lunch at Chartwell artist Bernard Hailstone, who painted the last portrait from life of W.S.C., was musing with Mary Soames (W.S.C.'s youngest daughter) on such strange phenomena as the Loch Ness Monster and Flying Saucers.

W.S.C.: I cannot believe them. I am more interested in looking

'ON THE OTHER HAND, HE DOESN'T LOOK VERY SLEEPY'
From Herblock's Here and Now (*Simon & Schuster, 1955*)

through the world's most powerful telescope to see that there is a Milky Way beyond our Milky Way.

Bernard Hailstone: Is it not true that the most powerful telescopes we make—the further we push our horizons—the more presumptuous is our belief that we are the only planet with life on it.

W.S.C.: I give you that—I give you that! Nevertheless I think we should treat the other planets with the contempt they deserve.

HONOURS | 1956-1965

11TH JANUARY 1956	Received the Benjamin Franklin Medal.
18TH APRIL 1956	Mr Bulganin and Mr Khrushchev began an official visit to London.
23RD APRIL 1956	Published *History of the English-Speaking Peoples*, Vols. I and II, which Labour's Clement Attlee suggested should have been titled 'Things in History which have interested Me.'
13TH JUNE 1956	The last British forces in the Suez Canal Zone were evacuated.
24TH JUNE 1956	Colonel Nasser elected President of Egypt
19TH JULY 1956	US and Britain's offer to finance the Aswan High Dam withdrawn.
26TH JULY 1956	President Nasser nationalized the Suez Canal Company.
31ST OCTOBER 1956	British-French troops land in Egypt.
24TH DECEMBER 1956	Last British troops leave Egypt.
9TH JANUARY 1957	Sir Anthony Eden resigned the Prime Ministership.
10TH JANUARY 1957	*New Government, Harold Macmillan, Conservative Prime Minister.*
15TH MAY 1957	The first British hydrogen bomb exploded at Christmas Island in the Indian Ocean.
4TH OCTOBER 1957	Russia launched an earth satellite, weighing 180 pounds.
14TH OCTOBER 1957	Published *History of the English-Speaking Peoples*, Vol. III.
3RD NOVEMBER 1957	A second Soviet satellite, carrying a live dog, launched.
17TH DECEMBER 1957	The US successfully fired an intercontinental ballistic missile.
31ST JANUARY 1958	The first US satellite, 'Explorer', launched.
23RD JUNE 1958	The US Congress approved exchange of nuclear weapon information with Britain.
14TH JULY 1958	American marines landed in Lebanon at the invitation of the Lebanese President.
	Headed trust to build new college at Cambridge called Churchill College.
	Cruised with Greek shipping tycoon Aristotle Onassis.
12TH SEPTEMBER 1958	Celebrated Golden Wedding Anniversary.
	Published *History of the English-Speaking Peoples*, Vol. IV.
4TH MAY 1959	Visited the United States.
27TH APRIL 1961	Published *The Unwritten Alliance*.
9TH APRIL 1963	Declared an Honorary Citizen of the United States by an Act of the full Congress and a proclamation by President John F. Kennedy at a White

House ceremony in which he was represented by his son Randolph S. Churchill.

19TH OCTOBER 1963	*New Government, Sir Alec Douglas-Home, Conservative Prime Minister.*
28TH JULY 1964	Presented with vote of thanks from House of Commons, which adopted a motion putting on record 'its unbounded admiration and gratitude for his services to Parliament, to the nation and to the world' soon after his retirement from the House.
SEPTEMBER 1964	With the dissolution of Parliament, ceased at last to be an MP.
16TH OCTOBER 1964	*New Government, Harold Wilson, Labour Prime Minister.*
30TH NOVEMBER 1964	Celebrated his 90th birthday.
24TH JANUARY 1965	Died at his home at Hyde Park Gate, ten years short of a century old, on the seventieth anniversary to the month and day of the death of his father, Lord Randolph Churchill.
30TH JANUARY 1965	Buried beside his mother and father in St Martin's churchyard at Bladon in Oxfordshire, near his birthplace, Blenheim Palace. It is said that he did not want to be buried in Westminster Abbey and share it with so many people he did not like. But set in the floor of the west door of the Abbey is a green marble stone inscribed: REMEMBER WINSTON CHURCHILL.

1956

EAR-WITNESS
While Hugh Gaitskell, Leader of the Opposition, was speaking in the House on economic issues, W.S.C., who was sitting on the Government Front Bench, suddenly began looking through his pockets and then on the floor, unconscious of the attention he was attracting and the confusion he was causing. Mr Gaitskell stopped, having lost the sense of his speech, and offered to help in the search.

W.S.C.: I was only looking for my jujube [a lozenge].*

JULIAN AMERY, MP
During a debate in the House of Commons, Bernard Braine was speaking from the second bench below the gangway, just behind W.S.C.

* Next day's Press referred to the incident as 'The Fall of the Pastille'.

W.S.C.: (*to Julian Amery*): Who's that speaking?

Julian Amery: Braine.

W.S.C.: James?

Julian Amery: No! Braine.

W.S.C.: Drain. He can't be called Drain. Nobody's called Drain.

(*Julian Amery then wrote down the name 'Braine' on the back of an order paper.*)

W.S.C.: Ah! I see. Is he well named?

Five minutes later.

W.S.C.: (*pointing at Herbert Morrison, on the other side of the House*): Who is that?

Julian Amery: Herbert Morrison.

W.S.C.: Who?

Julian Amery: Morrison, he used to be your Home Secretary.

W.S.C.: Are you sure? He looks very much aged!

CHURCHILL: TAKEN FROM THE DIARIES OF LORD MORAN

On a weekend in June at Marshalls Manor, Lord Moran's country house in Sussex, Norman Brooke, who had been a Deputy Secretary to the War Cabinet in World War II, recalled handing W.S.C. a report that did not meet his Chief's criterion, 'not over one page in length.'

W.S.C.: This Treasury paper by its very length, defends itself against the risk of being read.

also

Before the actual Suez Canal debacle.

W.S.C. to Lord Moran: It serves Anthony* right. He has inherited what he let me in for.†

1957   SUNDAY TELEGRAPH

When the British Army was reorganized and certain units were amalgamated, it was realized that W.S.C.'s old regiment was among those

---

* The British and French moved against Egypt October 31, 1956, avowedly to keep the Suez Canal neutral. After a censuring UN General Assembly vote, Prime Minister Eden ordered a cease-fire.

† Prime Minister Anthony Eden who, as W.S.C.'s Foreign Secretary, had negotiated an accommodating treaty with Egypt, much criticized from both Left and Right, in 1954.

doomed. General Montgomery was chosen to break the news of the economies that inspired the move.

W.S.C.: What about the Army's horses?

General Montgomery: Some would remain.

W.S.C.: What about the bands?

General Montgomery: You know, Winston, you are an extra-ordinary chap. I come to tell you about your old regiment and you talk about the horses and the bands.

W.S.C.: I want to make sure I get a good funeral.

and

First to Harold Macmillan, Minister of Defence from 1954 to 1955, and later to Duncan Sandys, his son-in-law, in the same Cabinet post in 1957.

W.S.C.: I hope you won't get rid of the regiments too fast. I want to have several brass bands at my funeral.[*]

1958

EAR-WITNESS

When he was told that Field Marshal Viscount Montgomery's Memoirs *were making more money than his* A History of the English-Speaking Peoples.

W.S.C.: I'm not surprised. The Field Marshal lived up to the finest tradition of Englishmen. He sold his life dearly.

EAR-WITNESS

At eighty-four, visiting his literary agent and friend, Emery Reves, in the south of France, they dined in a restaurant on his favourite roast beef and Yorkshire pudding. For dessert W.S.C. asked for a 'pudding.' The French chef, not quite sure what was meant by a 'pudding' but eager to please the great friend of France, produced what he thought to be a culinary triumph. Flanked by the waiters, he stood by waiting for the verdict.

W.S.C.: (banging down his spoon): Garçon! Garçon! Remove this pudding. It has no theme!

---

[*] Bands of the Guards regiments were actually kept intact and W.S.C.'s wishes for his funeral plans were filed away under the designation 'Operation Hope-Not'.

1959

SPEECH

In a twenty-seven-minute campaign speech to his constituents at Woodford.

W.S.C.: Among our Socialist opponents there is great confusion. Some of them regard private enterprise as a predatory tiger to be shot. Others look on it as a cow that they can milk. [Here he went through the motions of milking.] Only a handful see it for what it really is—the strong and willing horse that pulls the whole cart along.

EAR-WITNESS

On his eighty-fifth birthday, two Tory Members of the House of Commons were watching him from what they thought was a safe distance. One remarked to the other, 'They say the old man's getting a bit past it.'

W.S.C.: And they say the old man's getting deaf as well.

1960

ROBERTO ARIAS

Margot Fonteyn and her husband, 'Tito' Arias*, visited Chartwell some months after the 'Shrimp Boat Invasion' of Panama which sought to overthrow the Government of President Enrico de la Guardia. Señor Arias had taken a leading part and had been jailed. General Montgomery was also a guest. While Lady Churchill and Margot Fonteyn played croquet the men conversed.

W.S.C.: [to Tito Arias] What are you going to do now?

Roberto Arias: We shall go back to Panama.

W.S.C.: Don't use Montgomery in any of your revolutions. He will bankrupt you before you start. He will need 13 divisions before he'll ever make a move!

1961

HOUSE OF COMMONS

Sitting on the front bench below the Gangway he was straining to hear what was being said. A young man behind him leaned forward and told him, but got no response. Then Lord Hinchingbrooke,† who was sitting nearby, leaned

---

* Roberto Emilio Arias, husband of dancer Margot Fonteyn; Panamanian Ambassador to the Court of St James, London, 1955–1958, 1960–1962.
† Whose title was 'by courtesy' as eldest son of an earl, and could serve as an MP in the Commons.

back and said in a whisper to the young man, 'He can't hear you, he's very deaf.'

W.S.C.: (*without turning*) Yes, and they say the old man is gaga too!

1963

EAR-WITNESS

At eighty-seven, he broke his left thigh in a fall in Monte Carlo. On his return to his 28 Hyde Park Gate house in London to recuperate, he was carried over the threshold by an ambulance attendant.

W.S.C.: Not feet first, please!

1964

LETTER

He wrote to the Washington Branch of the English-Speaking Union upon learning that a nine-foot bronze statue of him by the American sculptor William McVey was to be placed in front of the British Embassy with one foot on British Embassy, the other on American, soil to celebrate the first Honorary American Citizen so declared by the full Congress.

W.S.C.: . . . It gives me the greatest pleasure that the statue should stand on both American and British soil, and I feel that it will rest happily and securely on both feet.[*]

ADLAI STEVENSON[†]

Ten years earlier, on July 29, 1953, at the close of a world tour, Adlai Stevenson lunched at Chequers with W.S.C. when he was again Prime Minister. Before returning to London to make a speech to the members of the English-Speaking Union he asked W.S.C. what message he might take from him to his audience. At that moment W.S.C.'s grandson Winston appeared, prompting the remark that the young boy was the sixth in direct descent from an officer (Lt. Reuben Murray) who fought in George Washington's Army, making him eligible for membership in the Society of Cincinnati.[‡]

W.S.C.: (*to Adlai Stevenson*): You can take back this message to your audience—tell them—tell them—I *am* an English speaking union!

---

[*] On the day W.S.C. was made an Honorary American Citizen, writer Vincent Sheehan cabled Lady Churchill, 'Congratulate Winston for saving England by annexing the United States.'
[†] Adlai Stevenson, 1900–1965; Governor of Illinois, 1949–1953; candidate for President, 1952, 1956; US Ambassador to UN, 1961–1965.
[‡] W.S.C. was elected a member of the Society of Cincinnati in 1947, and installed in January 1952.

TO
SIR WINSTON CHURCHILL:
KAY HALLE JOINS
ME IN BASKING IN
THE REFLECTED
GLORY OF YOUR
HIGH HONOR.
SINCERELY
Edward H. Kuekes

HONORARY CITIZEN
OF THE
UNITED STATES!

KUEKES
PLAIN DEALER
4-9-63

ON YOU IT LOOKS GOOD.

BLOODY YANK

MY DEAR MR CHURCHILL

On afterlife.

W.S.C.: And then there will be the cherubs. How strange it will be to have them around. Do you know the story of the French priest who was so holy that one day in his church he saw fluttering above him a throng of cherubs? He was not only holy, but polite, and begged them to sit down.

   '*Mais,*' replied the cherubs, '*nous n'avons pas de quoi.*'*

and

W.S.C.: I wonder what God thinks of the things His creatures have invented. Really, it's surprising He has allowed it—but then I suppose He has so many things to think of, not only us, but all His

---

* 'But we haven't anyting [to sit on].'

worlds. I wouldn't have His job for anything. Mine is hard enough, but His is much more difficult. And—umph—He can't even resign . . .

You know, most people are going to be very surprised when they get to Heaven. They are looking forward to meeting fascinating people like Napoleon and Julius Caesar. But they'll probably never even be able to find them, because there will be so many millions of other people there too—Indians and Chinese and people like that. Everyone will have equal rights in Heaven. That will be the real Welfare State . . .

and

W.S.C.: Some kind of velvety cool blackness. Of course, I admit I may be wrong. It is conceivable that I might well be reborn as a Chinese coolie. In such case I should lodge a protest.

and

SIR WINSTON
CHURCHILL,
HONORARY
U.S. CITIZEN

SIR WINSTON
CHURCHILL
HONORARY U.S. CITIZEN

WHEN EARTH'S LAST PICTURE IS PAINTED,
AND THE TUBES ARE TWISTED AND DRIED,
WHEN THE OLDEST COLORS HAVE FADED,
AND THE YOUNGEST CRITIC HAS DIED,
WE SHALL REST, AND, FAITH WE SHALL NEED IT---
-- LIE DOWN FOR AN EON OR TWO,
TILL THE MASTER OF ALL GOOD WORKMEN
SHALL SET US TO WORK ANEW!
- KIPLING -

AMID THESE STORMS

W.S.C.: When I get to Heaven I mean to spend a considerable portion of my first five million years in painting, and so get to the bottom of the subject. But then I shall require a still gayer palette than I get here below . . . There will be a whole range of wonderful new colours which will delight the celestial eye.

THE RIVER WAR

As a soldier at the age of twenty-three, his thoughts on dying in battle.
W.S.C.: I suppose, when we are ourselves overtaken by death, the surroundings of home and friends will not make much appreciable difference. To struggle and choke in the hushed and darkened room of a London house, while, without, the great metropolis is planning and contriving—while the special editions report the progress of the latest European crisis, and all the world is full of the business of the morrow—will not seem less unsatisfactory than, when filled with fierce yet generous emotions, to die in the sunshine and be spaded under before the night.
and

1965

EAR-WITNESS

January 24. At 90, as he lay dying in the 'darkened room of a London house' at 28 Hyde Park Gate.
W.S.C.:
I am bored with it all.
but
The journey has been enjoyable and well worth making—once!

EPILOGUE

Many biographies have been written of Sir Winston. None are more uncannily true of him than the words inscribed two hundred and sixty years ago on the Victory Column at Blenheim Palace to celebrate the glory of his ancestor, John Churchill, first Duke of Marlborough. By a beautiful irony the tribute was written by Viscount Bolingbroke, at the request of Sarah, Marlborough's widow. Though Bolingbroke was one of the great masters of English prose of his day he was also Marlborough's hated enemy who brought about his downfall!

The Castle of Blenheim was founded by Queen Anne
In the fourth year of her Reign,
In the year of the Christian Era
One Thousand Seven Hundred and Five
A Monument designed to perpetuate the Memory of the Signal Victory
Obtain'd over the French and Bavarians,
Near the Village of Blenheim,
By John, Duke of Marlborough,
The Hero not only of his Nation, but of his Age:
Whose Glory was equal in the Council and in the Field;
Who, by Wisdom, Justice, Candour, and Address,
Reconcil'd various, and even opposite Interests;
Acquired an Influence
Which no Rank, no Authority can give,
Nor any Force, but that of superior Virtue;
Became the fixed important Centre
Which united, In one common Cause
The principal States of Europe;
Who, by military Knowledge, and irresistible Valour,
In a long series of uninterrupted Triumphs,
Broke the Power of France
When raised the highest, when exerted the most,
Rescued the Empire from Desolation,
Asserted and confirmed the Liberties of Europe.

Two hundred and forty seven years ago, in the Summer of 1718, John Dryden's *All*

For Love was performed at Blenheim Palace. Its Prologue, addressed to John Churchill, the first great Duke of Marlborough, who was in the audience, contained this amazing prophecy in verse:

> *One shall arise who shall thy deed rehearse,*
> *Not in arched roofs, or in suspected verse;*
> *But in plain annals of each glorious year,*
> *With pomp of truth the story shall appear;*
> *Long after Blenheim's walls shall moulder'd lie,*
> *Or blown by winds, to distant countries fly,*
> *By him shall thy great actions all survive*
> *and by thy name shall his be taught to live.*

Herblock in
The Washington Post

ACKNOWLEDGEMENTS

✦✦✦

M y deepest appreciation and thanks to Martin Gilbert, author and Fellow, Merton College, Oxford, for his invaluable criticism and help; and to Elizabeth Beverly, for her devoted and tireless labours in assisting with the arrangements and typing of this collection. I tender thanks also to Bogoljub Jovanovic, of the Washington, DC, Public Library, for his swift and accurate research.

I found the volumes of memoirs, biographies, essays, periodicals, and histories from which I extracted certain examples for this collection to be gold mines of Churchilliana. Above all, Sir Winston's own vivid works.

A diligent effort has been made to obtain permission to reprint copyrighted material and to make full acknowledgement of its use. I am grateful to the publishers and others in the list that follows for having graciously granted their permission for the use of extracts and illustrations that appear in this book Any errors or omissions in the list are purely inadvertent, and will be corrected in subsequent editions.

Alden & Company:
SIR WINSTON CHURCHILL AT BLENHEIM PALACE. AN ANTHOLOGY, by David Green; copyright 1959, by David Green.
Appleton-Century-Crofts, Inc.; Division of Meredith Publishing Company:
THE REMINISCENCES OF LADY RANDOLPH CHURCHILL, by Mrs George Cornwallis-West; copyright 1907, 1908, by The Century Co.
Atheneum Publishers:
ANEURIN BEVAN, Volume One of a biography by Michael Foot; copyright © 1962, by Tribune Publications; permission also granted by MacGibbon & Kee Ltd.
FROM MY LEVEL, by George Mallaby; copyright © 1965, by the author; permission also granted by Hutchinson Publishing Group Ltd.
A. S. Barnes & Co.:
LORD RANDOLPH CHURCHILL, WINSTON CHURCHILL'S FATHER by Robert Rhodes James; copyright © 1959, 1960, by the author; permission also granted by Weidenfeld & Nicolson Limited.
British Book Centre, Inc.:
MY YEARS WITH CHURCHILL, by Norman McGowan; copyright 1958, by the author; permission also granted by Souvenir Press of London.
Burton, Richard:
From The Jack Paar Show of May 8, 1964; copyright © 1964, by Richard Burton.

Coward-McCann, Inc.:

MY 21 YEARS IN THE WHITE HOUSE, by Alonzo Fields; copyright © 1960, 1961, by the author.

Crowell-Collier & Macmillan, Inc.:

From *Collier's*: 'The Shattered Cause of Temperance,' Aug. 13, 1932; 'The Bond Between Us,' Nov. 4, 1933.

Dodd, Mead & Company:

ATLANTIC MEETING, by H. V. Morton; copyright 1943, by Dodd, Mead & Company; permission also granted by Methuen & Co. Ltd.

A HISTORY OF THE ENGLISH-SPEAKING PEOPLES, by Winston S. Churchill; copyright 1956; permission also granted by Emery Reves, by Cassell and Company Ltd., and by McClelland & Stewart, Ltd.

Doubleday & Company, Inc.:

INDEPENDENT MEMBER, by A. P. Herbert; copyright 1950, by Alan Patrick Herbert; permission also granted by Sir Alan Herbet and Methuen & Company Ltd.

Duell, Sloan & Pearce, Inc.:

THE DECLINE AND FALL OF LLOYD GEORGE, by Lord Beaverbrook; copyright 1963, by Lord Beaverbrook; permission also granted by William Collins Sons & Co., Ltd., London.

F.D.R.: HIS PERSONAL LETTERS, edited by Elliot Roosevelt; copyright 1950, by Elliott Roosevelt; permission also granted by George G. Harrap & Company Limited.

Evans Brothers Limited:

PROCONSUL, by Sir Bede Clifford; copyright 1964, by the author.

Eyre & Spottiswoode Ltd.:

F.E.: THE LIFE OF F. E. SMITH, FIRST EARL OF BIRKENHEAD, by the Second Earl of Birkenhead; copyright 1959, by Frederick, Second Earl of Birkenhead.

Funk & Wagnalls Co., Inc.:

I WAS WINSTON CHURCHILL'S PRIVATE SECRETARY, by Phyllis Moir; copyright 1941, by Wilfred Funk, Inc.

Harcourt, Brace & World, Inc.:

A BIOGRAPHY OF EDWARD MARSH, by Christopher Hassall; copyright 1959, by the author; permission also granted by David Higham Associates, Ltd., on behalf of the Estate of Christopher Hassall, covering the British edition published by Longmans Green & Co., Ltd.

LORD RIDDELL'S INTIMATE DIARY OF THE PEACE CONFERENCE AND AFTER, by Lord Riddell, 1934; permission also granted by Victor Gollancz, Ltd.

WINSTON CHURCHILL: AN INTIMATE PORTRAIT, by Violet Bonham Carter; copyright 1965, by the author; published in England as WINSTON CHURCHILL AS I KNEW HIM, for which permission has been granted by Eyre & Spottiswoode Ltd.

permission also granted by Fitzwilliam Museum.

THE WAR AND COLONEL WARDEN, by Gerald Pawle; copyright © 1963, by the author; permission also granted by George C. Harrap & Company Limited.

Little, Brown and Company:

A CHURCHILL CANVAS, by John Spencer Churchill; copyright © 1961, by the author; published in England as A CROWDED CANVAS, for which permission has been granted by Oldhams Books Limited.

David McKay Company Inc.:

MY TWENTY YEARS IN BUCKINGHAM PALACE by Frederick J. Corbitt; copyright 1956, by the author; published in England as FIT FOR A KING, for which permission has been granted by Oldhams Books Limited.

McLeod, Douglas:

ASSIGNMENT: CHURCHILL, by Inspector Walter Henry Thompson of Scotland Yard; Farrar, Straus and Young; copyright 1965, by the author. Published in England as I WAS CHURCHILL'S SHADOW.

New Statesman:

'Winston: a Memoir,' by Lord Dalton; Jan. 29, 1965.

Oldhams Books Limited:

THE AFTERMATH, by Winston Churchill; permission also granted by Charles Scribner's Sons.

A CROWDED CANVAS, by John Spencer Churchill; © 1961, by the author; published in the United States as A CHURCHILL CANVAS, for which permission has been granted by Little, Brown and Company.

FIT FOR A KING, by Frederick J. Corbitt; copyright 1956, by the author; published in the United States as MY TWENTY YEARS IN BUCKINGHAM PALACE, for which permission has also been granted by David McKay Company, Inc.

GREAT CONTEMPORARIES, by Winston S. Churchill; G. P. Putnam's Sons; copyright 1937, by the author.

IAN HAMILTON'S MARCH, by Winston S. Churchill; Longmans, Green and Co., Inc.: copyright 1900, by Winston Spencer Churchill.

LONDON TO LADYSMITH VIA PRETORIA, by Winston S. Churchill; published in the United States as A ROVING COMMISSION: MY EARLY LIFE, for which permission has also been granted by Charles Scribner's Sons.

THE RIVER WAR, by Winston S. Churchill; Longmans, Green and Co., Inc.; copyright 1899.

SAVROLA, A TALE OF THE REVOLUTION IN LAURANIA, by Winston Churchill; Longmans, Green and Co., Inc., 1900; see also Random House, Inc., below.

STEP BY STEP, by Winston S. Churchill; also see G. P. Putnam's Sons, below.

THE STORY OF THE MALAKAND FIELD FORCE, by Winston S. Churchill; Longmans,

Green and Co., Inc.; copyright 1898.

THOUGHTS AND ADVENTURES, by Winston S. Churchill; copyright 1932; published in the United States as AMID THESE STORMS, for which permission has been granted by Charles Scribner's Sons.

THE WORLD CRISIS, by Winston S. Churchill; permission also granted by Charles Scribner's Sons.

Pendar, Kenneth W.:

ADVENTURE IN DIPLOMACY, by Kenneth Pendar; Dodd, Mead and Company; copyright 1945, by Kenneth Pendar. Permission also granted by Cassell and Company Ltd., covering their 1966 edition; copyright © 1966, by Kenneth Pendar.

Frederick A. Praeger, Inc.:

THE CENTRAL BLUE, THE AUTOBIOGRAPHY OF SIR JOHN SLESSOR, MARSHAL OF THE RAF, by Sir John Slessor; copyright © 1957, by the author; permission also granted by Cassell and Company Ltd.

G. P. Putnam's Sons:

STEP BY STEP, by Winston Churchill; copyright 1939; by the author; permission also granted by Oldhams Books Limited.

Random House, Inc.:

SAVROLA, A TALE OF THE REVOLUTION IN LAURANIA, by Winston S. Churchill; copyright 1900 by the author, and copyright 1956 by Random House, Inc.; permission also granted by Oldhams Books Limited.

Reynal & Company, Inc.:

THE CLOCK WITH FOUR HANDS, BASED ON THE EXPERIENCES OF GENERAL SIR LESLIE HOLLIS, by James Leasor; copyright © 1959, by James Leasor and Leslie Hollis. Published in England as WAR AT THE TOP, for which permission has been granted by David Higham Associates, Ltd.

Russell-Volkening, Inc.

MR CHURCHILL'S SECRETARY, by Elizabeth Nel; Coward-McCann, Inc.; copyright 1958, by the author; permission also granted by Hodder & Stoughton Limited.

St Martin's Press, Incorporated:

COLLECTED POEMS, by Ralph Hodgson; copyright 1961, by the author; permission also granted by Macmillan & Co. Ltd. and by Mrs Ralph Hodgson.

Charles Scribner's Sons:

THE AFTERMATH, by Winston Churchill; copyright 1929, by Charles Scribner's Sons; renewal copyright © 1957, by Winston S Churchill; permission also granted by Oldhams Books Limited.

AMID THESE STORMS, by Winston S. Churchill; copyright 1932, by Charles Scribner's Sons; renewal copyright © 1960, by Winston S. Churchill. Published in England as THOUGHTS AND ADVENTURES, for which permission has been granted

NEWSPAPERS
The Daily Mail
The Daily Telegraph
The Manchester Guardian
The Observer
The Sunday Telegraph
The Times
The Washington Post

ILLUSTRATIONS

The Daily Express, London:
   No caption (My plans for the next 15 years).
Courtesy *The Evening News*, London:
   The New Britannia, by Low
   The Topper. Now, That's Something Like a Hat.
From Herblock's HERE AND NOW (Simon & Schuster, 1955):
   'On the Other Hand, He Doesn't Look Very Sleepy.'
Herblock, in *The Washington Post*:
   No caption (V for Victory).
   No caption (W.S.C.'s arrival in Washington).
   'Nonsense, Madam—All Babies Look Like Me.'
   'Season's Greeting!'
Illustrated Newspapers Ltd., London:
   First Lord of the Admiralty.
Edward D. Kuekes, *Plain Dealer*, Cleveland:
   On You It Looks Good.
   Sir Winston Churchill, Honorary US Citizen.
From the collection of Lord Lee of Fairleigh, who gave Chequers to the Nation:
   The Lion and the Mouse, by Franz Snyders and Peter Paul Rubens.
Reproduced from the Collections of The Library of Congress:
   Dream of World Conquest.
   The First Lord spent his birthday with work as usual.
   A Hornet's Nest, Poor Winnie-the-Pooh.
   Innovator W.S.C. converts Royal Navy from Coal to oil
   The Light of Epping Goes Out.
   No caption (F.D.R. and Churchill before 'Atlantic Charter' cake).
   No caption (F.D.R. and Churchill outside the Senate Chamber).
   No caption (W.S.C. walking beside the world).
   Two Cellars. 'I thought that would warm you, sir: I am sorry not to be able to

manage a little more coal as well.'

Winston Is Back.

Sir David Low and *The Evening Standard*, London:

All Behind You, Winston.

A Fine Team But Could Do With a Dash of Unity.

Imitation the Sincerest Flattery.

To Winston, with affectionate birthday greetings from his old castigator—Low.

Trial Grouping.

Winterton's Nightmare.

Bill Mauldin:

Bloody Yank, © 1963 by Mauldin.

Punch, London:

A Family Visit.

Hats That Have Helped Me.

Mr Churchill and Friend.

Neptune's Ally.

One Stage Nearer ('Privy Councillor at 32')

A Sea-Change.

Tenants' Fixtures.

Under His Master's Eye.

Ambassador James Roosevelt, US Representative to the Economic & Social Council of the United Nations:

Union of the pound and the dollar.

Vanity Fair Magazine, London:

The author of *Savrola* in 1900, by Spy.

INDEX

300, 301
Elliston, Herbert 10
Errol, Leon 4
Esher, Lord 68-9
Evans, Abel 3
Everest, Mrs (W.S.C.'s nurse) 14

Farouk, King of Egypt 278, 300
Feisal, Emir 75
Fields, Alonzo 244
Fisher, Admiral Lord 67
Fisher, Geoffrey Francis, Archbishop 236
Fitzroy, Captain the Rt. Hon. Edward 173
Fleming, Sir Alexander 215
Foch, Marshal Ferdinand 80
Folliard, Edward 176, 305
Fonteyn, Dame Margot 317
Franco, General Francisco 156, 248
Franks, Sir Oliver 246
Franz Ferdinand, Archduke 34

Gaitskell, Hugh 259-60, 274, 278, 299, 314
Gallacher, Willie 226-7
Gandhi, Mahatma M.K. 103, 107, 196, 239
Gaspari, Alcide de 301
Gaulle, Charles de 137, 138, 177, 197-9, 213
Gayda, Virginia 134
George III, King 85, 281
George VI, King 135, 138, 145, 220, 234, 239, 246, 247, 249, 278
Gibbon, Edward 20, 254
Gibbs, Dewar 69-70
Giraud, General Henri 137, 195
Gladstone, William 12, 13, 16, 94, 279, 284, 310
Goebbels, Joseph 134
Goering, Hermann 165, 239
Gordon, General Charles George, 36
Graham, William 107
Grant, General Ulysses, President of United States 12
Graziani, Rodolfo 160
Green, Colonel Edward 7
Green, Hetty 7
Green, Senator Theodore 281
Griffith, Arthur 75, 81, 83
Gromyko, Andrei A. 248

Guillotine, Dr Joseph 105

al-Haidari, Daud Pasha 246
Haig, Earl 246
Hailstone, Bernard 311, 312
Halifax, Lord 152
Hanfstaengl, Ernst ('Putzi') 111-12
Harcourt, Captain Cecil 245
Harcourt, Sir William 21
Hardie, Keir 286
Harriman, W. Averell 214, 246, 295
Harris, Sir Percy 173
Harrod, Sir Roy 142
Havenga, Nicolaas Christiaan 262
Herbert, A.P. 8, 10, 119, 174
Hess, Rudolf 172
Hinchingbrooke, Lord 317-18
Hitler, Adolf 100, 112, 122, 126, 128, 133, 135, 145, 149, 150, 155, 156, 160, 165-8, 176, 180, 185, 195, 204, 223, 224, 230, 306
Hoare, Sir Samuel 123
Hodgson, Ralph 11
Hollis, Brigadier Sir Leslie 293
Hopkins, Harry L. 181, 299
Hopkinson, Austin 203
Horder, Sir Thomas 85
Hore-Belisha, Leslie 165, 166, 188
Hughes, Emrys 286, 290-91, 292, 297, 300
Hughes, Hector 305
Hull, Cordell 211

Ibn Saud, King of Saudi Arabia 138, 229
Inönü, President Ismet 137, 202
Ismay, Major General Lord 146, 147, 159, 189, 208, 219, 232

Jacob, Brigadier Ian 203
James, Captain 16
James, Lionel 39
Jerome, Jennie see Churchill, Lady Randolph
Joan of Arc 197, 198, 291
Johnson, Very Rev. Hewlett ('Red' Dean) 290, 291, 294
Jowitt, Lord William Allen 46
Joynson-Hicks, Sir William 86

Kanellopoulos, Panayotis 192